[handwritten inscription: To [?], remembering some happy days in Camden Town, Carmel xxx May 89]

Penguin Books
In Camden Town

David Thomson was born in India of Scottish parents in 1914. Much of his childhood was spent in the country, in Derbyshire, and at Nairn in Scotland where his grandparents lived. After leaving Oxford University, he took a job at Woodbrook, in Ireland, and stayed there for almost ten years. Later he joined the BBC, where he wrote and produced many distinguished programmes, including *The Irish Storyteller* series, *The Great Hunger* (on the Irish Famine of 1845 to 1848) and a number of programmes on animal folklore. During his secondment to UNESCO he worked in France, Liberia and Turkey. Since 1956 he and his wife have lived in Camden Town where their three sons were brought up.

The author of *The People of the Sea* (on seals and their legends) and co-author of *The Leaping Hare* (on hares and their legends), he has also written three novels, the most recent of which is *Dandiprat's Days*, and several children's books, *Danny Fox*, *Danny Fox Meets a Stranger* and *Danny Fox at the Palace* (Puffin Books) and also *Ronan and Other Stories*. From his experiences in Ireland he wrote *Woodbrook* (Penguin, 1976).

David Thomson

In Camden Town

Penguin Books

Penguin Books Ltd, Harmondsworth, Middlesex, England
Viking Penguin Inc., 40 West 23rd Street, New York, New York 10010, U.S.A.
Penguin Books Australia Ltd, Ringwood, Victoria, Australia
Penguin Books Canada Ltd, 2801 John Street, Markham, Ontario, Canada L3R 1B4
Penguin Books (N.Z.) Ltd, 182–190 Wairau Road, Auckland 10, New Zealand

First published by Hutchinson & Co. (Publishers) Ltd 1983
Published in Penguin Books 1985

Printed and bound in Great Britain by
Richard Clay (The Chaucer Press) Ltd,
Bungay, Suffolk
Set in Plantin

To Martina

Acknowledgements

Most of the people who helped me with this book are mentioned in it but there are others whom I also wish to thank, among them Richard Bober, John Bunting, Sally Garnham, Robert Pocock, Raphael Samuel and Joan Thomson.

August 4th, 1980, Monday

Yesterday evening at about 6 we went through the park to the Rose Garden. Families leaving the park – their special slow pace and shuffling, small children in American-style hats and caps – some with stars and stripes on them. Lazy tiredness. It was hot and thundery, no rain, sun for minutes, then dark cloud.

Fat short Maria-like women streaming through Queen Mary's Garden gates unconscious of our wanting to get in – talk kept them and their men busy. Maria has no time to walk in the park on Sundays or on any other day. She has chosen Weds. and Thurs. as her days off from the Royal Free, gets time and a half that way and on her rest days from cleaning the wards she does our house and someone else's. Slave labour self-imposed. She is saving up for her house at home in Portugal which she will live in when she is sixty, twenty years from now.

The roses in large beds, curved or rectangular – yellow, white, orange, many shades of pink, some reds, so bright as to be dazzling in a mass. There was one kind – reddish orange with some pink petals and another that seemed to be two colours equally divided. Each rose has a scent of its own.

On the way across the park to the canal path, few people. A fat youngish woman in tight black trousers, her buttocks balloons on black sticks, was being pulled along by a large yellow dog on a lead.

As we walked on the towpath opposite the zoo, I spoke to

Martina of the dread, the sometimes almost physical horror, with which I often thought of my 'Camden Town' – the canal, my attempts at its history, my mass of notebooks, files of papers, card index, people I once used to talk to about it and now fear to meet.

She said

– Can't you put that into the book?

She suggested that I should start a Camden Town Diary. Here is the start.

I haven't thought how it will fit in, can be used. But she's right, that it will unstick me. At least I can bypass for a time my dread of opening the MS at the page where I left off.

She has noticed how fluently I wrote the Italian Diary. I finished it last Friday. I don't think it's well written but at least I carried on with it for several hours every day. And it makes me much happier.

On Saturday evening I met MacL. in the Windsor Castle, where I hadn't been for months. I had not seen him. He came up to me.

He said he had been to work in the Science Museum canteen kitchen that morning at 9. At 10.30 he told his mate he was going out to get a paper – 15 mins, he said, down Gloucester Rd he meant, I think. When he came back his mate said

– She's been asking for you.

That was enough to make him walk out.

– What about your pay?

– Don't bother. (Pay is by the hour.)

I said Mrs Thatcher would approve of him – his voluntary work. He screwed up his face in an expression of self-satisfaction and told me of another job he had left after 2 or 3 hours' work – scorning the pay because he wanted to come out top in a quarrel. In this, he has not changed at all during the past 10 years or more of our acquaintance. He has told me many similar stories in the past.

On Sunday night, after the Engineer, I noticed more than usually the pattern, from our bedroom window, of the lighted windows curving round at the back of the Glos. Crescent houses – the concave side: deep orange blind, bright yellow, pale yellow, white and ordinary elec.-light-coloured upright oblongs – unlit windows glistening in between patchwork.

Memory from BBC office windows of the first night the blackout was lifted.

Our tree is now a wide canopy of green, a translucent hood of leaves, its outer branches pendant and moving in the breeze across the pavement – you have to lean or stoop as you pass them.

When we first came the weeping leaves hung down to the grass of the lawn.

As I come in at the far end of the terrace watching our door which is now white, I sometimes see a shadow on the door moving like a person – someone leaving the house, someone looking out of the window of my room. It is the tree, the swaying leaves, the shadows of the lightest ends of its branches.

Today almost all day I've been thinking of our first visit to this house. I wrote about it years ago, about beginnings, the first day of anything that becomes a part of one's life. Find it. Put it here. Try bookshelf, bottom, with old Irish stuff.

Every beginning in all our lives is memorable – the first day at school, the first moments of love, the cold and fearful morning of a new job. The first sight of a city which by chance becomes your home can be indelible. It seems to belong to one day only and would fade like any other isolated memory; but, as its links with the future join each other one by one – as the city becomes familiar and beloved – that first sight settles down in the mind more firmly than a chance encounter never taken up again.

So it is with my first hour in Camden Town on the day when I crossed the extraordinary threshold of the house we live in now. Martina let me in, and maybe the very sight of her in a new setting has strengthened my memory of that hour, for in those days, while she was staying with her mother, I did not see much of her. I used to forget what she looked like and daydream about her at work, trying to force my imagination to re-create the image of her face.

It was a bright, sunny day in the middle of October 1955 but cold because a north wind was blowing, the sky pale with some clouds in it moving fast towards the south. It had been difficult to find the way. I took a bus up Albany Street to

Gloucester Gate, walked across the old iron bridge, leafy because that part of the canal had been filled in with gardens, over a railway bridge into Park Street, which is now Parkway, and I missed the turning and had to walk back. Regent's Park Terrace where Martina was waiting for me is hidden by trees and an old brick wall, behind a large garage called Henlys at the corner of Gloucester Crescent and Oval Road. At last I found it and knocked at the door. M. was glowing with cold and with excitement. The doorway she stood in faced south and as I waited for her to answer my knock I felt warm out of doors for the first time that day. The knocker was heavy, and round like a small wreath, made of iron and covered with the same black paint as the door, faded, chipped and blistered like the door itself. Behind me there was a beautiful tree, a weeping ash still in leaf; its leaves hung down almost to the roadway and touched in places the lawn it had been planted on.

As she opened the door I saw a blank wall facing it, behind her, and to this day whenever a stranger comes through it, the doorway seems to lead him not into the house but to a cell with a high ceiling. He must turn to the right before he sees how spacious the house is.

We turned to the right, to the east, and Martina led me on as though through a forgotten museum long emptied of furnishings, deserted for years, stripped even of wallpaper, with bare uneven floors that creaked as we stepped across them. The inner hall was long and wider than the cell, its ceiling even higher but in proportion perfect. She made me look up at its plaster mouldings, a ring of large leaves with fleurs-de-lys between them designed to hold the chains of a chandelier, and all along the borders of the ceiling rows of simplified daisies about five inches in diameter, each with a button in its centre, for a corolla, and on its circumference petals which had long been obscured by frequent painting, done over and over again in the last hundred and thirty years. On our left was a staircase with curved banisters lit by a tall sash window, its upper half arched. Ahead of us there was a door ajar leading into a room larger than any we had seen in a private house, about thirty-six feet long and twenty-one wide. The room faced east. Its wide windows which reached almost to the ceiling held the last slanting of the morning sun and were draped, as they now are all summer and autumn, with the leaves and spidery tendrils of Virginia creeper. The leaves were red, and some of them yellow, all shades of translucent red and yellow, the more faded leaves half yellow, others with blends of pink remaining in them.

The room was in two parts, divided not by doors but by a high arch from which in the old days curtains were hung. There were double doors to our right, tall and wide, opening into a front room.

'This is your room for writing in,' Martina said.

She showed me four bedrooms upstairs and a narrow old-fashioned bathroom, and then we went down a stone staircase to the basement and into a vast kitchen, like a farmhouse kitchen. In one corner it had a little lift for food and dishes which you could pull up to the dining room by rope – two other rooms in the basement, cellars for wine and a scullery door opening onto the garden. The basement smelt of damp. Its walls were wet and sticky. It was too cold to stay long in it.

I remember the empty cold stillness inside and the warmth of the air as we shut the door behind us and walked along the terrace slowly looking at the trees, still in leaf, on our right, and at the long lawn beneath them which had been laid out in an eighteenth-century style with a cobbled semicircle leading to a lichened stone seat halfway along. The twenty-one houses on our left – ours is number twenty-two – seemed to lead like the side of a ship towards the open (but of course we saw houses as we came near its end, and knew we would). All the houses of the terrace are four storeys high with basements below a black railing, except ours which has only two above the basement.

I remember only moments of our first few days in the house and each of them was happy, an unusual thing in memory. I remember of course our first night there, the night interrupted often by the baby and by each other, and, after lying awake in the early morning, going downstairs alone into the garden which that day was lit by a reddish, rising sun.

The way down to our garden is indirect and like our front door confusing to strangers. You have to open two doors on the ground floor which lead out from the inner hall through the north wall. Both have wide glass panels, the inner one of stained glass, a delicate leaded design of apples with leaves made by our predecessor here, Charles Moore, who was well known in England and the continent for his church windows; the second has a plain glass window set in rectangles of wood. You cross a stone-flagged landing between these doors leaving on your left the staircase to the basement, also made of bare York stone, and come out on to an outer landing, protected by iron banisters which lead you down fourteen gradual steps of the same stone into the side garden where the rubble then lay.

I walked through that over a beautiful green – once a lawn but untended for years – and came to a pair of gates, old and wooden, and pushing them open found I was in Gloucester Crescent. It was lovely to explore this large garden which we had seen only from the windows and to smell the fresh air, for the air in the front of the house was smoky from the railway. Beside the gates there was a little wooden garage with a rusty latch, which I did not explore, and a little way away, with its back windows facing ours, a small two-storeyed building, old blackened brick, with a vent in its slated roof such as hay lofts have. We had looked out on it before of course and knew there were people living in it, but now that I stood by it I saw it had been built in harmony with the larger house, not back to back with it but at a gentle angle so that its back window, ten yards away, faced ours and opened into a funnel which spread onto the wide green garden now wild and unlooked after. The trees were beautiful too; between this little house and ours an elder with twisting branches, to one side a sycamore and beyond the garden in the distance many larger trees too far away for me to name. They grew in the other back gardens of Regent's Park Terrace and in the gardens of Gloucester Crescent – an older road that curves behind the terrace, forming a half moon. The people were asleep, curtains drawn, and I walked round to the front of their house. Their front court was paved in the late-Victorian mews style – a black composition cut in two-inch squares to prevent horses from slipping – and seeing that, I knew that this had been the stables and coach house which went together with the house we had just bought. There was room enough beside the loft for a coachman and family to live; it was easy for servants and grooms to walk to and fro from our scullery door, and at the edge of the lovely garden, through the old double gates, the coachman could drive his carriage round Gloucester Crescent to the front door that had by so many chances become our front door.

Between the mews and our house our landlords had placed a single strand of wire on posts to divide the funnel-shaped patch of ground into two, advising us to come to an agreement with our neighbours on the type of fence to be put up. We were standing by the wire one morning, thinking we would rather not have any kind of fence, when they appeared and introduced themselves in a curious, and I thought snobbish, manner, shaking hands across the wire. The young man said, 'I am a gentleman and this is Mrs Gentleman.'

By their faces I could see they were not joking and stopped myself from laughing just in time. Martina of course had heard properly. His name was David Gentleman. We soon made friends and together we pulled up the posts and put the wire away, agreeing to share the whole of that wild garden. But a week or two later we discovered that the garden was not ours. We had not examined the plans. Nor had David and Rosalind Gentleman. They thought the garden was common to both houses – ours and theirs. It was not. It had been detached by the ground landlord's pencil, who intended to cash in on it, which he did a year later by building a two-storeyed doll's house, Georgian style. It was coyly named 'The Little House' and what remained of the garden was covered with crazy paving. Our first feeling was sadness at the loss of a green space and then I was angry at the greed and meanness of it, that our landlord should dare to spoil a design conceived in the 1840s by Charles Oldfield who built the terrace and the northern end of Gloucester Crescent. The Little House did nothing to ease the housing shortage. It was bought by an aged and wealthy stockbroker who did not even like it, or at least he did not like the district, squalid as most of it is, nor the people in the better kept streets – the kind of people Marc wittily lampooned ten years later in his *Listener* cartoons *Life and Times in NW1*, so wittily that we could not give our address to anyone without evoking a guffaw.

When I first saw the faces in Bosch, Breughel, Hogarth – alive as they are – I thought they belonged to the past, found no resemblance in them to any living person. Then gradually I began to see those faces on buses, at auctions, in markets, at fairs. For me it has been the same with Marc's cartoons. When I first saw them I thought Simon and Joanna String-Along were brilliant inventions, but now, just as you frequently see Socrates, the prophet Isaiah, Hamlet, King Lear, Malvolio, Voltaire, Danton and Mirabeau walking down Parkway in modern dress with Ophelia, Lady Macbeth and the Second Mrs Tanqueray, so do I see the String-Alongs and their friends every day. I suppose we are String-Alongs too in our way, or at least we are on the fringe of that noticeable tribe, but neither of us ever felt we belonged to it, and in fact its members never were typical of this large postal district which is mostly poor. And then, we came to Camden Town long before Marc made us all look so funny.

It was far less swish in the 1950s while gentrification was slowly tightening its grip. There were numerous cheap boarding houses in Gloucester Crescent, only one of which has survived, and half the houses in Regent's Park Terrace were occupied by several families, one of which with dozens of beautiful children was Indian, believe it or not. (There was a little frisson a few years after they had been persuaded to leave when we let our flat to a Jamaican man and his wife.) It was the hopscotch chalk on the pavement, the young mothers with prams, the crowds of children playing on the lawn that confirmed Martina's eagerness to live in the terrace. She saw all the favours of tenement life without the squalor.

All newcomers to London or to a strange part of it are at a loss until they discover a place in the society of one of the little communities of which that vast city is made up, and this takes a long time because dividing lines are almost everywhere invisible. But Regent's Park Terrace is on the western boundary of a region which has physical limits on three sides. It faces the railway, over which there is only one bridge within a mile; to the north there is the canal, to the east a main road like a race track for cars which no one crosses unless he has to, and to the south Delancey Street which is not a boundary in the same sense but there is no reason for crossing it either, because there are no shops, churches or pubs on the other side of it for more than half a mile. The area so bounded covers half a square mile and contains only six streets or sections of streets, all within five minutes' walk of our house. Even this small part of Camden Town held in miniature much of London's life: commerce, industry, a great railway and a once great waterway.

I remember our first walk when we turned to the right from our front door into Oval Road. By the Camden goods yard where Jamestown Road meets Oval Road, we saw sooty buildings, barrows on the pavement, lorries loading and unloading, many people in railway uniform, or overalls or ordinary working clothes. It is always shapes and sizes at first. You cannot get to know anyone for months and you never get to know the insides of buildings unless by chance.

Probably Martina's liking for all this – the polygon factory, all brick and long windows, which had once made pianos, a crowded blind alley leading to the railway station, the first terminus of the London and Birmingham line, the canal behind it once magnificent but at that time choked with filth, Gilbey's large whisky store with its high rectangular chimney – probably her liking was more real than mine. She had worked in a factory and taught in a small school, which I had not.

A wonderful discovery that morning was the iron hump-back bridge which carries the Chalk Farm Road across the canal. There is a magnificent view from there of Camden Lock and its watergates, a high curved bridge for barge horses, the towpath, Dingwalls woodsheds and yards, which were then stacked with timber, and several Victorian warehouses beyond. But those were the days between the death of commerce and the start of 'pleasure craft'. It was like looking at a memorial of engineering which left daily work to be imagined.

August 5th, Tuesday

Yesterday morning I walked for miles in that maze of poor back streets between Camden Road station and the canal. Cloudy, drizzling, not drizzling, cloudy. Canal black, with plastic cups floating on it, potato-crisp bags, Kentucky chicken and, I think, a dead cat. Had one drink in the White Hart, bleakly reading *The Times* and contrasting the place to the old days of even ten years ago when I left the BBC, thinking, how much have I changed and how much the pub? Is it my attitude or the atmosphere of the place that makes it so bleak? Only one other customer and he was about as dilapidated as me. And it was people's lunch hour.

Physically the pub is still agreeable. It is even more roomy without the partition between public and private bars. The mirrors have not been moved. The old double doors leading into the back room are still there, their leafy-patterned glass with the same one crack. I pushed them open. The piano has gone. Chairs with red seats, square flimsy tables have been put in, all as new and rickety as can be. But we never used that room except for the Irish variety of honky-tonk on Saturday nights. The saloon bar has been made a bit less pleasant by brewers' wallpaper, zigzaggy reds and lemony yellows. They employ experts to choose it. You need sunglasses. But the old blackened rexine and mahogany settees in the window niches are still there; too heavy to move I suppose.

The beer, which turned sour when Paddy Gorham retired, was excellent and I wondered why until I spoke to the barman. I couldn't help it because he was dying for someone to talk to, the old ruin sitting in the corner being of the silent kind. He is Irish, a Kerry-man I guess from his quick speech, and he is cellarman. The new manager, Birmingham English, has nothing to do with the cellars any more.

I was distracted by the wallpaper at times during this barman's life history but remember how he started in the job at the age of sixteen when he came to Dublin, then Liverpool and London via Manchester. He retired when he was sixty-five and got the old-age pension.

– Retirement can kill you. I heard that on the radio. That's why I took this job. Mornings only.

He thought there would be people to talk to in the White Hart. When I told him how crowded it used to be at lunchtime, he was loyal to it and said

– Pubs aren't what they were . . . in the West End or anywhere.

I knew it wasn't true of the West End, where everywhere is packed with shop and office workers, nor of Camden Town.

I was one of many, I believe most, of the old habitués who

left the White Hart soon after the present manager took over, some of them dating like the lamp brackets from before Paddy's time. He was a tenant. I can't think why modern breweries grab the leases back when anyone dies or retires. Perhaps they make, or think they will make, more money, but the managers they appoint on miserable wages and some commission haven't half the interest in the job that tenants or free house owners have. This one did the brewers' training course in which he learned not how to manage beer but to be afraid of customers. A glance at the *Morning Advertiser* any day will show why – 'publican assaulted with broken bottle', and all the rest. It was often a bit rough in the White Hart but Paddy had a presence, could quell a quarrel by one look.

August 6th, Wednesday

I'm much better at writing and feeling for writing and generally too – even early morning anxieties have nearly gone, but powers of concentration, of endurance such as I had in the past haven't yet come back. Today and yesterday I got the fidgets at home after 2 hours (10 to 12) at my desk – and now as soon as I'm in the pub (Engineer) I wish I was elsewhere. I think I miss people, friends to drink with. Yet often I hate the voices of people around me in a pub.

Yesterday, going to Primrose Hill, an angry man I know by sight, his hair long enough to cover his neck, but sticking out grey under his cap – angrily – hair on end. Hair usually stands on end from fear, but fear and anger are close to each other. It's gooseflesh that makes each hair stand up. I have only seen it on the backs of dogs and cats, but Brewer quotes an awful description: 'When the executioner put the cords on his wrists, his hair, though long and lanky, of a weak iron-grey, rose gradually and stood perfectly upright, and so remained for some time, and then fell gradually down again.' In childhood we used to say 'Keep your hair on!' when anyone was in a bad temper. How did that begin? Wigs?

This morning I saw a person on the terrace lawn with a white plastic bag. It was cloudy – not the weather or the time of day for people usually to sit on the grass. I didn't want to be seen staring. I thought it might be not a person, but two plastic bags dumped there, one large and black. Glancing out later once or twice I was convinced it was bags of rubbish; it did not move. In fact it was asleep – the brownish-black part – with the small white bag beside it. I knew because just before I left the house at 12, I saw a man sitting up, his hands clasped round his knees, in a brown suit, his possessions around him. I expect he had slept there last night – about opposite the Brandons' old house. I was glad no one had accosted or objected to him. Several must have seen him as they got into their cars.

I thought he would speak to me. He looked at me as I passed on the terrace pavement – a face red with the wind and sun, long chin and nose, exceptionally thin, not much hair. Scraggy.

I remember Rumpus burning the wooden door under which a tramp had sheltered for several nights or weeks. Repairs were being done in the terrace at the time and the builders had put up a hut on the lawn leaving an old rejected door beside it. The tramp had made himself a lean-to by propping the door against the hut to protect himself from rain at night. It was he not the door that was unsightly.

And then there was Martina and our two coal-cellar lodgers. They moved into our empty cellars with their bags and rags during one of those summers which we spent in Greece with the children; one of the two six months' sabbaticals I had from the BBC on half pay. I can't remember which one but when we came back in the autumn, raving about the glorious sun, everybody told us it had been just as sunny here. That should identify it.

I only saw one of them. It was when I was at my desk in the front room early. I saw his back in dark clothes like sacking, his grey hair sticking out over his collar, as he came up the steps from the basement area and limped away fast, but Martina says they both used to go out early like people leaving for the City. She says both had dark suits. I think it was perhaps the coal dust that darkened their suits, but she knew them well and spoke to them often. They were not at all shy when she discovered them there.

Sometimes she looked into their cellars when they were out. We have two, each about the size of a single room in Rowton

House but without windows, only a coal hole in the arched brick roof, its iron ring rusty with damp above one's head. The doors are full-sized like the doors of a room and you can stand upright inside when the coal is low. The cellars reach all the way under the broad pavement outside our front door.

When the time came to order coal for the winter Martina warned them, telling them to find somewhere else to stay, but on the morning of the delivery their possessions were still there and she had to make two bundles of them tied with string. She was struck by the difference in their ways. The anthracite cellar was beautifully kept; the one for ordinary coal was always in a mess.

Most of the poor are swept away with the insane, out of sight and out of mind. In those days more of them were visible in the streets near here. There was one old man I remember with shame who spent his last years on a bench just across the road from the convent, within three minutes' walk of our house. If you rang the convent bell in those days and told them you were hungry a nun would push a sandwich through the grill. He lived on those and on cartons of tea from the garage slot machine on the other side of the crossroads from his bench, but his legs were weak and painful and he never went any farther. MacL. used to fetch his pension for him from the post office at the bottom of Parkway and sometimes a quarter of a bottle of whisky out of it. The old man died of exposure, halfway between the nuns and people like us, in bad winter weather. Some of us felt to blame. No doubt the nuns felt to blame. Any of us could have taken him in for the night. We don't.

August 7th, Thursday

A German woman perhaps 70 – stopped me near the Smoke School to ask the time – an excitable, amused, flushed face, with bright eyes looking straight at mine then turning away to laugh.

– Twelve? Is it really twelve? Then I must have had lunch at 11. I knew something was wrong. But that clock has stopped and that one is slow. No wonder my tummy's rumbling. What can I do now?

On my way back I saw her, talking to someone else in the same exciteable manner.

She greeted me again

– Is it true it's ½ past 12 now? I had my lunch at 11, etc. What can I do? I'll soon be hungry again. Where are you from?

– Camden Town.

– Where?

– Just round the corner.

– Oh, I meant where were you born.

– India.

– India, oh! (laughing) No, I can't go as far as that. I've been to Istanbul – but not as far as that.

It was a cold bright day. She wore a tweed cloak and thick skirt, stubby brown shoes, a big scarf over her. Every loose end flew as she ran across the street.

Sue Gentleman fetching Milly and Sarah from that school once asked us why we called it the Smoke School. It is couthie now, with windows clear as water; you can see the mild red of its old bricks and its white stone cornices are white again; you can touch the ornamented railings and high iron gates without getting your hands black with soot. Anyone too young to have known it in the steam train years would hardly believe that the children used to run about the playground and sit through their lessons at the sulphurous mouth of hell. Regent's Park Terrace was smoky too, at about the same distance from the railway, but Primrose Hill Primary and Infants school was built near the coaling station where dozens of engines waited their turn night and day, pouring smoke from their funnels into the acrid air above them. Like many other railway dwellers, we thought it too much for the children to eat soot at school as well as at home and gave them a rest from it in the daytime, and also a much longer morning and evening walk, by taking them to the next nearest school on the far side of Primrose Hill.

It was our children, at their push-chair age, who introduced us to the history of the railway. The sound of steam trains was so exciting that anyone of any age would stop to look, and crossing the bridge at the corner of Park Street and Oval Road as we frequently did on our way to Regent's Park we always stopped to hold the children up. They wanted to gaze until the next train came and we gazed too. Every now and then we heard the thunder of an engine driving uphill through the tunnel below us. We were enveloped in smoke for a moment, and when that had blown away we looked down at the rounded roofs of carriages until the guard's van emerged, then watched the long train till we could no longer see it. It climbed the hill slowly. The trains fill my heart with restless longings to this day.

One terminus of the line is Inverness about nine hundred miles away and only fifteen from the little town of Nairn on the Moray Firth where I had spent part of my childhood by the sea. The others are at Holyhead, Liverpool, Heysham and Glasgow where I had often boarded ships to Dublin or Belfast. I came to know two men who shared my longing to be carried away from where we stood. One, a broad, grey-headed bricklayer in a ragged overcoat, without a hat, spoke of Mallaig and the rough crossing of The Minch. Another, who appeared to be younger, but thin and ill-looking, neatly dressed in a stained macintosh that fitted him and an old trilby hat, had been a publican in Manchester. I made friends with both in the years that followed, and although they replaced their clothes in second-hand shops from time to time they kept to the same style of dress until they died.

The view to the north was undramatic along the wide expanse of rails, some gleaming, some rusty, between the woody gardens of old villas in Gloucester Avenue and Oval Road, to the distant hills which are now hidden by the massif of the Royal Free Hospital, but in those days with their mists and changing colours made one homesick for the countryside.

The view to the south is startling and entirely made by men. If you cross the road at the end of the bridge nearest to the park and go into a mews behind the old riding school of Park Village East you look down into a canyon forty foot deep whose sides are faced with brick. The Edinburgh Castle stands opposite to you, on the brink of a precipice, leaning a bit as though it is going to fall in, and below you like a river running down the steepest part of the descent to Euston there is the widest stretch of silvery shining lines I know. Only those near the bank that lead into the Rat Hole tunnel are dulled by infrequent use.

I went there today, after writing this, and found that the wall of the mews like the parapet of our bridge has been made much higher. You would have to bring a stepladder with you to see what we used to see. The reason for the high wall is, I think, that nowadays people aim bricks and bottles at the engine drivers' cabs. Perhaps they always did, but the long engine in front of him and the small lookout windows on each side gave the steam locomotive driver more protection.

If you are tall enough you can still see the Edinburgh Castle over the wall on a level with your eyes and as I looked at it today across the railway, much cleaner, better painted than it used to be, I remembered how it almost did fall in or at least the railway side of it and where the billiard rooms were, below Michael Donovan's bedroom. When he and his wife Norma noticed a crack in the wall above their bed, he put a pin into it, when the pin fell out a matchstick and when that fell out a biro pen. When the pen fell out he rang his landlords – British Railways – and the Edinburgh Castle was propped up again. This happened during the electrification of the line.

When the canyon was widened about a hundred years earlier all the houses on the west side of Mornington Terrace, whose gardens looked down on the line, were demolished, except for the pub and its twin, a private house. These were supported by an enormous girder which stretched like a bridge above the trains. It got in the way of the electric wires and was removed. I don't think it was put back again, but something else was done in the end to keep the two lonely survivors upright.

This railway was the first to enter London, but to begin with it came no farther than Camden Town, the huge goods station two hundred yards from our house which was built in 1836 as the terminus of the London and Birmingham Railway. The speculators chose Camden Town for the terminus because Parliament had refused the permission they asked for to pull down houses and extend the line all the way across East London to the docks. They did not expect many passengers, but knew that their speedy carriage of freight would defeat the slow business of the canal. The Regent Canal had large warehouses and wharfs at Camden Town and beside these the railway company bought all the adjoining land for the transference of goods from Birmingham on to barges bound for the docks.

Two years later the London and Birmingham Railway Company succeeded in pushing through Parliament an Act permitting them to extend the lines as far as Euston Grove. All their activities, backed by big money as the motorway promoters are backed now, provoked opposition, sometimes violent, from landowners, and vain protests from people living in houses nearby.

The Railway Acts of Parliament ordered householders and farmers to let surveyors into their houses or land. Few knew the law and most of those who did ignored it. Anyone carrying a theodolite or plumb line was treated as a burglar or poacher, threatened by armed gamekeepers, harassed by landlords' tenants so fearfully that in one place 'the survey was only accomplished by night, by the aid of dark lanterns'. Even the great Robert Stephenson, who was said to have walked twenty-seven times over the proposed line, was scared away by Lord Sefton's men. Lord Denby's men threatened to duck him in the pond and 'guns were discharged over the grounds belonging to Captain Bradshaw'.[1]

Near Mornington Crescent while the Euston extension was being planned Robert Stephenson's surveyors were threatened with arrest by the headmaster of a school, on the corner of the great coach road to the north of England, now called the Hampstead Road, under which the railway was to run.

[The] annex of one storey, a hall or a breakfast room, with a flat-leaded roof, lay in the very centre of the line . . . it was necessary repeatedly to invade this gentleman's premises to cut holes in his garden-wall, and to make use of his very convenient 'leads' as a station for the theodolite. For the sake of . . . despatch the surveying party always carried a short and handy ladder. It was legal but it could hardly have been very agreeable for the worthy tutor who advanced towards the intruders. The amazed schoolboys, delighted with the 'lark', crowd in a semicircle; the half-scared, half-indignant mistress appears at an adjoining window; the pretty daughter makes good use of her fine eyes on the floor above; the giggling servants crowd on tip-toe in the yard below.

'Who are you, sir, and how dare you come on my leads?'

'Sir, I am an assistant of Mr Robert Stephenson, and I am engaged on a survey for the Euston-grove extension of the London and Birmingham Railway.'

'How dare you to climb up there, and to have the impertinence to look through my windows?'

'If you will have the kindness to look at this book, sir . . . This is an Act of Parliament by virtue of which . . .'

'Once and for all, will you leave my premises immediately?'

'I regret that my duty forbids me to do so, sir, but we will be rapid in our work . . .'

'Then sir, I shall instantly send for a policeman.'

'Perhaps that will be the most satisfactory course, sir.'[2]

Judging from Robert Stephenson's plan, which marks the doomed houses, I believe this happened at Mr Jones's Classical and Commercial Academy where Dickens added scraps to his meagre education when he arrived in London at the age of eleven in 1823 and lived for a while at Camden Town. He went back to look at his school in the autumn of 1851.

We went to look at it, only last Midsummer, and found that the railway had cut it up root and branch. A great trunk line had swallowed the playground, sliced away the schoolroom, and pared off the corner of the house: which, thus curtailed of its proportions, presented itself, in a green stage of stucco, profilewise towards the road, like a forlorn flatiron without a handle, standing on end.[3]

The walls Dickens saw have long since been sealed, but from the top of a bus, as it crosses the Hampstead Road bridge over the railway, you can still see the chopped-off shapes of the houses which remain.

Anyone whose dwelling is threatened by motorway plans can understand the struggle of wills that went on here in the 1830s. Landowners stood to gain from the building of the railway; they demanded excessive prices for their land and got them in the end. Yet naturally they hated the intrusion, the mess and noise of the works which they knew would continue for years, the splitting of fields, the spoliation of past and present. Merchants and farmers welcomed the railway so long as it did not come too near. The transport of goods by wagon between Birmingham and Camden Town took three and a half days and cost much more than the four hours by rail. In summer meat, fish and vegetables were putrid before they reached a distant market.[4] As passengers, too, even diehard opponents were quick to use the first trains, for stagecoaches, which had been welcomed for speed by that same generation, were forbidding: the jolting and crowded stuffiness within made people ill; only two on each side could look out of the windows; outside passengers were unable to move in frost, snow or rain; and any man young enough to ride a long distance preferred to hire a horse for himself at each eight or twelve mile stage. It was quieter, and riding keeps one warm.

The third-class railway carriages were crowded too, and roofless, exposing everyone not only to the weather but in long tunnels such as the one at Primrose Hill, just outside Camden Town, to red-hot coals and choking smoke, but hundreds of people put up with that for the sake of speed and novelty. Some even stood on the roofs of the first- and second-class carriages and lay down when they saw a tunnel ahead. Each train had two guards to prevent that peril, but they could not cope with all the daring passengers.

The two long tunnels at Primrose Hill and Kilsby had been made with difficulty and much loss of life, but the 'Euston Grove Extension', as the last mile was called, was said to be the greatest feat of engineering on the line – not mainly because of the exceptional depth of the cutting but from the gluey nature of the soil.

One mile of the Railway, between Euston Grove and Camden Town, has four lines of rails [it now has many more]. The passenger passes under several very handsome stone and iron bridges and galleries; the most extensive of which are under the Hampstead Road and Park Street. The whole of this length is excavated from the London clay; and the walls which form the sides are curved, in order to resist the inward pressure; they are as much as three bricks thick at the top and seven at the bottom; the number of bricks used in forming these gigantic walls was about sixteen million.[5]

The walls of the embankment, like the roof of Chalk Farm tunnel, which is nearly a mile long, were exposed to the 'creep' – a slow semi-liquid movement of the London clay – '. . . on the line of the resistance of the inverted arch'. Yet the clay is so hard that it could only be loosened by pickaxe. To cut through it was almost as expensive as cutting through rock and required more skill because the slant at which this clay would hold fast depended on its dryness when cut through: it 'has been made to stand at one to one, and has slipped at one to three'. The angle of repose was sought by trial and error.

The number of men and horses employed between our bridge and Dickens's school was prodigious and the number of accidents shocked contemporary observers. Navvies were notorious for reckless daring; young men would compete with each other in taking awful risks. At the Kilsby tunnel, near the Birmingham end of the line, 'two or three of the workmen were killed trying to jump one after another across the mouth of the shafts, in a *game* of "Follow my leader" '.[6]

But most accidents were caused by dangerous methods of work and by the hasty ruthlessness of contractors. On a deep cutting, such as that of the Euston Extension through Camden 'Bank' or hill, it was sometimes necessary to cause a landslide in order to widen the first opening which had been made by pick and shovel. The almost vertical face was undermined at the bottom, sharpened iron piles driven into the top until the section fell. This method was fairly safe if six or twelve feet were done at a time, but 'as more money can be earned by bringing down large falls of earth, a dangerous height is often adopted; and then men new to that form of work are frequently killed or permanently injured, by being caught under such falls.' Such accidents 'result from ignorant or avaricious mismanagement'.[7]

If the lie of the land permitted it, terraces called 'gullets' were made, step by step down, as the work went on, and tramways laid, along which the stuff could be drawn in trucks by horses to level ground at the end of the hill where it could be tipped out; but the Camden Town cutting, being deep and long, with a road and houses at either end, required a more dangerous method. Every bit of sticky clay, as heavy and more difficult to handle than rock, had to be drawn up to the top of the embankment in wheelbarrows. Only when the level of the permanent way was reached could tramways be laid and clay thrown into trucks by men with shovels. Till then the 'horse-barrow run' was used.

Planks were laid up the sides of the cutting to take the wheel of the barrow. These were called runs and the men who did the running – running up the plank and balancing the barrow as they ran – were always chosen from the young and most courageous of the navvies. Each wore a specially made belt round his waist with a rope attached to it. Out of sight at the top of the hill the other end of the rope was harnessed to a horse which, at a shout to show that he was ready, pulled him up as it was driven across the field on top. If the runner slipped off his plank, as many did in wet weather, his tumbling barrow fell on top of him; its contents imperilled the pick-and-shovel men below and unless someone saw him in time to stop the horseman, he was hauled, feet or head first or sideways, up the rough face of the cutting.

In working horse-barrow-runs, many men are seriously wounded and lamed, but it is principally thus: Strange men are anxious to try their hand at this, to them, new kind of work; and Englishman-like, the danger is its recommendation. They take hold of the barrow, get up a portion of the height, and then lose confidence, fall off, and are frequently seriously hurt; but still, 'it is the men's own fault'.

The engineer who made this statement, in 1845, was attacking railway contractors and directors who answered every criticism with 'it is the men's own fault'.[8] The runners' speed was controlled by the horses' on the way up, but freed from the rope some raced each other down with their empty barrows in an even more dangerous manner. The 'runs' were in sight of each other, fifteen or twenty yards apart. A contemporary engraving shows three at Camden Town which were almost perpendicular.

Navvies were reckless in their leisure too. Generalizations that were made about them are excusable because they came and went on to the next job in hordes, shared hardships and pleasures peculiar to their homeless life, helped each other in adversity, had a strong sense of justice, were loyal to the gang and to fair employers, and fiercely violent against those who cheated them of food or pay. Frederick Williams, praising the tact of a fellow engineer who settled what we now call an industrial dispute, said it was only 'such a decisive and judicious course that kept that mass of men from one of those scenes of rage, drunkenness, fighting and debauchery, which made them, in many cases, a terror to the people of the neighbourhood.'[9]

People feared them by repute. Some barred all doors and windows long before they arrived after tramping the roads for days with their shouldered picks and shovels and their camp followers. There was always a shortage of women. Some kept to one man at a time; others were attached to several. Many residents dared not go out in the evenings however well behaved the gang was during its long stay. They were like an invading army, but without discipline, tents, billeting officer, or commissariat, and, once settled in quickly built shacks or crowded into lodgings at the little cottages of the poor who welcomed a share in their wages, they invented their own leisure pastimes without direction, sympathy or help. They were constantly cheated by the holding back of wages and by the truck system.

Frederick Williams, who worked with them, wholly admired them.

> The navvies of Britain are distinguished by extraordinary power of body, and energy, perseverance, and courage of mind . . . and frequently manifest more courage than is to be found among any other race on the face of the globe; to which is often superadded cunning, which appears as characteristic of the race as shrewdness is of the Scot, and wit of the native of the sister isle.[10]

They were in no sense a race. Their vast numbers were made up of hordes of individuals of diverse parentage and background who found themselves sharing a common lot. The only men among them who had inherited a tradition were the fenmen from Lincolnshire and Cambridgeshire – the original navigators whose forebears had for generations been employed in similar work: drainage of swamps, reclamation of land from the sea and digging canals. The others came from all over Great Britain and Ireland, attracted by a chance, unique in their lifetimes, of knowing for certain where to find work – for the railways began during the depression of the 1820s and 1830s and partly eased the terrible distress among farmworkers that caused the 'Labourers' Revolt' of 1830. The majority of English casual farm workers were migrants anyway, tramping from place to place in search of seasonal work. Small farmers and fishermen from Ireland crossed the sea every year at harvest time. Fishermen and labourers from the Highlands of Scotland took their own roads to the Lowlands or England, the same roads, every year, trying farms where they were known, if they were old enough to have done it before. The Welsh did the same, seeking work in the English Midlands. When railway work began many stayed on and were away from home for years. The anonymous shifting gangs were a refuge too for people in debt and some who had committed crimes. Most of the navvies had nothing to hide but all lost the normal ties of village and home. They even lost their names.

> . . . from the nature of their employment . . . and utterly neglected state [they] have names, laws and customs, common exclusively to themselves. Many never hear their real names pronounced, but are entered in the contractors' books, and spoken of and to, as Gipsy Joe, Fancy Bob, Bellerophon, Fisherman, Fighting Jack, Brammagem, Long Sam, etc., etc. They have a marriage ceremony, which consists of the couple jumping over a broomstick, in the presence of a room full of men, met to drink upon the occasion, and the couple are put to bed at once, in the same room. I have known an instance of one woman, not twenty years of age, so married to six different men in less than three months.[11]

Doctors, engineers, lawyers, journalists and other professional people whose work brought them close to the navvies were able to give independent accounts of what went on. It was they, who had nothing to gain, and the navvies chosen for interrogation, who had nothing to lose, who between them provided evidence against employers which led, too slowly, towards reform. It was they who showed to parliamentary committees of inquiry that the system of contracts with severe time limits, of sub- and sub-subcontracts issued to get-rich-quick firms formed the root of evil. Their evidence convinced the government in the end that that was the cause of the loose and violent manners of the railway workmen. Ill-housed and often half-starved, deprived for weeks on end of wages due to them, they had to rob or beg with threats. Their normal working day was twelve hours but many did double or triple shifts of twenty-four or thirty-six hours, with only one hour for meals which usually included a long walk to a truck shop where they were overcharged on credit. When they were ill there was usually no way of getting medical help.

> Government interference may be objected to, on the ground that public works are not conducted in a worse manner now than formerly; but society having advanced in civilisation, this argument cannot be received . . . Can the crime, disease and danger now attendant on public works be abated?[12]

> No man cares for them; they labour like degraded brutes; they feed and lodge like savages . . . Being in a strange district they are only accommodated so long as they can pay and as there is no hospital provided for them when they are sick, they are thrust forth into the lanes and fields to shift for themselves or die . . . I have seen men with small-pox thick upon them wandering about in the lanes, having no place of shelter to go into.[13]

A missionary met a woman who asked him if he had been to pray for her man. She had been with the navvies for six years, 'and he is the twenty-ninth man I have laid out, and the first of them who died a natural death'.

The contractors and railway company directors made much of drunkenness and recklessness as the main cause of casualties which exceeded in percentage the official killed and wounded returns for the four battles of Talavera, Salamanca, Vittoria and Waterloo. Independent observers witnessed many accidents due to drunkenness but their evidence proved that most falls were caused by overwork. Drivers of tip trucks and men riding on the load to the tipping place were killed or maimed because they could not keep awake. They fell off, onto the tramway to be crushed by iron wheels, or down the whole height of the embankment. Often the whole train of heavily laden trucks was derailed because of badly laid tramways, and all, with its men and horses, would tumble to the bottom. One of the surgeons gave a ghastly list of broken spines and severed limbs for which no medical attention was available. Anyone killed outright was fortunate.

From what I have read, it seems to me that the dangers of horse-barrow runs were thought to be unavoidable. And of course it is easy to have hindsight a century and a half later. But tramways could have been laid from top to bottom of the embankment to take four-wheeled trucks hauled by rope and horses in the same way as the wheelbarrows. This would certainly have saved much labour. The truth may be that same truth which in the end persuaded Parliament to interfere, that labour was cheap, that the maimed and dead could be replaced within an hour, but that machinery needed capital expenditure and caused delay. A navvy's life was less valuable than a slave's.

Widows and incapacitated men were sent back, under the poor law, to seek support financed by the innocent ratepayers of their home parish. Employers had no liability. Chadwick believed that the 'principle of pecuniary responsibility' would prevent accidents and increase the real value of labour.[14]

Dangerous methods and equipment would be shunned if employers had to pay compensation for every man killed or wounded in any accident avoidable or unavoidable. This principle, applied to the shipper of pauper emigrants, had secured for every fatal casualty 'at least one sincere mourner'. 'Self-interest is the most constant – the most uniform – most lasting, and most general feeling.'

The abolition of the slave trade, the Factory Acts and the Catholic Emancipation Act of Great Britain, and also the first beginnings of an effective political fight against English oppression in Ireland, took place during the lifetimes of canal and railway navvies; and all were inspired and carried through by people who had no motives of gain. The three men who initiated laws intended to improve the railway navvies' lives were a surgeon, an engineer and a lawyer.

August 8th, Friday

I was sitting outside the Spread Eagle yesterday morning when Beryl Bainbridge passed. It was sunny and she looked nice – she has such an open, friendly face and manner, easy-going, but intensely interested in everything around her and in what people say. I had nothing to say except to offer her a drink. She wouldn't have one but sat down beside me on one of those spindly white chairs. After the 'How are you?' and the 'And you?', she said

– How are your boys?

I didn't want to give a description of their lives at present and said

– All right, I think. There's only one at home now.

She said

– Children are a nuisance. I've only one at home now, but she fell off a bus and broke her skull.

I thought of telling her how I broke my skull when I was 21, but thought that would be long and boring. But it did worry me. I thought how serious it is even though many recover perfectly as I did.

I said.

– Is she all right now?

Beryl said

– She drank a cup of vodka. She's 15. A whole cup and fell off the bus. She's perfectly all right. She came home from hospital, dyed her hair green, and off again.

She told this in an amusing way as though she was amused but without diminishing the serious implications she made her concern apparent – fear for her daughter's future I imagine to be among them. Her words, as I have just put them down, may sound like the brave Englishwoman – Mrs Trowbridge's 'silly old hysterectomy', Mrs Jolly's 'trifling cancer' – but they weren't a bit like that.

Beryl left with her packet of papers for the Photocopy place. 'I must get these photocopied' followed almost as one sentence after the green hair bit.

When she had gone I wished I had said something about her *Bottle Factory*. We had been sitting opposite it – G. Belloni & Co. Limited is over a gate large enough for the Italian juggernauts to back into but, the funny thing is, I think of her book in all sorts of places, not when I'm watching Belloni activities from the spindly chairs. Her *Bottle Factory* is such a lively, funny book. I have vivid memories of its people and places. I liked *Harriet Said* even more but both were spoiled at the end for me by improbable murders. I haven't read the others. But it seems to me in these early ones as though someone had told her 'you must end your novels with a murder'. That's what I wished I had asked her. She walked back from the launderette a week or two ago with four or five pillows hanging from her shoulder, chanting 'Pillows! Pillows! Pillows! Anybody want old pillows!'

I went to the post office for money – a fat forceful woman, sixtyish, edging her way in front of people in the queue, fully fleshed but with angular features like Mrs Gandhi, a roll of fat at the neck and two under each oxter at the back of her sleeveless dress. Her grey hair tied not in a pony- but a cart-horse tail, long, bushy, tapering in a few straggly strands. Some coloured plastic threads round it.

Outside the post office, on the pavement step of the closed-down cinema – a low step, six inches I guess, and obviously uncomfortably low to sit on – there was Davy Sloan – 'Tipsy Davy'. His face is still very thin. I asked him how he was.

– Not very well, Davy.

I have only once heard him say that before.

It is his leg.

– I should 'a been in the Royal Free at 9 o'clock this morning.

I reminded him of the morning I tried to take him.

– I remember it well. I'll never forget it, Davy. I'll no' forget your kindness. You know, an alcoholic is a very difficult person. Ye canna dae anything wi' him. I might say I'll go and I'll fully intend to go. But I must have a drink before I go.

I remembered that part of it too – a drink, then another bottle and another. It starts because of the shakes and the hangover.

I said

– I think you are scared.

– Oh, Davy! I am that scared I canny go. There's one trouble too – they can do nothing for ye when ye're drunk – send ye away.

– Can you walk on it? I said.

– Five yards. Then I must sit down.

– Does it hurt much?

– Sometimes I am crying with the pain. It has opened up again.

– If I go with you now, will you go to the hospital?

– I canny, Davy. Ye understand.

– But if you wait till you collapse, you'll be taken there – it'll be much worse.

– I know.

I am surprised he has lasted so long. It was in February, I think, that there was talk of amputating the leg.

Mary came up to us.

– Coo-ee Coo-ee. . . , and laughing.

– Have ye such a thing as a cigarette?

I reminded her that I'd given them up.

– Oh, aye, ye gave them up.

Davy had taken a butt from his pocket for himself and was waiting for a light. Seeing that I was about to go, he asked me for some money. He seldom asks, but always accepts it if I offer. Once or twice when he has stopped me in the street I've said

– I have no money.

– I'm no' asking ye for money.

A humiliating reproof.

I had £50 on me, but only about 17p in change. I gave him that. He needed 8p more. I said

– I can't. I've no change.

And as I walked away I was full of regrets wishing I had stayed to talk with him longer, very much wishing I had given him a pound. Felt mean. In the evening (Thursday) Ben saw an ambulance in the market near the Mixer, and a man on the ground and a lot of bloody handkerchiefs.

I think he would have recognized Davy – if it was Davy – but it is difficult if the man is lying on the ground.

I asked Ben later. It was a big man, like an Irish builder's labourer, he said.

I have known Mary and Davy for at least twenty years but only been on speaking terms with him since Christmas Eve in 1975, I think, or 1976. Whichever it was, it was sunny and freezing, too cold for snow. When Mary first spoke to me, years before that, she asked for sixpence or whatever the fare then was to Euston. The times were very hard on her, but if only she could get to Euston she would be all right. Some long etceteras after that made me think she had the return half of a ticket. It was nearly seven and the Glasgow train, which I often travelled on, went at half past. Next evening she was there again in Parkway asking me for the sixpence again with the same pleading lament. I thought her forgetful and stupidly unskilled in begging until I discovered that she meant what she said. She spends the night in Euston Station when places less exposed to police harassment are denied to her.

Davy never begged from me in those days and she seldom hooked me, because I used to walk fast to the bus stop and from it after work, but when I left the BBC I began to dawdle in the streets of Camden Town – so many funny shops crop up and die. There's one now with flowery bidets, a long gilded snake with a wide rose nozzle fitted to a porcelain showerbath, several sets of elaborate brass taps, and a square bath, the kind you have to sit up in, like the one in my Rue du Cotentin flat long ago but grander. Anyway, I was staring dreamily at something like that on a Christmas Eve when Davy came up to me and said that the off-licence was shut and would I go into the pub and get some cider. He had some little coins in his hand to encourage me. They are not allowed in anywhere and only into one café that I know of. I got the cider and some Guinness for myself and we went to drink it on a bench near the Buck's Head where in those days they liked to sit in the sun facing the end of Inverness Street market. No market that day. Beautiful sun, but weak. Hardly any traffic in the Chalk Farm Road in front of us. Mary and Davy were surprised that I felt cold. They spend their lives in such places.

It was on that bench that morning that Davy and I, between Mary's jealous interruptions, discovered to each other that we had spent much of our childhood near Inverness. He was born in a van on the Black Isle and spent his boyhood travelling on the roads of northern Scotland, and I spent much of mine at Nairn where my grandmother lived, wandering whenever I got the chance in the Grampians. My grandmother's windows looked out on the Black Isle about seven miles away across the Moray Firth, and black it was unless the sun shone on it. He knew Nairn harbour well – my boyhood treasure trove – and the danger signal there. He remembers landing fish on the quay, 'fresh fish for London in time for the night train from

Nairn', and I told him how my grandmother used to harangue the fishmonger, saying that his fish was yesterday's. 'All the fresh fish goes to London,' she said.

Davy's father dealt in scrap iron and could have 'bought the whole of Ross and Cromarty', but never a penny for the younger children. Davy would not go near him, now, for a thousand pounds, nor he near Davy for two pinheads. It was a large family. They travelled all the time, too many of them, and most of the children had to leave the van as soon as they were able to fend for themselves and too old to sell clothes pegs or beg with a childish appeal. Davy went fishing with the drifters and to Lowestoft and Yarmouth with the herring fleet. He went fruit and pea picking in the Lowlands and in England. He did hundreds of jobs in dozens of places, but says he would not have taken a steady one even if it came his way. It's more difficult, I think, for gipsies to fit into 'systems'. Davy gave up work gradually, as though by chance, while he was still in his thirties. He has forgotten most of his Romany, but often speaks travellers' cant with Mary and switches to English when he remembers that I cannot understand.

Neither he nor Mary has ever lived in a house, unless the derelict buildings they squat in can be called houses. Her parents' van was based in Paisley. They were tinkers and so she shares most of Davy's traditions. She was married for a while but doesn't know where her husband 'gae'd his way' to. She has gone about with Davy off and on ever since. I don't know the extent of their intimacy, but he treats her like a lover, takes care of her, is kind and humorous in his ways with her. In the old days, when I offered him money for drinks, he would say

– Give it to Mary. She's the paymaster.

One other morning when we met, on the bench outside the convent in February two years later, he whispered to me that she had 'the horrors'.

– Well, ye canny leave her alone.

She was trying to roll a cigarette from the tobacco I gave her. He watched her for a while with an amused but serious expression as one would watch a child determined to solve a puzzle, then took it from her laughing and made it properly with his steady hands. Hers were shaky with cold and hangover.

– She always gets it the wrong way round, sticky side out.

She was confused that morning but without pretence and her voice was soft and pleasant to listen to, as it always is when she's sober. To me she said

– Davy, could ye lend Davy one pound?

He changed the subject laughing, but all our talk for an hour was punctuated by

– Could ye lend Davy 10p, £2, 40p? all separately, and to her Davy

– Could we no' get a bottle of wine?

He told her he thought I didn't like wine and remembering the cheap sherry they buy I said

– Not much. It's too sweet.

– It's too sweet for him, Mary.

– Too sweet, she said absent-mindedly, and went on saying 'Too sweet' from time to time to herself.

Before we parted I gave him a pound, his so-called fee for the interview. I had put it in an unsealed envelope because I knew he was doing a suspended sentence for begging at the time. He liked the envelope and kept turning it over and said, without looking inside it

– I'll use that.

I told him to use the inside of it, anyway. He looked inside, much amused, as he is by almost everything, as he had been a few minutes earlier when I thought the 'green-liner' which stopped at the traffic lights near us was a school bus. It was, he told me, the toughest kind of prison van. He had ridden in one and advised me not to. He had broken into an off-licence once when drunk.

– He got into bad company, said Mary, He's no' that kind.

Which is true. I believe he has never been 'Drunk and Disorderly', but all the little begging and 'Drunk in a Public Place' offences are added up and he has to spend some days in gaol occasionally. In Parkway, the other day, a policeman caught him begging from a lady and came to charge him with it. The lady said

– I have just paid him for these postcards, and took two new postcards from her handbag.

August 9th

Mary came to the door. The burns on her face have healed up
– small marks only – and she looks well, weatherbeaten, older
than most townspeople look at 48. But both legs now have
ulcers that won't heal, both bandaged and seen to once a week
at Kentish Town Health Centre, and now her hand has a
festering cut, unbandaged, from a rusty nail on a boarded-up
house she was trying to break into to kip. I asked about Davy
and she shook her head

– I'm worried. D'ye think he'll live through? He's 56. Two
bottles of wine and he's drunk again.

She talks like a White Ribboner about him but you look for
the white teetotal bow on her dress and find none, he about
her like a Wee Free minister one of whose flock has strayed.

I asked if she was still taking her pills. She showed them to
me a fortnight ago, taking them out of her small plastic bag,
a spongebag she had found, blue and pretty. That was why
she showed them. She wanted me to look into it and see her
hairbrush, mirror, facecream – surprisingly dainty things. Now
she has lost the bag and the pills with it.

August 10th

Mary, dancing three steps on the Windsor Castle doormat
attracted by Irish jig on juke box and to tease the landlord,
didn't see me. Black stockings today hide, for the first time,
the leg bandages. She would always wear black stockings if
she could get and hold them, but everything she has in the
morning is destroyed or lost at night because she's nearly
always drunk by then, and in rough places. She wears
something different every day, mostly from charities such as
the WVS whose wardrobes she searches for stylish things, but
sometimes from private houses. She is well known in NW1
and NW3 and two or three women whose doorbells she rings
occasionally fit her out in almost new creations of the haute
couture. Last week when she called here in a new-looking long
red coat, I said

– Where do you keep all your coats?

She has many of them, of which the one she stole from Martina is the best. (The stolen one is never mentioned now. I raged at her, shamed her, made her cry, when I found out, complained to her so strongly about her unfriendliness that that's enough of that.) She took it from the hall peg while Tim was in the kitchen making her a sandwich. But then she's so forgetful – or is it 'innocence'? – that she turned up in it a few days later. I had told M. I could easily get it back, but by then it had a burn in it as big as a saucer and a long rent near the skirt. M. is really distressed but says Mary can't help taking stylish clothes – she's so dressy.

Mary has been in Camden Town much longer than Davy. She came from Glasgow when she was 18, worked as a char in the Park Street pubs, the Dublin, the Spread Eagle and the Britannia which is now a TV, etc., shop, on the corner of Camden High Street.

August 11th, Monday

Sitting on pavement – a change I think in Camden Town. Can't remember anyone doing it in our early days here. Now young people do – if waiting for a friend, and outside Spread Eagle drinking (there were no tables in the old days and now the few there are are not enough). Old people sit on the market pavement, especially on Sunday mornings and on summer evenings when the shops are closed.

The winos, including Davy and Mary, have found a real 'grandstand' – a huge wooden beam in front of the old ladies lav by the traffic lights at the bottom of Parkway. Here they sit in the middle of the road facing the Camden High Street traffic. When the green man starts walking, two streams of pedestrians cross the road in front of them within touching distance. But they do not touch. They greet me loudly, and I suppose a few others they know. (The lav has been closed for years – some sort of underground work.)

I used to compare the winos with animals in their awareness of the weather, in the way they always find the most sheltered place – but unless they must shelter, say at the Arlington Road side of the cinema, they prefer to be somewhere where many cars and people are passing. The Camden Town crowd at least do not like to sit drinking in the park. They stand or sit on plastic milk crates close together, passing the bottle from one to another.

M. spoke of the ones in Whitechapel sitting in a circle on a blitzed site, passing the bottle round. I don't think Mary would like that. She likes to see plenty going on about her. For that Camden Town is ideal. But twice she has said to me

– I don't like to always be in the same place. I like to get up King's X way or Kentish Town.

In this sunless summer when most people look pale the winos appear to be glowing with health – even Davy in spite of his leg.

August 12th, Tuesday

About 1 o'clock Davy called to me on the bridge. He was opposite Henlys garage, and had seen me from the seats where he was sitting with Mary. He was trying to cross the road, but I went over to him when the traffic let me. My first words were

– How are you? meaning his leg.

The real concern with which he answered

– How are *you*?

I told him I wasn't very happy.

– Why is that? as though it was impossible to imagine.

There by the curb on the pavement he spoke about the hospital – complaining about Mary visiting him drunk.

– That's no good. You know, there's only four in a ward. They don't like it.

Again he has walked out before the operation. He says it's her fault.

He crossed himself repeatedly, from below the chin and across his chest.

– There's only one thing for me – they'll have to measure me.

Without stooping he drew the shape of a coffin in the air above the pavement.

– It'll be that way. I'll see to it that it's that way.

I said

– Are you telling me you're going to kill yourself?

– I am only saying what will happen.

He went on for a long time about his hatred of those places, how he'd rather die than go in again. I said nothing. Then, entirely without prompting, he said

– Will ye meet me at those seats at 9 o'clock tomorrow morning?

I told him I would be there but he wouldn't, or if he was it would be like last time.

– I was in company by the cinema. On those seats – no company. I'll be there.

August 14th, Thursday

We had dinner on Tuesday at Diane's and Jimmy's with Paul Barker and wife who liked my seal book and *Woodbrook* respectively – had taken them to read on holiday.

As we left I asked Diane to drive me and Davy to the Royal Free at 9 next day.

She came here at 10 to 9. We sat in her car opposite the seats from 5 to 9 till 9.15. At first there was no one. Then a girl sat there – for a long time alone. I wondered why. Many people passed us on the pavement – mostly girls – going to work. That very tall girl who I once thought so attractive (just as she did), in the Dublin, came by looking earnest. They were all hurrying, uninterested, as one is, in anything except catching the bus. The place is leafy, the road damp and black from last night's rain.

Diane saw a man with a black sack approaching the seats. I got out to investigate. He crossed the road towards me on the island. No. I wished we had been sitting on the seats instead of the airless cramped car. Diane so patient and nice – to make me feel better about keeping her hanging about, said she loved sitting in the car.

– No telephone, she said, peace and quiet.

I said the off-licence would be open by now and if Davy got there – that was that. She suggested driving past it and we went down Parkway, turned left into Arlington Road and back by Glos. Crescent to opposite the seats. The girl had gone. A young man was at the end seat. No one else. And Davy had not been among the winos outside the Bingo – the only ones we saw on two rounds. At about 20 to 10, we gave up but had a long last look while Diane was getting petrol.

I went to the launderette and home with the stuff, looked at the seats again about one o'clock – none of them there. The bushes have grown high and thick – one with long cone-shaped purple flowers – the winos don't leave much mess here. Maybe it's cleared more thoroughly than the cinema, etc., by the roadsweeper. He was there with me, lingering a long time. One empty cider bottle by the railway wall.

After 2 p.m. on my way back from the Edin. the whole middle seat – there are 3 – was occupied by winos, rows of bottles at their feet – Davy at the lowest end, Mary beside him, all the other faces familiar to me. On the previous day he had said to me, when I gave him 20p,

– Don't give any money to that crowd if they come knocking on your door.

I was angry and more so when I thought of Diane and car, and said

– You didn't turn up.

He swore he'd been there waiting for me at 9.15. And in the old way of schoolboys in class, he said to a friend

– Wasn't I here? and the friend confirmed it strongly.

Martina thinks he'll outlive us all – and even now he has proved the doctors wrong. I mean he is still walking about on that leg that they threatened to cut off if he did not let them put a new pin in it.

August 19th, Tuesday

The old lame man who goes to the Spread Eagle doesn't easily
get up from his chair. He asked a young man to get him a
pint, gave him a pound, expecting change. The bar was
crowded on a Sunday lunchtime. The young man went
through into the big bar (the public bar) and did not return.

August 20th, Wednesday

Mike Ronan told me a parable. He had a very deaf woman
patient whose eyes were improving, when she left him and
didn't return for several months. When she did come back she
looked much younger. He thought she had had a face lift.
Her ear specialist had been prescribing stronger and stronger
hearing aids for years, until one day when she rang up for an
appointment, she was told that he had dropped dead. A young
American doctor took his place, and reduced the strength of
the hearing aid, more and more as time went on. Her hearing
improved. Her appearance improved. As she left Mike, she
said
    – You gave me a very strange look when I came in.
    – I thought you had had a face lift.
    I know I could improve my hearing by concentrating better
but to concentrate consciously is to strain – as with sight it is
difficult to achieve the relaxation, the receptiveness he believes
in. Relaxation, he says, is 'loss of self'. Emotional strain makes
my eyes ache, usually one eye at a time.
    The parable made me wonder whether I look deaf, as Justin
does. He is much deafer than I am, yet he hears better, still
goes to meetings and the theatre. His hearing aid is stronger
than mine but that's not why. He's not so lazy, that is all,
doesn't sink in private thoughts while people are talking.
    The deaf look is one of inexpressiveness. I can't remember
it much in Sam who used to talk most of the time whether he
heard or not.
    When I think of friends, how few I have now, I think of
Sam and the Ballroom Dancer, both dead. Davie Laing is still
here. But? The others if they are still alive were pushed away
by me, by my not answering letters and my reluctance to

commit myself on the telephone to any fixed appointment. Laziness does it and wanting to work does it – a fear of interrupting one of those god-given, unforeseeable days when writing is the only thing that matters. I used to see Sam almost every day without taking any trouble. I began to write about him in 1977.

The Edinburgh Castle soon became our favourite pub; but Martina could not come there often when the children were small. She used to make fun of the remnants of my Scottish way of speaking, the aspirated 'wh' for instance:

– Supper whill be ready when you whish to have it, she would say, and in the Edinburgh there was a temptation to resist in the form of the largest roast of beef I have ever seen, cooked by the landlady's mother – a new one cold every Monday after the family's Sunday dinner. It was the most comfortable and friendly pub imaginable, very large yet warm in winter and pleasantly cool in summer, and furnished with Edwardian and late-Victorian stools, tables and settees. The saloon bar, which we usually went to, is shaped like a long S, with many decorated mirrors and patterned panes of glass about it, and a staircase curving up from it to the landlord's premises. In those days, in the winter time, there was a great coal fire in it and another in the public bar, which you could stare at from a distance, so that everyone in the public or saloon could stand with his back and his front to a fire at the same time. At weekends there was a third fire visible from the saloon in the first of two billiard rooms beyond a mirrored door which was usually kept open.

The only part of the Edinburgh Castle that has been lost and that I regret nostalgically, as Betjeman regrets large nineteenth-century structures such as the Euston Arch, is the wrought-iron arch above the double gates which lead into the garden and the saloon bar. Fixed to it there was a board curved like a horseshoe hanging over your head, which said in gold letters on a green background 'The Edinburgh Castle Gardens'.

On summer evenings the sun shines down the garden into

the saloon and through the doorway you can see flowerbeds and broad-leaved trees.

The flowerbeds were looked after during my first years there by Sam, a retired policeman. The landlord paid him for it every week with a little money and free beer and because he had been brought up to it – he is described on an enlistment paper dated 1911 as gardener – every kind of flower flourished on that jaded London soil. When I first knew him he was also Ralph Richardson's gardener at a house in Hampstead near the Spaniard's Inn.

He is now eighty-five, or 'fifty-eight the wrong way round', as he said this year when he was celebrating his birthday. Then he took off his hat to show his hair, which is white with grey strands in it, thick, full and beautiful, and, looking at my bald head, he said for the thousandth time in his deliberate Wiltshire way, 'Grass won't grow on concrete and 'air won't grow on brains!'

Sam is my oldest friend, the only man I grew to know in the days when I was shy of talking to strangers. When I got off my bus in summer for a drink on my way home from work in the West End, he was almost every evening in the garden with a watering can or stooping down to weed. Our friendship began with talk about plants and has continued for twenty years. Like many old people he has an excellent memory of the past and a poor one for what happened yesterday. In the winter time he sat inside at the bar for hours on the same high-backed stool and in the same corner that he likes now, but nowadays he stays only for an hour and drinks at the most a pint and a half a day.

The other habitués we knew in those days are dead, like the landlord; or have moved away. Public-house friendships are transient anyway, except amongst those who work together in the daytime and go drinking together at night, and few people know each other's address even after years of acquaintance. If you miss a familiar face for a few weeks, you say you haven't seen so-and-so lately. Sometimes someone has read of his death in a local paper. Sometimes someone who knew him intimately tells you how he died or why he left the district, for gaol perhaps or retirement to a bungalow by the sea. By convention no one asked or gave an address.

Public-house society was distinct; like that of the old-established London clubs, it was detached from domesticity. Nicknames were more usual than they are now, and though they remain essential to cockney speech I think they were used in pubs to preserve anonymity. The wittiest were never used in the vocative, but of course in the end you got to know your own. I have been known as 'the streak of pump water', because I am long and narrow, but to my face I am 'Professor' because of my bald head and spectacles. Only close friends knew each other's real name.

There was, in the Edinburgh Castle, a mortuary attendant named 'The Shroud' and sometimes 'The Black Shroud'. He wore long black overcoats of different weight according to the season. He was tall and bald like me, but his face and pate were pale, exceptionally so, his skin smooth and all in one pallid shade from the chin to the crown of his head, like the skin of a baby two generations ago when sun and wind were thought to be dangerous to the very young. The Shroud was much liked for his wit and his knowledge of racehorses. And so was 'The Neighbour', an antique dealer who is still remembered with awe because he once put on a bet of £100 and lost it philosophically. The Edinburgh was a great betting pub in the days before licensed bookie's shops; the landlord knew more about form than any newspaper tipster and folded slips of paper were secretly passed to bookie's runners all day long.

Sam says when he first came to the Edinburgh Castle there was one section of the bar where he had to stoop to make his order heard. The whole saloon bar was screened with patterned glass you could not see through set in a frame with a long, low gap below it through which drinks were passed. At the end where he still likes to sit the screen was fixed from top to bottom, but all along the rest of the bar there were small panes, the size of his face. These were on swivels and could be pushed open 'if you thought the bar-maid worth a squinny'.

Sam joined the army in 1911 at the age of nineteen when after seven years of gardening he could find no work and then, in 1919, the police, with whom he tramped the streets of Kentish Town and Camden Town so long that he frequently recognizes middle-aged people he knew as children. He had one friend whose first baby had been born under his care in the middle of a rainy night on the pavement of Royal College Street. He carries old snapshots and keepsakes such as army papers in his breast pocket, in a wallet which is now as worn and split as the papers themselves – photographs of his comrades in the First World War attending to horses on a picket line, one of himself with his back to the camera and his gun team of horses facing it, taken just before the battle of Ypres, one of his wedding and several of his son.

According to his army papers, his eyes were grey in 1911 and blue in 1919; he was five foot nine all the time, his hair brown and his complexion fresh. I have more difficulty in describing him. His hair was beginning to go grey when we first spoke in the garden; he was strong and weatherbeaten, and the skin of his rather thin face looked young. If I had been a recruitment officer I should have put down his eyes as green. But there is no room on the form to describe their clarity, their awareness of small detail – the slight failing of a little plant, the cunning or candour of another person's eyes – nor for his intelligence, nor his soul, by which I mean an inner quality of calmness, derived from experience perhaps, the kind of calm and uninformed wisdom that some people get from religion, all of which comes to you through his eyes.

Sam left school at the age of twelve and his pure Wiltshire speech was never tampered with. Fifty years of London life have not speeded it up and even if they had, he never could have parried cockney wit and repartee. He did not envy it or try to compete with it as I do sometimes, but startled the crowd around him into laughter with words which, if anyone else had said them, would have come too late. His voice and almost stately presence were unique in that pub. When the Shroud said to the Ballroom Dancer, 'Never mind, mate, we'll soon have you on the slab,' only the Ballroom Dancer laughed; the rest of us half-smiled because the Dancer looked frail, but Sam said, 'You best leave your beer on the bar then and go home to the deadhouse, to start making one to hold him. He's some weight.'

Then everybody laughed. Both jokes seemed cruel to me then, but they were not. The Dancer, the Shroud and Sam were close friends and their sense of humour was of the kind that allows you to greet a one-legged man as Peg-leg.

The Ballroom Dancer took a great liking for Martina. On the very first day she came with me to the pub, he would not let us leave until she had accepted a tiny bottle of scent which he had in an unopened packet in his pocket, and now and then for years he gave her little treasures from the many pockets of his well-made suit; cosmetics, make-up compacts, lipstick in gilded tubes which were in fashion at that time. He gave them with Edwardian grace and his conversation, mostly reminiscent, was good because, though never shy of speaking of himself, he listened. He worked in those days as a packer, underpaid, in a wholesale chemist's two streets away. He was married, but his wife did not allow him to have beer, so he took a room opposite the Edinburgh Castle and only went home at weekends. I thought, when he first told me that, that she lived in the country, but their flat was near Baker Street tube station, ten minutes' walk away across Regent's Park or the shortest stage fare by bus.

His fondness for Martina increased the instinctive liking I had for him, for I had often said to her of him that she should meet my double, perhaps ten years older, to get an idea of how I should look in ten years' time. I am bald and short-sighted like him, and as tall and narrow, and though I can walk straight-backed as Sam does, I usually stoop a bit. The Dancer's stoop was forced on him by something that had gone wrong with his neck; he could not raise his eyes from the ground, his chin was tucked into his chest and while he was standing he could only see another person's eyes from the corners of his own by turning his head sideways. That was why he preferred to sit down in a pub, while most of his friends stood for hours. By leaning back on the bench he could face them or anyone who sat opposite to him. Martina saw why I thought him my double. It made her laugh. But really he had an elegance I don't possess; his gestures and walk were graceful, his manners perfect with women and never coarse to men even if one was rude to him, which once I observed. His shirt was always white and newly laundered, his tie dark and neat; he wore a waistcoat summer and winter in the old-fashioned way; his suits and shoes were old-fashioned too; he liked fawn or pepper-and-salt materials and patent leather shoes, all of which had been made specially for him in his prosperous days, when for successive years he won ballroom dancing contests, many times in England and twice internationally. He often picked a rose from the Edinburgh gardens in his lunch hour and wore it till it faded late at night. His feet were too large for his long narrow legs. His fingers were long and well manicured, his manner of speech quick and sharp. I cannot remember a moment's tedium in his company.

Justice Shallow also wanted to dress well but had nowhere and no one to keep his old good clothes. He had been living in Rowton House for many years and when he died there in his cubicle, in 1974, no one could be found to inherit his tiny suitcase of possessions. He had some savings in the post office when I first knew him which, with an old-age pension, was enough on most days for beer and a meal in a café. It was not the Rowton House food he objected to; it was the crowd, and especially the breakfast queue which still at weekends fills a corridor fifty foot long. And then, because of his comparatively prosperous youth and upbringing, he felt out of place as one of a thousand poor and homeless men. He would not or could not speak to any of them. He shunned the pub next door – the Good Mixer – where drink is cheap, and once when I met him outside the Windsor Castle and asked him in, he said with disgust, 'But that's an Irish pub!' and we had to walk up to the Edinburgh, into the saloon bar. The only 'Irish pub' he tolerated was the Dublin Castle where English, Greek and Irish people mix but are marked by one of those tiny class gradations, imperceptible to strangers; to this day you seldom see Irish labourers there, only gangers or contractors, the Greeks are mostly shopkeepers and the English range from house agents' clerks to barristers and journalists. All these, with Justice Shallow, used the saloon bar. Beer in public bars was a penny cheaper everywhere, and an old large penny was worth a lot to him – a cup of tea, a newspaper, a little bar of chocolate. His pride made him angry when anyone bought him a drink on a day when he could not afford to return the compliment; the friendly intention seemed patronizing to him and this in itself made him solitary in the Edinburgh Castle whose landlord, Michael Donovan, gave free beer to regular customers on the day before pay day and would always draw a pint without charging for the extra half for any pint drinker who ordered a half. Shallow used to say proudly, as so many English people do, 'I keep myself to myself.'

I have never heard anyone of any other nationality, however shy or lonely, believe in such a made-up principle. But it is consoling to catch hold of a principle which fits one's nature. Justice Shallow had not chosen to be alone, to hate groups of people, to be silent in the presence of anyone he thought beneath him. His isolation began with a tragedy that came upon him at the age of nineteen; complete loneliness and successive financial failures, which were probably one of the results of loneliness, overcame his spirit in his twenties. His only escape was inward. The outward bitterness, apparent to others, was concealed from him. He was thought to be snobbish for speaking only to people of my sort of upbringing – the 'professional classes', he put us down as – but he was never servile, and because he found no interest in other people's lives or jokes he felt at ease only in the company of people who told him of their work, the books they liked or anything they had read in a newspaper he had not seen. Also, like most lonely people, he took to anyone who expressed an interest in him, in his thoughts and opinions or the story of his life. It had to be a private conversation. He had long been cursed by privacy. I never heard anyone call him by name and I never addressed him by any name, which was why I gave him my own private nickname. It was impossible to describe him to Martina, to recount what he told me, without one.

I named him Justice Shallow because of his physique, not his character, because of his coat-hanger shoulders and long skinny neck, his thighs that under worn-out trousers looked like railings bent with a knob at the knee, his narrow, sad, lined face, his concave chest, the wristbones which were more prominent than the tiny wrists above them, the long, rather beautiful fingers and their five distinct tendons, which seemed to me like wires beneath red tissue paper, and the blue veins of his hands. He always wore a long raincoat, unbuttoned in summer, torn at the seams below his knees, and spattered with stains. His suit was well kept but too thin for the winter, his ties sombre, narrow, tied too tightly in a little knot. He probably had two shirts or more, white with the old-fashioned collar and studs. He washed them himself and they were always clean.

'. . . a' was the very genius of famine . . . you might have thrust him and all his apparel into an eel-skin.' Falstaff's physical description fitted him and I suppose I named him Justice Shallow because of that; but though he had Shallow's timidity and took each rare opportunity of speaking of his youth, he never boasted of wildness, nor claimed to have been friendly with the great. His talk of youth was so sincere, so loving towards his parents and his wife and of the country of north Norfolk where he was born, that I knew it was truthful.

The talk came slowly. At first there was so little of it that I could as well have named him Justice Silence. But many things he said about childhood in the country reminded me of mine and my reminiscences opened a way for his. He was born in 1891 near Holt, the son of a publican–farmer, and brought up in one of those little public houses, once numerous, which made little profit but formed the only social centre for country people. Small market gardeners and farmers, retired postmen and policemen rented or bought them as a place to live in and added a little to their income or pension. But Shallow thought the more important benefit to his parents was that in old age they were at the very centre of rural life, knew all the people young and old. It was to him a distressing contrast to his own isolation in old age.

He had had a happy childhood. Before he left school at the age of twelve, he helped his father on the farm in the evenings or his mother behind the bar.

'The best thing I learned, and I liked it, was how to look after beer.'

It was also the only learning that promised him a good career. As his father grew older, he did more and more work in the pub, became a favourite of the customers and an expert at its management. Then, when he was eighteen, he fell in love with a girl of seventeen and married her with his parents' blessing. They had enough savings to buy them the tenancy of a small public house in Cumberland, where leases were at that time cheaper than in Norfolk, although even in those days there was more of a living to be had from summer visitors than from local people. It was a strange country to him and his wife, and they might as well have gone to France or Italy, for the language used by their regular customers was incomprehensible at first.

But his wife was pretty and much liked, and from what he half told me I think he was once curious and generous enough in conversation to be liked too. He hid much from me as he told me of those early days; my Jewish and Irish friends of the 1950s were more ready to expose their warmth of heart, tell more of their loves and lives in half an hour, than he could tell in a year. His heart was warm, but you had to learn his code words to get at it, which took years of occasional encounters.

When I felt broken-hearted as a young man in love I thought it impossible to die from it, as so many people died in the old novels I read. I have learned since that it can happen, not by suicide but by despair, that extreme of despair that makes you shun friends even of your own sex and go utterly into yourself, so much alone that you cease to care about work or social intercourse, or about life itself; you cannot imagine falling in love with anyone else and even to speak to a girl who attracts you seems like sacrilege towards the one you have lost. When I was nineteen a friend of mine hanged himself, successfully, in that state of mind. If I or anyone else had been there to stop him, he would be alive now, and possibly happy with another girlfriend or the succession of them which most men find. Justice Shallow's spirit died of the same cause and at the same age, nineteen, when his wife died suddenly soon after her eighteenth birthday. From that day onwards he began to fail. His first thought was to walk off on the day after her funeral, but he did not do so rashly; he waited on in Cumberland until he had sold the lease of the pub for less than his father had paid for it. With the money he got he bought a share in a Manchester pub, in a good position at a corner of one of those narrow old streets near Piccadilly. That failed too. He said his partner cheated him. But I think he had lost heart, and found himself unable to hold his own in the partnership or speak to customers agreeably, which is an essential part of the pub business. The whole of his living after that, until the age of sixty-five, was gained by casual work in restaurants or bars. From then on he lived on his old-age pension and the diminishing post office savings bank account into which in his youth he had put some hundreds of pounds.

He was gently censorious of everyone and most matters, so much so that I often wondered what faults he found in me or even in Martina, who for a long time he took to be my daughter. His expertise made him critical of barmen – the way they drew a glass of draught or poured a bottle, the way they washed up or dried their hands on the glasscloth afterwards; he knew every tiny fiddle practised in that underpaid job, to which any sensible publican turned a blind eye. His muttered oaths were reserved for cellarmen. And usually there was no real cause for any of this, especially in the Edinburgh Castle where Michael Donovan kept the cellar himself. Sometimes after watching me speak to someone else, he would say, 'That man's a nuisance to you. I can see that.' Often he warned me against mixing with 'bad characters'.

Sam warned me of another danger he imagined I was in – the danger of putting my hand in my pocket too often.

'Now I see you with that crowd at nights and all those pretty girls I don't blame you. I watched you often when you bring them in, there might be a baker's dozen some nights, all waiting for you to put your hand in your pocket.'

He still goes on about it sometimes twenty years later and will not accept my truthful explanation. The baker's dozen he occasionally saw me with, near closing time at night, were members of the band and cast of whatever radio play I was producing, for in those days the Camden Theatre was a BBC studio. It was the custom for the producer to buy the first drink after a long day's rehearsal – those who could afford it bought one back for him and the others took turns to buy their own in little groups. One or two members of the band had cars for their instruments and friends and as soon as I introduced them to my favourite and spacious pub they began to go there, taking me and as many actors and actresses as possible with them sitting on each other's knees or crouching, for the short journey. I remember eleven of us in one small car.

Justice Shallow died in April 1974. I had not seen him for a month, and only found out by going to 'The House' and asking for him. He was said to be eighty-three but could not vouch for it himself. I knew him intimately during the last five years of his life, because after I left the BBC in 1969 I often went to the Edinburgh Castle in the middle of the day, on weekdays, and sometimes we were the only people who used the saloon bar there. He had always kept to his room at Rowton House in the evenings, gone to it at four o'clock every day and stayed there reading until bedtime. No one, however old, is allowed into his cubicle or room between 9 a.m. and four, and often in the early seventies, when chronic bronchitis had set in, I was frightened for his health in the mornings when I met him at a street corner in the mist or sheltering in his wretched raincoat from a storm under the canopy of the cinema doorway. He could not bear the canteen or the common rooms, had tea and bread and margarine for breakfast in a café, and dinner in the same one after three in the afternoon when the pubs close. In bad weather, he sat over his after-dinner cup of tea until five minutes to four; and then walked back to 'The House' glad to be allowed to go upstairs to his monastic cell.

Something had softened his bitterness by then, it seemed to me. In his last years, he began to speak of the future, to dwell less upon the happiness of childhood or on his present misery and to question us about our holidays which we usually spent with the children in Norfolk about ten miles from his birthplace. He liked to hear about the state of daffodils and bluebells, roses, chrysanthemums, blackberries, in the seasons of school holidays, about the effect of weather on farm crops and the look of the land and of villages he once knew. He regretted as we did the closure of a little railway but took the news of a North Sea gas plant at Bacton well.

After Easter, two years before his death, he spoke more than ever about Holt, the nearest market town to the pub where he was born, and said he would go back there if he had the money. We compared the rent he paid at Rowton House and the price of his Camden Town café meals with board and lodging in the country. The country was cheaper. We could find the fare. He asked us to look for a room for him in Holt, and wrote his name down for the first time, saying how well it was known there and that any old person with a room to let would favour him.

When we reached Holt in August we were given at news-agents' and pubs addresses half a mile away from market-town life which would to him, with his slow walk, have been a sentence to solitary confinement. We walked to these good bungalows and spoke to their friendly owners who had rooms to let, feeling all the time on roads, with cars chasing us and no pavement to shelter on, the sense of desolation every city dweller who likes the country feels. Bungalow land seemed to us, without a car, as it would have seemed to Shallow, though not to its inhabitants, a prosperous desert. Our one-day search was a failure, so we put a card up in the newsagent's window saying, 'Holt gentleman, retired, leaving London, seeks room in Holt', etc. We gave our own London address instead of his disgraceful one, and paid about sixpence a week for four weeks to keep this pitiable thing up there. I have never known a mean newsagent; they usually leave cards up until they have to make room for new ones; and ours must have been shown for six weeks because it was nearly the end of October before we received a reply.

I saw Justice Shallow only two or three times during that month. He had spent all his savings I guess, and it was only after persuasion that he would consent to come with me to the Edinburgh Castle for a pint in the warmth. I knew the low walls he sat on on sunny days and occasionally sought him out. We did not speak of Holt or the advertisement until the day of the one reply. I searched the streets for him that morning and found him leaning with his elbow on a telephone engineers' green cabinet at the corner of Arlington Road and Inverness Street. These upright metal boxes are conveniently placed in Camden Town at the right height for one's elbow and broad enough to spread a newspaper on. I was surprised to find Shallow at this one, because it was usually occupied by Rowton House men studying form before a visit to the bookmakers, an occupation he despised. But it gets the sun in the mornings and he was there alone. He was reluctant to open the letter. He said he was sorry for putting me 'to all that trouble'; then he read it and handed it to me in silence. It was a pleasant letter offering him a room at an address we both knew, five minutes' walk from the main street, but the actual prospect, even the sight of the unopened letter, inspired him with such fear that he would not even let me go to see the house. He never went there, never moved from London or from Rowton House.

August 21st, Thursday

2.30 Moving shadows of weeping ash on wall to R. of my window, slants of sunlight, sloping, moving all the time, sometimes like the shadows and light of small waves of the sea by a flat shallow shore.

I looked at the weeping elm opp. No. 8 today which has the Dutch elm disease and must be felled. All the leaves and branches near the ground look healthy, but high up and drooping over the terrace towards the houses, the leaves are withered, blackish green and crumpled.

Early this week I saw from my desk two women come up to our door, one holding a book, and I thought 'Jehovah's Witnesses' and thought I would be polite in refusing to buy the book. The book was *Woodbrook*! Would I sign it for them? They had walked all the way from Euston and the older one in her fifties said they deserved my signature.

– We love you, she said.

I saw a letter from me in the book – a reply to a fan letter from the older one – the other wasn't young enough to be her daughter and was a friend I guess. But both said 'we' all the time.

On Wednesday I went to the launderette. I like it. I don't think many people do. I mean I like it when I'm in a good mood. So many people who go bustling about elsewhere sit down in there and read or talk while they wait for the moment of hasty activity between the washing and the drying. Some stare at their washing swirling round, with a TV expression, a dull acceptance of whatever is given you to watch. I like that too, but only for a minute at a time – the white whirl of soapsuds keeping pace with bright clothes. In the dryer, which has a larger screen and no interference from soap, I watched Ben's trousers chasing Martina's shirt; reds, blues, yellows, white streamers from the ribbon of her nightdress, dark blotches of my jeans, all flying in a circle, blown by the fiery wind. The hot wind is made by gas. When the coin slot goes wrong, Beardie opens a door on top, sets it off by hand and displays the blazing furnace. He used to be a seaman, which is why he can't stop swabbing the floor and polishing the metal for a second. On Sundays, when I usually go, he seizes the hose from the council man and washes the whole of the empty market street and pavements, and some of the parked cars, like Merlin in a frenzy, then comes back to his launderette, dancing, tripping, singing, finding fault. He's kind too and helps a lot of people, including me, and lately he has made the place beautiful with geraniums and a hundred potted plants. I once dropped a match on the floor. He shouted at me to pick it up. Martina said once, to calm my rage, that a launderette she used to go to was awash with dirty water and rubbish. She says there is one thing I must like about Beardie, must feel for – his love of women. Yes. He has nice cats too.

The standard of beauty has gone down in there. Haven't seen the Greek sisters for a year. No one to fold the sheets with me. It was like a stately dance, folding sheets – walking up to each other and away again.

One tall mermaid occasionally, that's all.

I wandered in the market while the clothes were cooking. Not many people and the few who were there were strolling, as I was, with no intention of buying anything. But I did buy some roses, orangey pink with a strong lovely scent. The flower stall was specially beautiful, built like a high bank of blossoms shelving up from pots on the ground. It and the cats' meat are the only ones shut off from the pavements with high wooden backs. Most face the street, but you can buy fruit and vegetables from the pavement side as well. The father was there, but I got the roses from his elder son. I remember him and his brother as little boys when they first came out to help; we bought Christmas trees from them when they were smaller than the smallest tree.

That's a pleasant thing about the market – continuity. Nearly all the greengrocers' shops, the grocers', ironmongers' have been turned into supermarkets or boutiques, but the stalls have been kept by the same families for generations. The King of the Market, chieftain of vegetables, as famous a figure in Covent Garden as he was here, died several years ago, but now his son grows more and more like him, as tall, as broad, as strikingly dressed and wearing the same kind of round, short-brimmed hat. The King's handsome grandchildren, two girls and a boy, help on Saturdays.

On my second outing, while the dryers were at work, I went

to the top of the street to look at Reg's things. He has had junk stalls there for over thirty years outside the pub on the corner of Arlington Road – alongside his father to begin with. Jim Robbins who has lived here since 1953 remembers his father's stall. It was called the penny stall. Everything on it cost a penny and there was always a crowd round the elder Mr Stone, Jim says, listening to his witty non-stop patter. Unlike father unlike son, for Reg is taciturn.

A few books, but not the kind I like. Asked him why so few.
– Can't get 'em.

Last year, in one of his rare bouts of speech, he said there was none of the good old stuff about. I think that began when Dingwalls market and the pricey antique shops cropped up. Reg has never charged much.

We bought most of our crockery from him when we first came, and cooking pots, wooden spoons, sieves, corkscrews, all of the old strong kind, bread bins, coal scuttles, rubbish bins, chairs, a huge coal shovel, several spades and a graip. I've just been upstairs, trying to remember. You can't go into any room without seeing something of his. My favourite table came from him, the low, round one behind me with three curved legs, a beautiful cabin trunk bound with metal, now filled with relics, a dolls' kitchen dresser with a willow-pattern teaset on its shelves, a dainty oval teapot, milk jug, sugar bowl all in willow pattern and all, by a miracle, unbroken, for every child who has come to the house in the past twenty years has played with it. Then, there's a whole family of polar bears who have been asleep in a drawer upstairs ever since Tim, Luke and Ben grew up. Many books but, except for the two great Bibles, I can't remember which ones came from Reg. I do remember carrying the Bibles home; I'd never imagined that any book could weigh so much. Neither of us had ever seen inside a lectern Bible before and these are magnificently printed, with some coloured pictures and hundreds of full-page engravings. Both are heavily bound in leather patterned with gold leaf with gilt paper fore-edges and the one in our bedroom has a gold lock as well, though the clasp was broken before we bought it; on its spine there's a red vellum title plate. M. remembers what we paid for them – five shillings each. It was written in chalk on the cover.

When I asked him 'Why so few books?' he was standing by his stall, as he usually is, like the master of a ship, looking ahead impassive but alert, a cigarette in his mouth which he never puffs at. He has the dignity of a ship's master and the silence. He is not very tall, but lithe and still, and emanates a power of command without effort. His head seldom moves but his eyes do, watching everything. Eight or nine customers, mostly old men and women, stood round his stall turning over the small objects, their hands like hens' feet scratching gravel, or picking up garments from teachests on the ground. All his large objects – TV sets, electric fires – are on the ground.

I saw a woman asking him the price of a coal hod she had picked up.

– 75p.

– What?

– 75p.

She tried to say something.

– 75p! Put it back. That's right.

She put it back. He asks a huge price of people he has argued with or doesn't like. Martina once heard him ask £3 for some little thing that had been 20p to start with. The man had quibbled, offering 10p, then 15p. Reg wouldn't budge from 20p. The man walked off but must have wanted the thing badly, because he came back having changed his mind with the 20p in his hand. It was then, at the sight of him again, that Reg asked £3.

I guess this woman had been stealing from him. He told me many do and I saw one the other day dropping a roll of red rubber tubing into her shopping bag. This woman had long grey hair tied back, an aggressive angular grey face, a white dress unsuitably and noticeably short for her, white with a grey uncomely pattern. She walked quickly on from Reg's to the back of the flower stall, picked up a bunch of white daisies from under the green canvas canopy. No one was looking. Father and son were at the front of the stall. But the father appeared unexpectedly:

– What are you doing, dear?

First she abused him. Then (I thought) he forced her to buy 2 bunches for 20p.

August 22nd, Friday

Dr Haas this afternoon. Last time he said he thought I wasn't
behaving naturally about getting old, not accepting it – that I
couldn't expect to be as quick or as spontaneous as I used to
be. *But*, said he, to keep my morale from sinking any lower,
that doesn't mean that your faculties, your mind, your power
as a writer have diminished. (!)

Today he asked whether I had any 'blockage' during
Woodbrook. I remembered one at which I was saying to myself
that I would abandon the book. I told Dr H. that I thought it
came when the famine section turned out to be too long and
difficult to handle: too much material, too much research – all
out of proportion to the book as a whole. But now I am not
sure where the blockage came and suspect it began with a
mood, not with a practical difficulty.

He asked me to describe the mood that led to fluent writing.
I said about self-confidence, as the uppermost necessity, a lack
of self-criticism *while* one is writing – that it is OK to hate
what you've done, next day, to cross it out or re-do it. But to
lack confidence in oneself for several days, even, or a week,
may lead to months of blockage.

That is the upper layer.

The essential layer is deep and accessible rarely. But if you
can reach it, get down inside yourself to it, you can start.
Once you have started the flow, it gets easier and easier to
resume it next day, to start again each day. I had to attempt
a description of this deep-lying mood.

While you are asleep and dreaming you are deeper than it.

If you can sit still in silence by yourself and recall a forgotten
dream you are near it. You can in this mood remove yourself
entirely from what is going on around you – or I suppose not
entirely because you are conscious of cars outside the window,
footsteps upstairs, children playing (and yet if somebody comes
into the room and speaks suddenly it makes you jump). But
you are removed from outside things. More important you are
removed from all the bitty scraps on the surface of your mind.

I told Dr Haas how, often all my life, I have felt compelled
to write – not for money, hope of fame, etc. – but for itself.
This mood, almost religious, in which I wrote during school

holidays as a young boy and from time to time throughout my teens – sometimes in the drawing room at my parents' house in the presence of other people talking – seems remote from me now.

How I must (at least for a day's start) recapture this mood so as to resume *Camden Town*.

He said

– But you are going on with your diary? and I told him, yes, not every day but more and more, that it's better than the abyss of last year but it's not the book. I described the book as a monstrous growth on the brain; often the thought of it makes me physically sick. I can't get rid of it. Nor can I write it.

August 24th, Sunday

Last night when we walked on the terrace lawn, Martina noticed that some of the leaves have gone brown – on the trees and a lot on the ground. (Today she smelt and saw a bonfire of leaves.)

I said

– You make it sound so sad.

– It is sad.

Then at night a large but, she says, wintry moon. Even years ago, as soon as the longest day was past, she noticed earlier darkness. This summer especially with its weeks and weeks of cloudy evenings.

Both girls and men, this cold and rainy summer, carry jerseys. But the usual way nowadays is to tie the sleeves round the waist and the jersey hangs like a short apron over the buttocks.

On Saturday, by the builder's hoarding near the Catholic Church, a very drunk man, 50-ish, propping himself up, said in a Belfast accent

– Can you tell me where St Patrick's Church is?

– It's just there, two doors along.

– I'm not a millionaire. But I have money (meaning – due to me or in the savings bank). Give me some money for a drink.

– I can't do that.

He accepted my refusal without emotion. M. thinks he really wanted to go to the church. The drink a separate wish.

August 26th, Tuesday

Yesterday was Bank Holiday and a beautiful day, sunny all day and a slight breeze. We walked over Prim. Hill to Finchley Road tube. We had walked this way at the same time, about 9 a.m., in the spring. It was lovely – I much less sad now than then, although I was melancholy on the way home. M. said about me walking in parks only when depressed

– It couldn't be worse than anywhere else.

Why did we walk together there early this year? A bus strike? We saw the row of dead trees on top of the hill to our left and she remembered seeing small hopeful leaves on them. She says I thought them dead and I was right. Near our path to the right a large dead elm and farther on another tree, withering leaves, which I thought was an elm but on the way back a plane tree. The huge white skeleton of that elm without bark.

Huge amount of paper and tins all over Finchley Road and pavement, as at Cam. Tn. M. remembers Cam. Tn *much* cleaner when we came. I left her at F. Rd station looking out at the sky blue and light through the booking hall. All the way back after Swiss Cottage I tried to follow our footsteps, crossing the road where we had crossed.

Later I met Davy and Mary the Short and the Tall, both limping, he briskly she with longer strides, alert, cheerful, his hat, her white hair, both well dressed – a highly respectable couple calling me from across the street. I waited on the bridge until they crossed. I asked how they managed to get money for drink every day. I said

– You must need an awful lot of money.

– All by begging, Davy said, and Mary

– It comes in bit by bit – you've got to persevere. A bottle of wine is £1.20.

– We had 3 bottles of wine this morning, Davy said. There was too many in the crowd.

When I gave him 60p he was disappointed, said he thought I'd give enough for another bottle.

– You're a heavy drinker – you know what it's like.

I said if I was it made it worse – to keep them in drink as well.

– Well, if everyone gave me as much as this (it was in his open hand) I'd no' be doing badly.

I thought of 60p because it is what he often asked for. Unlike some, he is good natured when you disappoint him.

Yesterday when he asked Martina for 50 or 60p, while he was sitting in the market in the afternoon, she gave him 20p. She said she had spent nearly all her money on shopping, which was true.

– I have no money to spend, Davy said.

M. reproached him for not turning up to meet me to go to hospital – after 'getting me up at crack of dawn'. He misunderstood her and said

– I have to be up at crack of dawn because I have no place to sleep.

In the Engineer unhappy on that beautiful sunny Bank Holiday Monday, I saw a group of young people sitting down to drink unhappily in the garden. It's easy to forget how unhappy one can be at 18 or 20. I walked from there all along the canal towpath to St John's Wood – many families having picnics on benches – a newly peeled boiled egg in sun.

My friends were surprised when I joined the BBC Angling Club in 1960-something. I didn't want to fish, but in those days all the gates to the towpath were kept locked and anglers had keys, and it was an exciting place to take the boys. Towing by horses had stopped about 1956 but there were still a few narrow boats with cargoes and the banks through the zoo and as far as St John's Wood were even wilder than they are now. The boys took fishing rods, real or homemade. They never caught anything, but when fishing bored them it became adventurous – the long curving towpath to run on, dark echoing bridges, steep bushy banks to hide in here and there and one or two climbable walls.

The walk in the other direction past Camden Lock and Dingwalls timber yards, past the old Camden brewery in Jamestown Street which backed on to the canal, towards St Pancras and Islington was treeless, sooty and frightening. Very few men sat down there to fish. There was a grim high wall on our left and across the canal to the right ancient factories, warehouses, goods yards, wharves appeared round each bend of the towpath, one after another all in pitiful condition. These, once grand and hopeful, are the remnants of a risky speculation which Nash and his assistant James Morgan set afoot in 1811 for the making of the Regent's Canal which led from the Grand Junction Canal at Paddington Basin, through Islington and Bermondsey to the Thames in Limehouse. In 1967, on that long stretch of the towpath with everyone else locked out except one lonely hunched-up fisherman now and then, you felt cut off from living things, murky water one side of you, the black wall on the other, no vegetation, no dogs, no gates so far as I remember between Camden Road and Islington Tunnel where the towpath stops. In the old days the horses were taken off there. The boatmen legged their boats through, lying on their backs, and by pressing the soles of their feet step by step against the roof or walls of the tunnel, they pushed the boats along.

In my last year at school, when I was fearful about Higher School Certificate and Smalls, I had a private tutor for a while, a scholarly eccentric, thin, witty, often angry, with lots of grey hair, one eye that worked, the other a whitish-blue blur. He was very poor. He lived all alone in Lyme Terrace, that curved alleyway near Camden Road overhead railway, high above the canal. From his window you could see the water and the horses pulling barges and across to a large timber yard. I forget its name. There are only a few houses in the terrace and his was a gleaming strip amid decay. His landlady was a Bretonne and cleaned everything all the time. She believed that his books bred dust. He had thousands in his tiny room, mostly on the floor, and gave me dozens when he left, including the six volumes of Walter Thornbury's *Old London* which I've still got. It was one of his interests, the history of London. He was a good talker and aroused my interest in it, starting with the canal below his window. I never explored the subject then, but after we came to live here I learned a bit more.

At a time before railways diminished canal traffic and fourteen years before any railway reached London a link between the Thames docks and the north of England seemed essential and profitable. Almost every canal company was profitable. People scrambled to buy shares. But the Company of Proprietors of the Regent's Canal almost failed from the start. Both land and water were denied to it at first. The Crown rejected Nash's proposal to bring the new canal through Marylebone Park which he was then ornamentally converting into the Regent's Park. He believed that a navigable waterway and especially the sails of barges moving through copses would embellish the park, and by channelling the Tyburn river which traversed it he would have had a cheap and constant water supply. By refusing to share their water, the Grand Junction forced the Regent's Canal Company to build a reservoir nine miles away on Finchley Common. Three great landowners – Portman of Marylebone, Agar of St Pancras and the Bishop of London – refused to part with any of their land and because of 'violent and unforeseen opposition' the Act of Parliament enabling work to start cost the company £12,724 instead of £4241 which had been the maximum estimate.

A ceremony of delving the first spadeful of soil was grandly performed on 14 October 1812 but the millions of other spadefuls made between Paddington and the Thames cost more in lives and money than the most pessimistic of the engineers had guessed.

Portman's forbidden territory was flat, the Eyre estate hilly and required a longer tunnel through Maida Hill. Its proprietors, having fleeced the company before any work began, forced it to build splendid villas along the Maida Vale canal banks on the stretch now splendidly called Little Venice. Mr Lord loved his cricket ground so dearly that he had to be paid £4000 to move it, turf and all, to the other side of the road where it is now – his patch was worth about £100 – but then he had only just moved it from its original site which is now called Dorset Square. The Crown's forbidden park would have needed normal excavation. Skirting round it was deep, laborious and slow.

It is difficult to find out much about the diggers of the canal – the navigators – homeless thousands of men who carved the channel out by hand using those horse-barrow runs that were later used on the railways. They were busy ants in an anthill, industrious bees in their hive, according to one writer.[15] The living and the killed were sometimes numbered. But until after 1825 no one wrote about how they or any other workmen lived or died, and where there were no houses there are no hints, except for reports of rioting and theft. Several times in the late eighteenth century, when huge numbers of migrants were employed, riots in which constables and employers were killed led to public inquiries which incidentally showed that their food, shelter and the conditions of their work were as wretched as those the railway navvies were to suffer later. The newspapers reviled them in just the same way, and never mentioned them till trouble started.

During the making of the Regent's Canal between Paddington and here there was only one accident, so far as I can find out, serious enough to be mentioned in *The Times* and in *Bell's Weekly Messenger*. It happened in August 1813 very near to Camden Town on a stretch where the cut had reached a depth of twenty-five feet. A large gang was undermining the bank with spade and shovel to make it fall and widen the channel. It fell too soon 'with a dreadful crash' and completely buried twelve men. 'Eight were dug out alive, but four with their arms and legs broke, and the other four much bruised and cut, six of the eight are in such a state, that their recovery is not expected.' Four others were dug up dead.

Herbert Spencer[16] says that there had been a bad accident earlier that year halfway through the tunnelling of Maida Hill when the navvies encountered a spring of water with running sand, not noticed in the survey, which caused serious casualties, loss of equipment and much delay.

Much money was lost in such ways but even more was stolen soon afterwards by Mr Thomas Homer, superintendent of the works, a much respected man who had launched the whole ploy but put no money into it. He embezzled the company's funds – cash intended for the purchase of materials and all that had been paid personally to him by investors. He was questioned about it and fled by sea. He was caught and sentenced to seven years' transportation but that was no use to the company because the money had succeeded in escaping.

The steep decline into Camden Town was excessively costly too. They tried caissons at first for the Hampstead Road lock but they leaked and had to be abandoned, steam engines and all. They were replaced by the ordinary twin locks which are still there. And this was done in a hurry because the Prince Regent's birthday – the day appointed for the opening of the first section of his canal – was very near.

On his birthday, 12 August 1816, at noon, two 'elegant barges' decorated with flags and attended by two regimental bands of music set out from Paddington with a number of ladies and gentlemen on board. They were preceded by three navigation barges, loaded with people, and martial and sentimental music was played all the way along. They were towed not to Hampstead Road but down the branch line parallel to Albany Street whose terminus at Cumberland Basin was ready, where the ladies and gentlemen were with difficulty conducted through a huge cheering crowd into a marquee to partake of an elegant cold collation at half past one o'clock. The navvies, wearing purple favours in their hats, were presented with several hogsheads of beer which they enjoyed outside the marquee. Plenty of quart and pint pots had been provided but, not finding these large enough, many of them held out their hats for a fill-up and drank copious draughts from those.

Before work began on the ordinary twin locks that are still there excavation had proceeded under the high bank now topped by Lyme Terrace and on into Somers Town where Agar's estate with its fine mulberry trees and trim hedgerows lay across the chosen line. When James Morgan, a surveyor, approached the gates with a contractor and a gang of navvies he found them barricaded and manned by a posse of gardeners under the command of Mr William Agar, KC. Morgan grouped his men who were well armed with spades and shovels behind a front line of wheelbarrows and ordered a charge. A breach was made, the gardeners retreated and digging began. It went on all day unopposed but next morning the gardeners, reinforced by stablemen and scullions, made a surprise assault. Work stopped. The fight was stopped by a Bow Street runner who arrested Morgan's assistant and the navigators' foreman. At the trial some months later these two and Morgan and Lyons, the chairman of the company, were found guilty. Agar was awarded generous damages for the spoiling of his park and the course of the canal was diverted to the circuitous route we know.

In 1820 the canal at last reached the Thames. It was opened for traffic in August that year but even ten years after that the shareholders' money continued to sink to the bottom while half-starved boatmen and their families worked their laborious way up and down on its surface. Act upon Act of Parliament was passed to buoy up the company's finances. Dividends fell and debts to the Treasury rose. A long spell of prosperity came when the railways reached London and I suppose the company felt the irony of that; but their waterway was close to five main lines, those ending at Euston, Paddington, St Pancras, King's Cross and Liverpool Street, and one minor line which runs through Camden Town to Broad Street station. The Regent's Canal was the cheapest and speediest way on which the heavy materials the railways needed could be carried. Millions of tons of clay and rubble were removed on return journeys. Having used canals for this all over England, the railways stole their trade and in London succeeded so well that in 1845 the Regent's Canal Company proposed to convert their canal into a railway line. They did not do that but they did agree to sell it to some speculators calling themselves the Regent's Canal Railway Company. The deal flunked for lack of investors and the waterway somehow survived.

The canal boatmen also survived but suffered rather more than the shareholders. They too were inadequately paid. And from the start they had missionaries climbing on to their boats. The shareholders, so far as is known, had none.

For three years, from 1829 to 1832, the missionaries based on Paddington Basin issued a periodical called the *Canal Boatmen's Magazine* which if you push your way through a dense shrubbery of self-righteous verbiage gives a glimpse month by month of the way canal workers lived, of their opinions, what they thought.

Dear Sir, . . . one clerk in a large establishment told me, that for upwards of six months he had only been at liberty on two Sundays, and that was when the canal was closed for cleaning; at all other times he had been at work every Sabbath morning . . . I have also been informed that the Boatmen, Porters and others, so employed, do not receive any adequate remuneration. I do not know exactly how or what they are paid; but I understand it has been the practice of the establishment . . . to give the men nothing for their labour on the Sabbath day but a constant supply of drink, which in many cases has caused them to add the crime of intoxication to that of breaking the Sabbath . . . I am happy also to inform you that *memorials* have been prepared to be presented to the Regent's Canal and Grand Junction Companies, praying them to close the whole of their locks on the Sabbath Day.

Your most obliged and obedient servant,
E. Carpenter, Boatmen's Chapel, Macclesfield Street, City Road

A Description of the Boatmen's Chapel (the Paddington one)
By Tom

Last Sunday our boat lay in the basin and in the morning some persons came and asked us if we could read; we said, yes, some of us, Master, then they left us some of their books, and asked us to go to their Chapel . . . The front was just like our Master's stables, only 'Boatman's Chapel' was written on at the top . . . I had a good look at the place; there were some benches for the gentlemen and ladies and some plank ends for us to sit upon . . . After a bit the place got nearly full and then some one got up and read a little, then we all stood up and they began singing, but were soon tired . . . Then a nice old gentleman in black said 'Let us Pray' and he asked the good God to look down from heaven on the boatmen who were present; then I was afraid, but he soon prayed to God to give us new hearts, and after death to take us to heaven. When he had said 'Amen' he sat down, and the people opened their eyes again: and all looked so comfortable. He said we were all great sinners. Thinks I, some of the fine people won't like that; but they all kept quiet.

Outdoor Preaching to Paddington Boatmen and Carmen

The people were more quiet than on the preceding Sabbath, with a few exceptions . . . Many from the Lime Wharfs and Dust Wharfs appeared very anxious to attend to the preaching . . .

Perhaps there are some poor mechanics here who have lost their work. You said when you were busily engaged that you had no time to see to religion; and now God has taken away that work, that you may attend to these things, and not have it for an excuse. O, poor mechanics! Who have no work, and but little to eat; and some of you have only stepped in to hear what the babbler would say. Hear what Christ says to you. 'Arise, shine, for thy light is come.' O, go to him, fall at his feet, and say, 'Lord Jesus, shine into our hearts, and take us to the mansions of glory.'

Every month the magazine had a page called 'Journal of Attendance' from which it appears that canal men were outnumbered in chapel by 'fine people'. For example,

> Sunday, 26 [April] Nearly two hundred persons present, sixteen canal-men.
> Sunday, 31 [May] The chapel full – eight canal-men . . . In the evening ninety persons – ten canal-men.

In winter many more 'labouring persons' came – the accounts give figures for coal and kindling for the chapel fire – and deep frosts such as that of January 1830 made more boatmen accessible.

> Sunday, 17 [January] 1830. Twenty-nine boats were up this morning and all frozen in.
> The severity of the weather, it appears, enabled many a boatman to hear the sound of the everlasting gospel.
> January 24th – This morning we found many of the boatmen busily engaged in breaking the ice. There had been a partial thaw, but now it was freezing again, notwithstanding which, news had arrived that Pickford's boats, from the City Road basin, were on their way to the Paddington canal. This intelligence aroused the men; they set to work, and were enabled, after much difficulty, to proceed to the stop, or house where their cargo is weighed, lest the City Road boats should take the lead, which by their accounts they considered to be of great importance. We exchanged their tracts, and gave up the hope of obtaining many at the chapel today . . .
> – 'We have but just done work,' said the men, 'and have got to have something to eat, and to clean ourselves; but we'll come in the evening.'

No figures could be given about attendance at open-air services but each was carefully reported. The most difficult opposition came from Radicals who chose to hold their meetings as near as they possibly could to the crowd the preacher had assembled. But there were interruptions by individuals too.

On Sunday morning, June 14, 1829, a sermon was preached in the open air . . . As usual on such occasions, a mixed multitude assembled, – men, women and children, and many workmen. The congregation was annoyed by some, who standing by the public house on the other side of the way imagined they could disturb with impunity. One half drunken man came by with a sheep's heart in his hand, which no doubt he had been buying for his breakfast or dinner. The minister's preaching offended him; he held up the heart in his hand, looked at it and said, 'I've a good mind to throw this in his eye, that I have.'

But looking at the minister, and then at the sheep's heart, he walked on.

The Infidel's Confession

To tell you the truth I am against the bible because the bible is against me. It commands what I hate and condemns what I love . . . How can a criminal love a prosecutor who accuses him, and the judge who condemns him?

Coachmen, Guards, Waiters, and Others

Sir, That sailors and boatmen have been proverbial for wickedness is so notorious, that no one is disposed to contradict it; and the fact that the latter have been left for half a century, and the former for a much longer period, 'no man caring for their souls', must be admitted.

It is equally evident, that coachmen, guards, hackney-coachmen, chaise-drivers, porters, waiters, ostlers, boots, sailors, boatmen and wharfingers . . . become an easy prey to Jews, crimps, publicans and harlots . . .

A good preacher can alter people's attitudes and sometimes even their conduct but it is hard to believe that canal missionaries succeeded. Of all the delusions they worked under, usually on the Sabbath, the notion that reading the Bible improves one's morals was the greatest. I read it a lot. I read of warring, polygamous societies in which men were by law allowed as many concubines as they could afford and consorted with harlots as well. I read how Samson, possessed by the spirit of the Lord, set fire to three hundred foxes and burned down his enemies' vines, olives and corn with them, and soon afterwards at Gaza saw a harlot and went in unto her; how King Ahasuerus put away his wife because she would not come and show off her beauty at his feast, how Mordecai deceived him into making Esther, the orphan, queen instead; how Laban tricked Jacob into marrying his elder daughter instead of Rachel, the younger, whom Jacob loved, and then gave him Rachel as well next week; how Lot's daughters made their father drunk and took turns to seduce him in the darkness of the cave he had taken them to hide in; how Abraham's wife Sarah, believing herself to be barren, persuaded him to lie with one of her slaves and then, when at last she did have a child of her own, drove the slave and the slave's son, Ishmael, out of the house.

By nineteenth-century standards the customs and deeds condoned or praised by the authors of the Old Testament are unspeakably wicked. And as to the New Testament, judging by the *Canal Boatmen's Magazine* I don't think the missionaries would have countenanced those sinners whom Jesus Christ took to His heart.

The Fly-Boatman

These are what are called 'Fly-boats': they convey goods to and from Manchester, Liverpool, York, Coventry etc. and they travel as fast as possible – hence they are called 'Flys'. There are usually four men employed in these boats – two rest while the others lead the horse and steer the boat. And, like the stage coaches, they have their regular stages, where they change their horses, and proceed on without delay. The captain takes with him his passage bill, on which is the date and hour of his departure from London – and he is of course answerable for any delay in his passage.

But let us see who is in the cabin – O, here's one of the men asleep on his table – that is, the door of his cupboard, which has hinges at the bottom, and falls down like a flap, and then rests on brackets, so as to avoid useless furniture, and taking up too much room. Let us awake him.

'Hollo, there – what! Asleep in the middle of the day?'

'Ha Master!'

'I say, are you asleep in the middle of the day?'

'I believe I were – and right sleepy I am too.'

'Why, how's that?'

'We've not been in but about two hours – and travelled all night – we work just like horses.'

'On Sundays as well as weekdays?'

'Why, you know, if we stopp'd, others would not; and so they would get their goods down before us, and get all the custom.'

'Well, you can come to chapel to-day.'

'I fear not, Master; one is so tired and dirty, that it will not be possible.'

Now, this is not an over-rated picture: the men who work the fly-boats are little better than slaves; they toil and work, day and night, week and Sundays – for what? to enrich their masters.

The boatmen are usually in smock frocks, neatly worked, and which are to them what finely worked collars are to ladies. They bear fatigue and hard labor remarkably well. But the great feature to be deplored in their character is ignorance. Many do not attend a place of worship for years together – many cannot read. At present this is their occupation; they arrive with their boats in London, and unload them; then re-load, obtain what drink they well can, lay in their stock of meat and peck loaves, and off: – thus they live.

The usual speed of the fly-boats was two and a half miles an hour. They were owned by canal companies or firms such as Pickfords. Each captain, or steersman, was under contract and chose and fed his crew of three. The slow boats, slower because they were moored at night, belonged to the families who lived on them.

It is true that fly-boatmen were 'little better than slaves', but I don't think the lightermen, stevedores, carmen, stablemen and porters who worked on the wharfs were any better off. Even the mechanics – skilled workers, comparatively well paid – were frequently unemployed with no relief unless some small private charity helped them.

But if all these people worked 'to enrich their masters' they did not succeed, for throughout the nineteenth century wharfingers and boat owners kept going bankrupt or turning to other trades. The survivors were great firms like Pickfords who had long been in the road transport business and whose capital assets enabled them to adapt canal work to the needs of the railways. Pickfords had large canal stables near Camden Lock. A block in Oval Road, almost opposite our house, was still being used by railway horses when we came here and of course the Camden Town warehouses were conveniently placed for railway goods.

Such firms and the Regent's Canal Company itself benefited too by the completion of the Midland Railway in 1868 with its terminus at St Pancras. Beside St Pancras station a large canal basin was made to enable the coal trains to be unloaded into barges and taken to the docks. Coal from St Pancras was always a reliable source of income. Explosive and inflammable freight paid well too because the railways were reluctant to carry it and asked enormous sums for it.

Early in the morning of Friday, 2 October 1874, a train of six light barges pulled by a steamer tug worked its slow way through Camden Lock and got up speed on the straight between the Zoological Garden and Albert Road (Prince Albert Road). The first barge, *Tilbury*, carried sugar, nuts, straw-boards, coffee, some barrels of petroleum and about five tons of gunpowder. 'It is stated to be a common practice', wrote the *Illustrated London News* reporter, 'to send gunpowder and petroleum in the same barge.' *Limehouse* came next; *Susan* behind it had 'a little gunpowder on board'. As *Tilbury* was passing under Macclesfield Bridge which links Avenue Road with the north gate of Regent's Park it blew up. The men on *Tilbury* were killed; it was broken into fragments and another barge was sunk.

The bridge was entirely destroyed. Several of the neighbouring houses were half-ruined, their roofs and walls being greatly injured; and in hundreds of other houses, a mile east or west of the place, the windows were broken and many fragile articles of furniture. St. John's Wood and Camden Town were thrown into great consternation. It must, however, be confessed that the effects of such an explosion might have been much worse, if it had taken place at any part where, as in Kentish Town, the surface of the water is near the level of the adjoining streets. The fragments of the barge and cargo would, in the latter case, have been hurled right and left, a hundred yards or more, with terrible force and effect; instead of which they were mostly confined to the deep cutting of the canal. The sensation was that of a sudden shock and lift, and then a perpendicular fall, quite unlike the vibration caused by a passing railway-train in a cutting near one's house. The sound, which followed one or two seconds later, was a single sharp bang, like that of a huge bombshell, with a rolling clatter of echoes . . . But this sort of disturbance was nothing to the experience of some families inhabiting the houses in or near Albert-road, about the corner of Avenue-road, and the streets behind, in Portland Town, St. John's-wood. Not a few were fairly tossed out of their beds by the force of the shock, which really amounted to an earthquake in that part. Women and children rushed out of the houses, screaming for help, some in their night-dresses, others wrapped in blankets, and were not easily pacified by those of cooler mind whom they met. People soon hastened up from every quarter of town. The police, the Fire Brigade, and a detachment of Horse Guards (Blue) from Albany Barracks, presently arrived and kept order, while the task of saving what remained and searching for the lost was actively begun. A watchman who had been upon the bridge all night had fortunately left it . . . In the streets behind Park-road inhabited by small tradesmen, the contents of shops were lying on the pavement, the insides being perfectly gutted. A portion of stone was hurled from the canal into a garden in Acacia-road, a distance of five hundred yards, where it embedded itself in the ground. Lower down, towards the park, the destruction was still greater. The canal was obstructed by a heap of rubbish 20 ft. high, amidst which were to be seen the columns which supported the arches of the bridge, and other pieces of ironwork. The arch over the towing-path had fallen in, The girders supporting the midway were torn away and hurled high up on the slopes at the sides. The fluted pillars – shells of iron filled in with brick – which had supported the structure on each side, were cast down, and lay in the midst of heaps of earth, with a mass of puddle, broken stones, pieces of planking, and metal pipes formed a passage to the other side. A main of gas and one of water here crossing the canal were broken. The gas was on fire, and the water ran to waste; a drain or sewer was also burst open. A barge lay at the side nearest town; a couple of barges and the wreck of a fourth were visible at the other side. The trees on the canal banks were torn and scorched by the fire.

The sad work of dragging the bottom of the canal to find the dead bodies was watched by a multitude of spectators. The first two, those of William Taylor and the boy, were found at an early hour, beside the sunk barge Limehouse; that of the boy was lying on the canal bank. The body of Charles Baxton, steerer of the Tilbury, was found near four o'clock in the afternoon, under one of the other barges. These dead were removed to Marylebone Workhouse . . .

The animals in that part of the Zoological Gardens which is nearest the canal, and in which is also the house of Mr. Bartlett, the superintendent, were very much terrified. The elands and antelopes, the giraffes, the elephants, and a rhinoceros, showed great excitement. Some glass was broken, and the frames of the wirework in one of the aviaries, so that a dozen of the little birds escaped.[17]

Politicians never have had foresight except when they find themselves in the Opposition and if they are ever self-critical they take care not to show it, yet both qualities are essential to good government, which is why there never is good government. Most ordinary people have foresight and many are willing to express in public another useful virtue – fear. But in England, at least, there must be a calamity before their rulers listen to them. The dangers of storing and carrying explosives had been known for years. In 1864 a huge powder magazine at Erith blew up. In 1873 Bromley rice mills caught fire and a gunpowder barge moored in the canal beside the factory was showered with burning embers which by a miracle went out before they burned through its tarpaulin covers. There was a public uproar after the Macclesfield Bridge explosion. The newspapers were full of protests and special meetings were arranged to press the government into passing safety legislation, which they did in the following year when the first Explosives Act was promulgated.

In exactly the same way north London has now been waiting for years for an Act to control the transport of nuclear materials. All of us have watched the long sinister trains passing through Camden Road station on their way to the thickly populated East End. I guess we shall have to wait for a disaster ten thousand times worse than the 1874 one before those of us who survive can persuade any government to bother about it.

Now that the towpath gates have been unlocked, hundreds of people walk on it every summer under Macclesfield Bridge; some people still call it 'Blow-up' Bridge, the name the boatmen gave it after that disaster. I go in the winter too and once or twice I have passed another person. The bridge looks as it does in the old engravings of it because the pieces of the broken pillars which support it were welded together before a new roadway was made. I read somewhere that the lower parts were put the wrong way round; grooves made by towlines in the cast iron, such as those that remain on the Camden Lock horse bridge banister, have faced the land instead of the water since 1874.

Pickfords in the early days painted their boats to advertise themselves. British Waterways about a hundred and fifty years later did the same in blue and gold, which looked good to me but distressed the families whose homes the narrow boats were. I remember speaking to some of them in 1947 when the change began, while they were moored by Camden Lock at weekends. The outer panels of their boats had for several generations been painted in bright colours with roses, diamonds, daisies, towers and castles, which all made me think of Tarot cards and fairy stories. The boat I was invited into for tea had similar decorations inside. Their teacups and plates had roses on them. Their brass rails and chimney bands shone. Seven people, including four children, lived in that tiny cabin and it was more orderly than any house I could remember. It was the grandmother who spoke fiercely about the official colours which were to be forced upon her family. Her daughter resented any change at all. She had never been to school and didn't like her children going. She said they were learning bad ways from the Gorgios.

Cargo boats like theirs soon disappeared from our part of the canal and for several years so far as I remember there was no traffic on it at all except rubbish barges which were loaded at the council's wharf by Jamestown Street and were surrounded by a floating mess. I am surprised to hear that *Jason* began its pleasure trips as early as 1951 when horse-drawn narrow boats were still sometimes to be seen. British Waterways started the water bus between Little Venice and the zoo in 1959, St Pancras Basin was opened for yachts and during the sixties and seventies the number of pleasure boats, private and public, increased until now, in the summer time, the canal is as busy as it ever was.

The past keeps turning round to face us everywhere. There

are pictures of crowded pleasure boats at Paddington as early as the 1840s. *Jason* is painted with castles and roses. The cast-iron columns of 'Blow-up' Bridge are back to front like a turned shirt collar, the worn part inside.

August 30th, Saturday

Davie Laing in the Edinburgh had fixed to meet me no earlier than 2, because he thought today would be Friday – to give him time for lunch at the Hillwood Centre. His hair was even shorter than before and shows hollows in his temples, as deep as the hollows in his cheeks. He was much more cheerful than usual, more like he used to be when I first met him with Jack Winocour, in the days when Jack had just left his PRO job on the World Jewish Congress and spent more time in the Edinburgh Castle, a little way across the road from his house in Mornington Terrace.

Today, Davie spoke affectionately of Jack and I remembered what an impressive pair they were – equal in height, contrasted in character, Jack like a lavish film producer with his Scottish-American accent and hefty build, Davie as stern and starved as an eighteenth-century dominie. They shared reminiscences of Scotland, their Scottish-Jewish parentage. Davie was only half Jewish. His mother was a Presbyterian. But both their fathers were refugees from Eastern Poland. Jack's father was strictly orthodox and married a Glasgow orthodox wife, but he made his living by peddling Christian artefacts in the Outer Hebrides.

Arlington House is better for Davie at this time of year – half empty, most of 'the yobbos' are away on holiday jobs, and the new manager is very nice. Davie went to the optician Mr Johnson and was very thoroughly examined by a young lady with every kind of equipment – and was told he had no cataract, no glaucoma. Old age was all that's wrong with him. This cheered him up, although it meant she could not prescribe reading glasses. He went to the doctor, and by good luck the old English one was away. A young Indian took a lot of trouble, and decided there was nothing wrong with him physically. Depression was all that was wrong. This cheered him up. He was given anti-depression pills but they gave him diarrhoea. I said they had the opposite effect on me.

– I can't imagine why you would get depressed.

What reason would anyone with a family, friends and enough money to live on in a comfortable house have to be depressed?

That was his attitude years ago, too, when I was unhappy and told him so, told him that you don't need to be poor to be unhappy.

He has given up alcohol and drinks tonic water or tomato juice. He gave me a lecture on the poisons in the bitter I was drinking and it didn't strike him as funny when I pointed out that he had been drinking it with me happily a few weeks ago when we last met. He is less nervous in the mornings since he gave up beer. Even 2 pints affected him next day. His hand shook, and he had no appetite for breakfast. Now he has a boiled egg, or 2 if he can afford it, toast and 2 cups of tea. At Peter's. Peter's is the best café, clean, and it's mostly elderly people who go in there – 'no yobbos'.

I said apropos of how he spends his day

– You're very much alone.

– By my own choice. I keep myself to myself. I'm better on my own.

Which is a change from the past, when he was distressed at having no one to talk to – when he so much longed to see me as the only one.

Another change was that he said he had 'no difficulty at all in passing the time': Shaw library, for big print books, Lincoln's Inn Fields to walk and sit and 'if it's raining I'll take any bus anywhere, anywhere at all'. He likes to sit on top and look out of the window. When he gets to the terminus he doesn't go walking or do much. He takes another bus back. His eyes were alert, his face expressive. His appearance and everything he said showed he has got over the depression. Consequently, and this is an unfair fact in physical illness too, I no longer found him tedious. When he most needs companionship and is lonely and sad, I hate to be with him – his complaints about his circumstances, his sorrow for himself make me more grumpy than I normally am. He has a new and healthy habit of drinking 'pure orange juice'. He gets it at the Pakistani shop, as he calls the Inverness St supermarket. Then a bottle of milk at the dairy – and that is what he has in the evening. He gets back about 4 – and never goes out because he's afraid of being mugged. As we parted he said he had a few messages to get before going home.

August 31st, Sunday

From the Edinburgh Gardens M. and I saw the smoke from a huge fire. It was far away across Paddington across the park but it darkened the sky to the west and seemed to be blowing upwards and towards us. We talked about that day last month when night came over London in the middle of the day – about the doomsday feeling. I had taken a note to Luke in the pouring rain and first saw it as I turned out of Arlington Road. Car lights, then street lamps came on at noon – yellow grey-green foggy low clouds turning black over Edinburgh Castle, and coming lower like a fog as I looked from Delancey Street and then from Parkway over the trees of Glos. Gate and Reg. Park.

Martina seeing it from the house was reminded of smog. And when she said that I remembered the great smog – the last? – which was when she was with Richard – how she was excited by it, enjoyed it, and how doom-like I felt it to be because I knew she was with him.

September 1st, 1980, Monday

I started a new MS book this morning, the patterned cloth one, wrote six lines and broke off as nearly in tears as I have been since last winter. I can't sit still, am terribly nervous and my thoughts are scattered. After listening to D. Laing on Sat. I am inclined to blame drink – 4 pints of bitter yesterday.

And now I have lost the six lines. I know I wrote them in the flowery book but they are not in it now. Panicky search. There's a page torn out in the middle, roughly torn. I do it with a knife and if I start writing I start on the first page. Besides, I'd remember, wouldn't I? And I hid the book. No one else in the house. Whatever I wrote was probably no good, but it's alarming to have forgotten it because usually one can say anything over to one's self for a day or two almost verbatim, can't stop revising it in one's head all the way down the street, which is annoying. It was about Martina's pyromania. I remember that much. And her first bonfire in the garden here.

September 2nd, Tuesday

> I saw a frisky fox-tail of fire peep out of a garret-window and shake itself in the air, speckling the night with large fluttering sparks that fell to earth slowly and unwillingly. The beauty of the fire excited me. It was as though some red beast had sprung suddenly out of the moist, warm darkness into the window under the roof, had arched its back and was gnawing furiously at something . . . I thought: Someone ought to go and knock at the windows, wake people up, and cry: 'Fire'! But I felt incapable of moving or shouting: I just stood, captivated, watching the quick growth of the flame: the hue of cock's feathers had begun to flash on the edge of the roof, the top branches of the tree in the garden became pink and golden, and the square began to light up.[18]

If Maxim Gorki had lived long enough and known Martina, he would certainly have put her in his diary together with Nikita and Zolotnitzki whose passion for fire was greater than his own. Zolotnitzki had been imprisoned for thirty years for heresy and left prison a fire-worshipper. He was very quiet. He

> grew animated only when he was allowed to light a wood-pile in the stove and sit in front of it, watching it. Seating himself on a low little stool, he lit the logs lovingly, making the sign of the cross over them . . . He pushed the burning logs gently with a small poker, swayed backwards and forwards as though about to poke his head into the fire, while the wind drew the thin green hairs of his beard inside the stove.

When the Tartar soldiers arrested Nikita during a forest fire they accused him of arson, of dragging the fire from one place to another.

> 'I was only lighting my pipe.'

'. . . we saw you set fire to a branch and carry it along.'

They thrashed him.

The bailiff said, 'Don't strike him . . . Flames go to his head like wine to a drunkard's. Whenever there's a fire he's the first to rush there like a madman. He'll come and open his eyes wide and stare dumbfounded, as though he were nailed to the ground. It never occurs to him to help.'

Gorki himself lay that night

on the dry, hot ground and watched the purple flames swell and balance in the sky over the forest as though bringing a sacrifice to propitiate the Wood-Satyr, incensed with thick smoke . . . At times the fire crept slowly out of the forest, like a cat on the look-out for a bird . . . The air grows more and more stifling and acrid, the smoke thick and hot; the earth smoulders . . . one can feel the hairs of one's eyebrows move with the hot blast. It is impossible to stand the smoky air which tears one's lungs any longer, yet one feels strangely unwilling to go: when shall we have the chance again to watch such a magnificent feast of fire?

I have known Martina stay half the night alone by the great bonfires she makes in the country, circling round with a long rake in her hands, watching each flame separately as it leaps and glides down again into its red bed of cinders, coaxing the cinders gently into a new rising flame, stirring the dull ashes to redden them again. It was to make sure the fire could be safely left alone for the night. Yet she kept putting new things on and whenever I came out to see her long after dark on summer nights her eyes were on fire, but she looked serious and peaceful like a religieuse in silent hidden ecstasy.

She made her first bonfire here out of builders' rubbish a few days after we had moved into the house. The side garden, that long cold narrow strip beneath our north wall, was heaped with laths and dry-rot splinters which burned well. It was a Saturday or Sunday and from the backs of the houses in Oval Road and Gloucester Crescent people stared at their new neighbours and slammed their windows angrily down. The side garden is lower than the basement floor but the flames at times sprang up to the level of my eyes as I watched from the open staircase window which is just below the first floor;

whenever they dropped, clouds of smoke, grey and blue, enveloped Martina and the windows of the houses round about. She soon cured that by piling on fuel. The fire went on from two in the afternoon till midnight.

While I was looking after it and she putting Timothy into his cot upstairs a window behind me was thrown up and I saw a fierce head above me which shouted

– There's a law against that!

It harangued me for a while with the sarcastic kind of anger the Scots are so good at and then the window thudded down. I am always terrified by other people's anger. I had never made a bonfire in London before, except on Guy Fawkes nights with crowds of people joining in. And then I thought the man might be right about a law and how bad a beginning it was to raise a smoke screen between us and our neighbours. I tried to quench the fire a bit. When Martina came down again and heard what had happened she took it lightly, even laughed. She said the man was probably teasing me, trying to frighten me to see what I'd do; I looked so odd, she said. I said

– We'd better let it go out now.

– Yes. May I just put on these little bits?

Little bits kept going on until it was as big as ever.

Years later a stranger spoke to me

– I'm the man who shouted at you. I was pulling your leg.

His name is Jock. I got to know him well. His house in Gloucester Crescent was pulled down about a year after our fire.

M. came in for the telephone book just now, silent, not wanting to interrupt me, but I didn't want her to go. I was angry about what Pillicock said – me not keeping accounts, losing receipts. It's true, but I don't want a sermon. He's missed his vocation. Should have been a parson, not a tax accountant. I was wishing I'd told him that. She glanced at my face and this diary and said

– How's Mrs Thatcher getting on?

She welcomes Mrs T. as my scapegoat. When I told her I was writing about her affair with Maxim Gorki she seemed pleased but I think she would have preferred Dostoevsky. Her love of Russia comes mostly from literature but is much deeper than mine because of her father.

September 18th

Getting old under state surveillance is somewhat like the
change from winter to summer time or summer time to winter,
sudden and unreal. Just as you read in the newspaper one
evening that the clocks will go forward or back at 2 a.m. that
night you hear from the government that their 'records show'
that you'll get the old-age pension in six months' time. It has
been decided officially that you become old on a certain day,
just as it is decided that it will be dark at six instead of seven.
You can have your first coach trip to the seaside on that day.
You will be taken care of, even pitied, from then on. The
natural, gradual change is not allowed.

Sho-Sho doesn't know how old she is. She pauses and looks
for a second more than she used to before jumping the long
jump from my windowsill to the next-door doorstep, but she
roams about on her adventures every night all night and at
home she still plays as she did when she was a young cat.

Mrs Lunnon didn't know how old she was until she met a
school friend on the bus who had been drawing the old-age
pension for seven years.

But I am not old. I am a Senior Citizen. I don't get the
OAP. I draw a State Retirement Pension. I no longer go to
the Deafness Clinic at the Royal Ear Hospital. The word has
been crossed out on my appointments card and Audiology
Clinic written in in ink. It is all so beautiful.

September 19th (After Brittany)

Returning from Tréboul Sables Blancs was sad in a way I
remembered from childhood but had forgotten till the moment
of parting from the *femme de chambre*, *patronne*, etc., on the
steps of the hotel.

In childhood there had been desolate holidays – one at
Worthing, I remember, and sometimes even at Nairn when
gloom or boredom prevailed and frequently we longed for the
day of departure. On the day, I was suddenly overwhelmed
with regret, felt I loved the place, had wasted its beauty in
bad moods; remorse made me look at or think of every detail

that I had ignored. I wanted, like all those old men I have listened to, 'to have my time over again'.

Tréboul wasn't desolate at all. But even M. was saying
– It's only 5. Two hours till dinner.

So it was often boring, sometimes pleasantly boring. And when it ended, I had terrible regrets about the whole of our Brittany – the first two days of which were really near to desperation. But mainly in the taxi to Quimper Aeroport, it was the thought of Tréboul, the hotel and the people in it. I wanted to go back and have more of it.

And I am surprised here at home to find how much the hotel occupies my mind. M. thought of *M. Hulot's Holiday* and I think of old illustrated magazines, but someone said the hotel was unique – only one other something like it farther south. *Salons vitrés* – vast glass dining room, breakfast room with glass roof and walls. Our room, the end one of many looking on the sea and beach and bay. Nothing in between, steps from main hall on to walled-in sand, and from there to public beach. The cliff path, the path to Tréboul Port by the little church. I remember it all and the people there vividly as I wake up or lie half asleep. And now we are away from it it reminds me of other places or people one can't go back to that one could have known better at the time. One lovely thing I miss very much is being together night and day all the time for a whole week. And now with the St Albans course M. will be away at work 4 days a week instead of three. When I was writing properly I used to love to be quite alone in the house. Now I cannot imagine being able to sit at my desk from 6 a.m. Early a.m. is the worst time.

September 21st, Sunday

Last night with the Jamiesons in the Engineer we were surrounded by young people, who packed the pub full of enjoyment, light-heartedness, and looking at a table full of them I thought the untrue thought that I had got old in a day – that it really was quite a short time before they would be old. But, immediately, I worked it out as a long gradual time.

I had been wondering for a moment whether one of them

could see himself at my age. But of course he would not or could not.

September 23rd, Tuesday

Last night I met M. at St Pancras after her first St Albans day – she doesn't get back till about half past eight. I was waiting for her in the bar called the Shires Bar – all the buffets and bars have been changed since our wedding reception there. It was so long since I had been alone in town in the evening that for the first time I had a sense of fear – e.g. I thought two men were staring at me, then realized that they were watching another man, on a gambling machine behind me, and that I was blocking their view.

I was remembering with regret how fearless I used to be and how I used to enjoy being in much rougher places than a railway bar.

September 26th

On our way home from Mornington Crescent we stopped to look at the old Camden Theatre which was renamed the Music Machine when it became a pop music centre about five years ago. Its old green dome and yellow pillars are unchanged but above and around the doors there are psychedelic lights and lettering, which make it look like an old lady, in stately hat and bodice, who has stepped into a young girl's glittering mini.

Said to M. as we walked on how glad I am that it has been opened for people's pleasure again after all those private years as a BBC studio.

Several punk girls came walking fast towards us, and it struck me again how like space fiction their get-up is; their make-up is inhuman too; some give the impression of *Grand Guignol*. The first we saw took long strides in long legs closely fitted with yellow stockings to the knee and tight black satin breeches to above the waist. A top of some bright colour, hair cropped and scraped with top knots sticking up. She had passed us in a flash, and as I looked back I had the impression that she was wearing a sword at her waist. It may have been a long cane, or an umbrella as tightly rolled as herself. Then a few yards behind her came the others straggling but with rapid steps like speckled glaring lights.

In spite of the bright clothes and the greens, yellows, scarlets of the hair in streaks, in patches or whole – sometimes a blotch of white on dark hair reminds me of a long-healed saddle sore on an old horse – in spite of the showy flash, there is a puritanical severity about the punk look, male and female. The skimpy scrimp of the boys' clothes – tight jeans often not long enough to cover the shins, jackets pinched at the armpits and chest with sleeves stopping short of the wrist – give them a poor and meagre look, especially if you compare them with the long-haired boys of a few years ago whose clothes were more amply cut. Then, since facial expressions can be designed and worn to fashion, the majority look as grim as any Wee Free Minister. It is startling to see such a look of severity, especially on the girls' faces in the evening outside a pleasure dome, but this I guess is fashion too.

September 27th, Saturday

I have started to write about the smell of bonfires and the way it rouses old emotions and works on memory. Sounds and tastes do the same. It seems when you first think about it that all three would have to be experienced rarely to have such effects, yet petrol fumes, which like everybody else I breathe in daily, sometimes evoke the most poignant memories of setting out in a car, when cars were rare and we were children, to the country from Nairn. And the strange thing is that usually I hate the smell. I sometimes have to shut my window if I'm writing at my desk on a summer day and cars are starting or queuing up to park outside it. Until recently we had never met anyone who disliked the smell of leaf or woodsmoke – but neighbours' complaints about our own bonfires are common. Rimple-Pimple used to make an awful fuss in the autumn when leaves were being burned in the terrace. The Henlys garage men once rang the police when the smoke was blowing their way. In the suburbs I have heard of people complaining about cockcrow, people who hate the smell of stables, cowsheds, boiling tar. And now that the last horses have gone from the railway buildings – Gilbey's coach horses were the last – M. and I have only a ghostly experience to share. When I first told her I smelt horses at the Henlys Corner traffic lights, she said

– You're lucky, and laughed about it.

I knew it must be an illusion too. But one day when we were together there, she smelt it too. And now we often notice it when we are together. She has an idea that traffic lights may smell like horses, but we have neither of us experienced it anywhere else.

So how about a new cult – the Ghost Sniffers? Have you had this exciting experience or are you still chugging along in low gear without knowing it, like most other people, without knowing that you are living with your handbrake on? The Community of Smells will teach you to release your brakes. Emanations from the past are trying to reach you. The Community will guide them and show you the way to them.

September 28th, Sunday

Yesterday, Saturday afternoon with M. on her way to her driving lesson, we passed many people of a kind we never used to see in Camden Tn before, people connected with the markets – buyers and sellers from the newest one by the Bucks Head and from Dingwalls Lock – the new name for Camden Lock. They were mostly young and there was a carefree feeling about them – some sitting and standing outside the Elephant's Head, which we called the Boxers when we first came. They are very unlike the Inverness Street market people, some of whom are also very young, and unlike any group one sees on weekdays – crowds enjoying themselves here at weekends, as strangers to us, and to most local people, like tourists. (Those are Martina's observations.) Our new markets extend to side streets on the right of the Chalk Farm road and to the forecourts of the Round House. The one outside Swiss Cottage library grows and grows.

M. saw a young girl on a 31 bus with things she had bought and was going to sell elsewhere – filled with excitement and enjoyment. It was the sense of enjoyment outside the Boxer that struck us yesterday, and the very fact that they were enjoying themselves openly in the street is something new too. For, some years ago, no Cam. Tn pub and least of all a working-class one like the Boxer would have had tables outside on the pavement.

Martina thinks Loup-the-Dyke is like Don Quixote – especially when he described the Café Royal dinner which he attended while he was a patient at Barnet. He had special permission and was given an allowance of £4 for the evening.

– For some reason I thought it better to get out of the tube at Camden Town. I ran all the way from there to the Café Royal. I thought it better to take my sweater off. I was in a blue shirt. No one said a word. I was shown to my place – it was halfway through the dinner.

He took a taxi back, but got out and walked long before he reached Barnet – not having enough for the whole fare.

M. thought how English it all was – the dinner – the wrong clothes.

September 29th, Monday

It is 20 past 9. Martina left before 8 for St Albans. I am alone and am surprised to find myself uneasy to be alone. For a long time now Ben or M. have been here. Yet I am also glad to be alone. The long-lost feeling that I can write, at least a little bit, and that my imagination is working again – at least intermittently – consoles me as soon as I open this diary and I remember the devoted interest I had in writing and the occasional pleasure or at least satisfaction. Last week (on the 23rd) I wrote about the punk girls and my unfounded fear in the St Pancras bar. I guess it was unfounded. But there does seem to be more to fear in London than there was when we first came to Camden Tn. And yet remember Martina's dark railway footbridge on the way to Tanza Rd, and there were Teddy Boys, Mods and Rockers and what else? A succession of warring groups or gangs.

Doris Lessing's *Survivor*[19] has gangs of marauding children. I don't think we ever considered that possibility until we read the book. But talk to any school teacher and you know how adults can be terrorized. We were sitting on the terrace, last year I think, Joan, Martina and me, and three little girls, the eldest 7 or 8, came to torment us with demands – I forget for what, but I remember their complete insensitivity to our feelings of annoyance, their blocky persistence. One started pulling things out of M.'s bag, stopped when I rebuked her, but started again surreptitiously. And last week two boys in school uniform stopped me on the canal bridge in Kentish Town Rd and one said

– What's the time? in a threatening tone with a thick tight expression on his face, ungiving, seemingly incapable of smiling, yet only 10 yrs old. It annoyed me, their lack of grace, the aggressive tone, the way they regarded me as a clock instead of a person; it annoyed me so much that I would not look at my watch, but guessed the time. When I had passed them I saw I had guessed half an hour wrong, and I thought of the boys in Doris Lessing's book.

October 1st, Primrose Hill

Smoke School Infant Sch. Assembly for reading of *Danny Fox*. Little children, very quiet, walking in class by class and sitting on floor. Piano. Sun and sky through windows. The whole thing made me sad in a way I can't define for a reason I couldn't think of. The playground too afterwards – all pleasant, happy looking. On the way home I found M. had felt sad too. She had been thinking as we sat behind the children – 'What happens later? What goes wrong?'

October 4th, Saturday

A report of an inquiry into the working of the railways published this week says most of the cancelled commuter trains are cancelled because drivers and guards don't turn up, take days off without warning, etc. 'The practice of taking unofficial days off is so well established that staff have special names for it – "Awaydays" in S. region and "Blow-outs" in Eastern.'[20]

M. and I were talking about it last night – as something new, an attitude to work that didn't exist 10 or 15 years ago. And in our experience – theatre, BBC, farm, etc. – it wasn't the fear of getting the sack that made people turn up for work, nor a feeling of duty towards a superior. It was just that one did turn up. M. said it was the same with social engagements – that I wouldn't let down Bob Marriott. And that reminded me that I think he must be dead. It was just before Christmas last that I saw him in the MDDX, and then went again and heard he had been discharged. I have never inquired about him at the Southwell place, and he never wrote about the little Adrian Boult book I sent for Christmas, which is unlike him. He was always writing letters.

My old notebooks and diaries are sprinkled with him.

I have known Bob Marriott for thirty-five years, but anyone who knew him for as many minutes would be struck by his selfish and dictatorial nature, and also by his love of music, for he never wants to talk about anything else and as he talks he sings, with perfect memory, bars from the works of Sibelius, Bach, Beethoven and from his favourite composers who are Elgar, in the lead, and Walton second. In the wartime blackout, and especially on foggy nights, his voice in Portland Place was a guide to all who heard him on their way out after work from the BBC because he, like me and my colleagues, was making his way to the nearest pub, the George, with more confident steps than ours. He had known the district since his young days at the Queen's Hall which was a blitzed wreck by then. The George had survived the bomb and kept most of its old clientele, who were musicians. Bob lived for years near us in Camden Town at Rowton House and then, because he couldn't help wetting his bed, he was moved to an old people's home which he doesn't like at Southwell, five miles away, south of the river. He still comes here frequently to see old friends, thanks to the old-age bus pass.

Like several old people I know, especially women, he cannot go anywhere without a heavily loaded bag in each hand. His are filled with newspapers. He buys *The Times* on Saturdays only, for its concert page, keeps all the back numbers in one large plastic bag together with out-of-date copies of other papers which his old Camden Town newsagent gives him. In another bag he has more papers, a large thermos, hairbrush, nail clippers, sandwiches often, a transistor radio about twelve inches by three, and an old-fashioned alarm clock. The radio and clock are presents from friends. The clock was given to him by a violinist in February, but he was delighted for months by its novelty, stooping with difficulty from his chair every few minutes to take it out of its bag, when we met in May, look at its face and put it back again, although he was in no hurry and never is.

'That clock's an hour slow,' he said, pointing to the pub clock.

He will not believe that his gains ten minutes a day and is cross with me because he thinks I am late for our meetings.

'I know you're a very busy man. Some people are lucky.'

I had asked him his age that day in 1977.

'Let me see. 1894 I was born.'

I worked it out as eighty-three.

'I didn't know I was over eighty. No. 1897 I was born. Royal Marines 1914, that's right. They had a good band, that's why. We went to the States and Norway. I wasn't in it, they wouldn't let me in it. Private soldier, that's all. The only friends I made was in the band. Always at rehearsals when I got the chance. I went to Netherhall last week, met Whatd'youmacallim – good trombonist – commissionaire now. Now he's been very good to me, got me tickets for the Elgar.'

His manner of speech is sharp and clipped, without flow, each phrase detached, and so to speak without gracenotes. Bullets of speech issue from a tiny mouth, an imperceptible slit between immovable lips. When he smiles or laughs it is his cheeks that move but only a little bit now that he has grown fat; when he was thin they were like sheets of starched pink linen on which God had dabbed with a paintbrush two minute bright blue dots for eyes.

He has had many friends in his long life, Barbirolli, Hubert Parry, Constant Lambert and Alan Rawsthorne amongst them, and yet some people found his very presence repellent. Louis Macneice, who always took about five years to tolerate a stranger, used to embarrass me by turning away whenever Bob came up to speak to me in the George, but Bob was unconscious of that situation. In those days I had him for short spells only with other people joining in. His jerky monologues exhaust me now and I have to find excuses for a rest. Also, he is severe with me, strictly critical of my ways. My ignorance of music annoys him, especially when he tells an anecdote about a composer whose name he has forgotten, hums one bar and expects me to know who wrote it. He is very popular in the Camden Town post office where he used to draw his old-age pension, the only money he has had since his sixty-fifth birthday, and he still goes there to talk to the clerks to the great annoyance of customers behind him in the queue.

He was born in the City of London a short walk from St Paul's Cathedral where his father for many years sang alto in the choir. He went to St Paul's School, on a chorister's scholarship, where he sang treble or soprano until his voice broke. It was then that his father introduced him to the Baltic Exchange. His voice and lungs, long accustomed to projection, made him acceptable at once as a 'caller'. His job for many years was to stand dressed up in uniform on the rostrum of the exchange calling out people's names in chanting tones that could be heard by every member of the concourse in that vast chamber, by the shipping men in front of him and the cereal men farther back. Each one, when his turn came to speak, stepped onto the rostrum and whispered his name to the caller who had to catch the name quickly, invent his own chant for it and call it out at once. He cannot and never could write the names. He learned them as he learns and remembers music, at the first hearing, and his memory of the most difficult of them has lasted to this day. 'Giorg Bounapopholous. I stumbled on that first time, but not next day. And worse, his brother Eustasius Bounapopholous.' He pronounced these names fluently to me but could not spell them. I have written them phonetically.

'It's a long time ago. Who was that man whose wife got mixed up with Edward VIII? I knew him well. After a while he'd come up on the rostrum and look at me. It's a long time ago. You know the name.'

'Mr Simpson.'

'Simpson Spencer Young. That's right, I knew him well. If

93

I waited for him to say his name, which I was supposed to before I called it, he'd say, "Come on, Master Caller, you know me by now." Then there was – it's a long time ago – what's his name, that rival to Onassis? That was a difficult name.'

He speaks French fairly well, and when I asked him how that came about he said St Paul's was 'strong on it and then I was with the First Secretary in Paris. British Embassy.'

'What was your job with him?'

'Looking after his shirts and suits and everything. We ate downstairs. We ate well. Beautiful house. Rue Whatsit. You know the place. No, it's Place . . . It's a long time ago. Well you had a job over there. In Quartier Whatsaname. You know it. I'd been with him at the Foreign Office here when I'd come out of the Royal Marines in 1922. Met him in Pompey, that's right. Our ship was in the dockyards in Pompey. Nice place. It was a gunnery ship. Our band played on the seafront all summer. Beautiful.'

When I asked why they wouldn't have him in the band, he said he wasn't good enough.

'I could play several instruments for my own pleasure, but never good enough. When I was with the First Secretary he gave me tickets for concerts when he could. *Faust* – that was something special all my life, the chance to have seats at the L'Opèra. I heard the Elgar last week. Had a dozen complimentary tickets. Sold them for £1 each, except one. I've got to live. You've always been very good to me, David. I remember once, I'll never forget it, you couldn't get comps. You walked out of the George. I thought I'd said something wrong. You bought two tickets from the agency next door. I took the canteen lady from Bruce House along.'

She was his only friend in Bruce House. In Rowton House he had none, and has none now in the old people's home, but by his own energy he has saved himself from Justice Shallow's loneliness and from the creeping apathy that overcomes most people living in institutions. Justice Shallow was ashamed to ask for money and had no friends. When Bob has been unlucky for a long time be begs either for cash or comps, but in a code which only those who know him well can decipher. Thus:

Dear David, I was laying in bed this evening thinking of the 'Gluepot' [the George]. I turned my transistor on at 7.30 p.m. Radio 3 Scottish National Orchestra conductor Alexander Gibson. Programme Holst Suite The Perfect Fool (another Planet) Aurora a new work by Ian Hamilton (very modern) *and* Elgar Symphony No. 1 in A flat op. 55, some people are lucky, Yours truly . . .

By 'some people' he meant himself.

Dear David, I called on you this morning and was informed you were in Norfolk. I enclose the programme of the concert of the 23rd, Yours truly . . .

Dear David, I was *not* in Camden Town this morning *but* I received Prom Tickets for the 23rd and 24th July practically the *first nights*. All the best. Yours truly (Bob) E. L. Marriott.

Dear David, I was listening to Man of Action (2 p.m.) Michael Ayrton. He mentioned The George. He knew Constant Lambert, Cecil Gray, Lizzie Lutyens, William Walton. I wish you well. Yours truly . . .

Dear David, I listened to a magnificent performance at 8.30 of Elgar's symphony No. 1 in A flat. BBC Northern Orchestra conducted by Sir Charles Groves, also last night a tribute to Mrs Edwin Clarke – many people spoke of her as a personal friend Yours truly, (Bob) E. L. Marriott.

He sends these discreet and nostalgic *cris de coeur* by second-class post. His thank-you letters travel first.

I feel I must thank you again for that £5. When I saw you this morning outside the post office I had £1.17.6d on me to last until *next* Thursday. I only wish we could have had a 'session' in the Dublin Castle.

I had been in a hurry that day but even when I am not I try to escape chance 'sessions'. I need a little time to compose myself beforehand into a humble and receptive mood. Without it he angers me, and I him, or my attention wanders from him. He is jealous and possessive; no one is allowed to speak to me in his presence. There was a lovely Irish barmaid in the Dublin last year who ran across the road to buy a paperback of one of my books and came back to get me to autograph it for her sister as a birthday present. She took a little time reminding me which sister it was – there were five whom I knew – and I tried to introduce her to Bob. He turned his head away grumpily and would not speak until her unwelcome presence was withdrawn. If I wear anything unusual – I mean anything he has not seen before – he jeers at me.

'What's that on your head?' he said in Camden High Street once and laughed aloud at the sight of a black corduroy cap. And years later, 'You remember when I saw you in that funny cap? Now that day I meant to tell you . . .' (he had his revenge by telling me whatever it was for twenty minutes at the street corner). 'Well you're a busy man, I don't blame you. Always in a rush.'

Some of his letters were reproachful too in veiled or open terms:

I was on a 68 bus this morning – going to Kingsway to have lunch with a girl friend and I saw you in a light coat and your peaked cap – seeing a lady on to a bus behind me! I must say you looked well. Yours truly . . .

I rang your bell yesterday and a lady opened the door. I asked if you were in – but got no answer. I noticed the blinds were down. I was also in the Dublin Castle from 11.30 to 12 but didn't see you.

We were away and Maria must have been tidying up the house. She does not like my disreputable acquaintances.

Some years before that, when I hadn't seen him for some months, he told me he had passed down Regent's Park Terrace once or twice.

'Are you still living in that big house?'

'Yes.'

'I saw a motorbike outside. Expensive things, you know.'

In fact there were two, belonging to our sons Tim and Luke who bought them with their own wages. Tim was working in the sewers at the time and Luke in a factory. Ben was still doing music at Morley College, but saving up for his bike.

October 5th

Until today which is cloudy we have had beautiful warm sunny weather – people sitting out in the park, on the seats opposite the convent, on the low Henlys' wall and bus stop walls, and outside pubs whether the pub is open or not. And many men leaning on the wire fences by the traffic lights, à la farmyard gate. On Henlys' low green wall a reincarnation of Justice Shallow has been sitting reading a paper for hours day after day. He is thin and wears a stained ancient mac and when he walks his hands are clasped behind him, the fingers curled like claws, the palm of one hand outwards. His walk – a bit splayfooted – is very like J. S.'s, his skinny slightly hunched shoulders too, but his face is not so thin, not I think so sensitive.

Susan says the weather is always beautiful like this at this time of year. It makes her sad because it's the end of the summer. It makes me and Martina sad, just as spring does, but not for such a clear reason – it's more like yearning – for Paris? For some past autumn, or some ideal autumn that never happened? Martina reminded me of the *vitres* being put up in the cafés in Paris – the excitement we felt at this time of year.

October 7th

A wild day – broken branches in the road and on the pavements – the leafy branches of plane trees with green sea-urchin fruit on them.

October 9th, Thursday

What I long to regain, if I ever had it, is the ability to enjoy autumn, spring, etc., while it is going on. I am sure I did once. Perhaps I still can. But I have an idea that enjoyment is never felt while it is happening. After a dance or game of tennis, people say 'that was good', but if you consciously think 'this is good' or 'I'm enjoying this', while it is going on, you have stopped concentrating on it, interrupted your enjoyment. Compare not knowing what you are doing in a crisis – when often you do the wrong thing; lose your head. (M. said about Brittany in Sept. that it 'distilled' into something good.) And I'm sure my yearnings have nothing to do with age, with wanting a return to youth. I had them throughout my youth and at school. But this autumn is peculiar; it's haunted by last autumn, weather and our daily journeys across London – the trees, the fallen tree in the pond, the bus stops, the hospital grounds, and the trees wildly waving in the wind outside the Ward F windows.

Last Tuesday, Oct. 7th, was just such a wild day, a heavy storm of rain from 11 for an hour or two, then bright sky with clouds quickly passing. I walked through Primrose Hill to Maida Vale – the pavements littered with leafy branches, mostly plane trees and bunches of prickly green nuts.

October 10th

In the Spread today, Alf – I think it is – spoke to me in just the way I hate

– How's that Camden Town book coming on? That must be four years ago you were talking about it.

It's my own fault, but I thought at the time I had to let people know what I was doing, to explain my questioning and in the hope of volunteers with memories and opinions. I've got out of the habit of talking to people and wanted to bury my head in the newspaper which, these days, is more depressing than anything he could think up. But he was depressing, and bitter about his past: unemployment in the thirties, an employer cutting his wages down, what he said to the employer, how he was cheated after the war by a building contractor for whom he worked on the 'lump', how the landlord of the White Hart – Paddy Gorham I suppose – who was no better than him before he got the pub, insulted him when he ordered a pint by saying

– I thought you'd want something from the top shelf by now, meaning spirits. Gorham was a builder's workman, just as Alf was, but became a Big Digger and made enough to buy the lease of that pub. Then we had the Tories, much against those bloody fools in the working class who voted Thatcher in

– 'Now they've got their deserts' – with which I agree, but it has often been so. I remember the dockers cheering their arch-enemy Enoch Powell, and marching behind him to Parliament just because he made one of his anti-black speeches to them. We had much against the young, too, for not 'sticking it' at work, which may be true of some; one cause I think is drugs which in my youth and Alf's were a privilege reserved for the rich. But I hate the sentimental pride with which he boasted about there being no social security when he was their age, as though there is a virtue in suffering.

I said nothing except hoom and hum all the time, and wished I was somewhere else.

Maybe he was just in a bad mood this morning, with a different way of coping with it than mine. He was funny at the Parkway zebra crossing the other day, waiting endlessly with me on the pavement as the cars rushed past.

– D'you remember how we used to help old ladies across the street? Now we have to wait for them to help us.

I find mothers with push chairs even better, but for real safety make sure there's a baby in the chair not a bundle of washing from the launderette. Cars spot that kind of deception from a distance.

October 11th, Saturday

Davie Laing met by chance in the Edinburgh has gone back to beer which he lectured me against last time we met when he was drinking tonic water.

October 12th, Sunday

In the garden of the Engineer I mistook a man's gestures for rage. It was his way of dealing with a wasp – unsuccessful until a woman with a long scarf came to the rescue and I suppose struck it to the ground. I still think our childhood way was best, to sit still. They don't sting unless you attack them.

October 27th, Monday

Warm – clouds – leaves flying. Some fly up. They cross each other's paths like birds.

November 3rd

Armistice Day. Poppies. Very few people wear them nowadays and I evade the sellers not from meanness, but from revulsion formed in childhood. I knew even then that they raised money for disabled soldiers, etc., but they and the whole occasion were inspired by self-righteousness and sentimentality – and in my young boyhood at Norfolk House by bellicose patriotism. Now it is worse. It is used by the British Nazis and the South Africans for their own propaganda.

Norfolk House taught me to dislike the Union Jack at the age of 8 or 9. It has now become the English Nazi flag and it's difficult not to think of that when you see it.

Two years ago the old Australian badger was much influenced by the Kentish Town Nazis, young and middle-aged, who flattered him by listening to his adventurous life at sea, etc. – he can be a good raconteur. He used to go about saying, in his Aussie accent

– Are you English? Who's English here?

To people who obviously were not – McL. for instance, and pointedly Nathan, who responded with a dignified silence.

The Nazis persuaded him to march to the Cenotaph in their special group, which wasn't officially allowed. At that time he kept on talking about Hitler's birthday, etc.

November 18th, Tuesday

David Laing died on 4 November and I went to the funeral yesterday at St Pancras Cemetery, a vast place shared by Camden and Islington councils in East Finchley. I have never had even a similar experience. The question is – although I want to – can I sit in my room and describe it?

When the letter came, signed Jean Graham, I thought I had never been to East Finchley before, but at breakfast M.

reminded me of going with her and the children often to the Finchley baths, the open-air ones. Nomansland begins miles before you reach the cemetery; as the tube emerges from the tunnel you see how it begins. I came out of East Finchley station at about quarter to nine in the morning, warm, rainy but not raining then, and was told by a cheerful ticket collector to cross the road and turn left up the hill. I crossed it through those sheep-dip railings they now use to guide one through traffic lights and walked, for twenty minutes, Jean Graham said, but I thought half an hour, with huge traffic on my left and lonely closed small shops and cafés, cheap clothes for unhappy churchgoers, 'mini-markets' with tins at bargain prices, black print on yellow posters pasted on their windows, a Wimpy, two little kebab shops looking long disused – 'Large or small kebabs. Take-away'. More take-away shops. The tiny clothes shops were the saddest, as though they had been set up with pride and now dust and out-of-dateness lay on them.

I saw a man locking or trying the lock of an off-licence, then trying or locking the house door of the shop, a man's handbag hanging from his wrist – a small dark hunched man in an old IRA mac fiddling and peering at a bunch of keys of many sizes. He was startled when I asked him the way to the cemetery, but he recovered himself and told me to walk straight on. I thought, Is he a burglar? The handbag has a gun in it. Will he have to shoot me because I saw him at it? It is the kind of street at that hour for that thought and everybody said 'Walk straight on', which I could not believe. I asked many because I could not believe it was so far with no sight of an open space. I believed I should have turned to the right where the roads looked level in the distance. I would have asked more people but most of them were safe from me in cars or lorries.

The main road forked, little houses on each side, no more shops and at last an open space beside me on my right, but it was 'Allotments No Admittance', then playing fields, then after the brow of that long hill, as the road sloped gently down, round a curve which gave no warning of it, the cemetery, 'The St Pancras Cemetery and Islington Cemetery' in black letters on a white board, a drive with wide white gates leading in and a big Victorian gatelodge on my left. A man in uniform came out of it and touched his car as though he would have got into it if he hadn't seen me. He was in traffic warden colours, a dark suit with yellow bands, and he was smoking a cigarette, noticeably smoking it. I asked for the English chapel.

– That's it there, he said, pointing with the cigarette to a spire among trees half a mile away.

– I'll be down there shortly myself.

He asked if the funeral I 'wanted' was a Camden one.

I said

– St Pancras, because the old-fashioned name on the notice board was just behind us.

– I call it Camden. What name?

He knew David Laing's name at once, and that the funeral was at 9.30, and again he said he'd 'be over at the chapel directly', as though I would blame him for being late or might be afraid to wait there alone.

I walked on along a wide roadway lined with graves and little shrubs, with side roads leading off it, graves on either side as far as you could see. A fork to the left led to the chapel and as soon as I turned towards it an old sense of reverence came back to me, a sense of being in a place where people had been buried and mourned; I had not reached the intimacy of a graveyard but at least I was out of the tidyness; the symmetry till then had been like a stonemason's display. I was soon in the oldest part, but saw no grave earlier than 1880. They were rather grand and ornate. A favourite style had a flat stone roof held up by pillars and in the middle of that four-poster bed lay a thick carved cross with its head on a pillow and its foot sloping down towards the roadway. One of these, to a woman, was inscribed 'Gone but not Forgotten'. Her husband's name below it, five years later, was carved without a saying. Much better. The worst thing about sayings is how people use them ready-made. How could he have forgotten her however long he lived? And anyway he must have decided on the inscription soon after her death.

Nearer still to the chapel there were modest attempts in the mausoleum style.

By these old graves and beside the chapel there is a sacred grove of huge old trees which I took to be yews as I approached it, but they were strange to me entirely: one with leaves like an oak, but elongated, narrow and I think evergreen; another, more beautiful, with a great reddish trunk had dark, shiny leaves, laurel-shaped but narrow and smaller. The others I cannot remember but there was one yew. They had been planted roughly in a circle and their leaves formed a canopy over the bare earth beneath them on which lay twigs, scattered leaves and bits of bark, russet-coloured like the trunks of the trees. I felt calmer. On my way there, from that moment I turned into the drive, I felt I was in a desolate housing estate among miniature houses for the dead. I had not expected to find a sense of holiness in a vast borough council cemetery, but the grove and the chapel were made by the St Pancras Vestry a hundred years ago, when the Camden Town churchyard in Pratt Street overflowed. The grove and the chapel are the oldest parts, I think.

The little chapel was of whitish and grey stone with a grey spire pleasant to look at but rather too tall for it. There were privet hedges with pathways that seemed to lead to north and south doors but, trying to find a notice to show it was Church of England and thinking that Davie's funeral should have been in one of the Scottish churches, I walked between the privet narrowly and came to an old public lavatory built into the chapel wall. A broken board with faded print exhorted me to hygiene.

The front door of the chapel had no notice board at all, so I opened it and was looking round the inner porch when I saw a young woman sitting in a vestry reading under a bare electric bulb. I asked her. She said it was the right chapel.

– I'll be back, I said, because it was still too early, too long to sit and talk to a stranger, though I guessed at once that she was Jean Graham. I walked about the graves and the grove again expecting to see a hearse, a parson or at least the traffic warden man. Slow solitude. Then I went back and introduced myself, saying that I had heard a lot about her from David Laing.

– Oh, that's not me. That must be Margaret.

I had not remembered the name of his friend.

Margaret had known him through her job with the Royal Scottish Corporation for seven years and certainly it was she he spoke of so affectionately and often, but, said Jean, she had left her job about seven weeks ago. Jean took over at that time and had only met David Laing once, about six weeks ago – about five weeks ago? And then only because his wallet had been stolen. I remembered then, but did not say so, how in the Edinburgh Castle on that day together he had had a 'windfall' from the RS Corporation and was pressing me to a large whisky 'to return a little bit of all your hospitality', and how I had disappointed him, almost angered him, by having beer instead. When I said I'd have a muckle dram next time we met, he shook his head.

– My pocket won't be strong enough to hold it.

Jean Graham comes from Inverness so we had a flimsy bond through Nairn where she spent her childhood holidays, or if not at Nairn then on the Black Isle across the firth. She was lively, fluent, insistent, and showed real sympathy for Davie.

Jean and I were waiting, talking, glancing at our watches, not knowing that we had arrived too early, when the traffic warden or coffin warden came in with a lighted cigarette in one hand and a large parcel of lavatory paper under his other arm. He said something I didn't hear and threw the parcel into a large cardboard box some distance away from him. There were lots of cardboard boxes and other junk against the wall of the vestry, disordered, sordid – the whole of the little room uncared-for and smelling like a pub when he had gone. But it was a bright room, with large windows and a high ceiling slanted at the corners like an attic, all newly painted in white and pale green.

Then Margaret came in – a lively, amused-looking girl with an east coast Scottish accent (the wee Dundonian, Davie called her in one of his letters), dark short hair, serious humorous round face, dozens of Fair Isle jerseys, which she took off rapidly, and a short coat. She was just in time, for at that moment the warden came back without his cigarette and ushered us into the chapel – a tiny cruciform room which had also been newly painted, but in white and blue. We sat in pews on the southern arm of the cross, short pews made for four, and only about six of them, divided by a narrow aisle. The girls sat in the front row on my left, nearest the altar, and I in the front row across this aisle, nearer to the door. There

were no pews facing the altar and nothing in the little nave
but two high trestles. On the reading ledge before me there
were two pink books, disagreeably shiny and stained, each
containing various funeral services, and a black book which
in the short time before the service began I thought contained
the Church of England Book of Common Prayer one, but I
wasn't sure because I haven't looked at a funeral service since
my father's death nearly thirty years ago.

The parson and the coffin came in without music because,
as I discovered later, he has to switch it on. He was about
forty, with dark brown hair, thick and full, and a reddish but
not unhealthy weather-beaten face. How could that be in
London – the remains of a holiday or from standing many
times a day reading the burial service on the edge of an open
grave? There was something coarse and bored about his face,
or so I thought then, but now I remember not to trust such
momentary judgements.

Beyond the trestles in front of us in the northern arm of the
cross where I had expected to see more pews, there lay a
higgledy-piggledy mass of indescribably large boxes or boards
painted grey and slotted like the acoustic equipment in a
studio. The parson stood behind a simple wooden lectern,
looking expectantly down the centre of the nave towards the
door. Then three mutes walked in slowly with the coffin on
their shoulders, two grey-haired men on one side, one at the
head and one at the foot, and on the side nearest me a young
man with his shoulder under the middle of the coffin. They
laid it on the trestles dexterously by stooping, turned and
walked out. It was dignified. The young man looked more
gloomy than he need have, but had probably only just finished
his training.

When they had gone the parson began his gabbling: 'Pink
book, page this, paragraph this, line that . . .' and he ran
through each passage rapidly. I was afraid we would be
expected to sing the psalm ('The Lord is my shepherd'), but
that and the Lord's Prayer were spoken by the girls trying to
keep pace with him. I muttered bits I think, but could not
make myself join in. When he came to the end he stretched
his right arm out and pressed a button for the funeral march

and, hearing this, the mutes came in and shouldered the coffin again. The parson followed it out, then the girls, then me.

I had been imagining during the service what Davie was looking like, what dressed in, inside the coffin, not a pleasant imagining. I then wondered whether it really held his body, for by now my mind had fashioned a skyscraper mortuary run by the council to supply so vast a cemetery, and in it the corpses would go by floors and numbers and easily get mixed up. I thought he should have been buried with his walking stick by his side, as men were once buried with their swords. He could scarcely let go of it even while he was eating, or drinking beer. And then, the coffin seemed too short for so tall a man.

I looked at the sacred grove again as we came out of the chapel and then at the three men sliding the coffin into the hearse. The hearse is fitted with rollers. The pale unvarnished wood of the coffin was already speckled with rain.

Fortunately Margaret had a little car. The grave was so far away that no mourner on foot could have reached it in time. After passing through acres of gravestones and unadorned graves, which got poorer and smaller as we went on, the hearse careering ahead of us down the sandy roads, a glass balloon framed in black, we came to a flat open field – the rest of the cemetery is slightly hilly – and slowed down to a stop by a rusty iron-netting fence which separated us from the Great North Road where a stream of juggernauts, lorries and cars roared and shook. The rain had become a small drizzle and the wind blew strongly in our faces as we left the car and waited for the men to take the coffin from the hearse. They were fitting long straps of greenish khaki webbing to it.

We followed the bearers of the coffin up a muddy slope. The grass showed through in places and, treading it, we made it disappear, and where the way was muddiest there were planks to walk on or sections of weatherboard paling laid flat. We were on the much trodden route to the most recent 'public graves', as paupers' graves are called, for the rest of the field below was green. The bearers were sure-footed and balanced the coffin skilfully over the slippery way.

As our procession went along by the railing, a juggernaut passed only a little bit faster than us and I could feel it shuddering through my body, shuddering through the coffin in my mind. Then we turned from the railing down the slope to the grave – a long pit, deeper than I thought it would be, so deep on that dark day that it looked bottomless, its perpendicular walls precisely cut and glistening without a spademark, the blackest of black topsoil for several feet and, farther down, the yellowish shitty London clay which also lay in clotted heaps round the rim of the grave. There were planks and boards to walk on and these were so slippery with wet clay that I thought the bearers might fall with their heavy load, but they found firm footholds and lowered the coffin on its straps. When it reached the bottom the straps released themselves – I don't know how – and were pulled up to be used again.

The parson stood far from us, above the head of the coffin and was completely inaudible to us at the other end, even to the girls. Jean walked round to the side to be nearer to him, keeping her balance with small steps on the slippery board.

'For as much as it has pleased Almighty God of his great mercy to take unto himself the soul of our dear brother here departed, we therefore commit his body to the ground; earth to earth, ashes to ashes, dust to dust . . .'

At the right moment Jean stooped, picked up some clay and threw it down onto the coffin. It was hard and sounded like a stone. Not hearing a word, I did the same too late and mine sounded duller.

She had brought a bunch of flowers done up in transparent plastic, but quite invisible because of the rain. In fact funeral flowers are nowadays always invisible; instead you see plastic bags shining on top of the coffin, on top of the hearse. On our way to the grave I had noticed probably a hundred of these packages heaped up against the fence, unopened with the withered flowers inside them. From a distance they looked like the scales of a giant fish, and as we came nearer like translucent fan-shaped bones, quite flat; I think it is the bones near the gills that I mean. They reminded me, too, of dead bluebottles' wings and of mother-of-pearl fans with thick, uncomely handles where the stalks of the flowers were. Whatever image they make you think of, it is old and dusty and thrown away. I suspect that the grave-diggers neglect to lay them on the grave at all and that David's would be thrown on to the pile as soon as we had left.

The rules are strict. As we left, I holding Jean by the hand, both of us intent on not slipping into the grave, one of the older undertakers distracted my attention dangerously by tapping me on the shoulder and handing me a printed card – 'London Borough of Camden. Saint Pancras Cemetery . . . Public Grave No. 246. Section C H 6.' Only the figures were filled in in handwriting. The name of the public corpse was not given, but on the back were rigorous instructions to the mourner, starting:

The only memorials allowed on public graves are as follows:
a) A bronze plate which can be had on application to the Cemetery Office, Town Hall, Euston Road, N.W.1.
b) A stone flower vase not exceeding seven inches in height, length and width . . . Your stone mason must apply to the cemeteries Manager for permission to erect the vase and, after approval, pay the Council's licence.

Davie Laing has no relatives, no one who cares about him more than Margaret does, more than I do, or the people at the Hillwood Centre whom she expected at the funeral but who didn't come, and none of us is likely ever to revisit his grave. He left no one to be personally distressed by these rules.

The parson said goodbye, still bareheaded in the rain, the undertakers piled in, and the hearse raced away empty. It and the parson's car were out of sight before we started.

Margaret drove us back through miles of Nomansland as far as Tufnell Park tube station.

As we said goodbye to Margaret there, I told her how often and affectionately Davie used to talk about her.

– Don't believe a word of it, she said.

Rain, sodden papers, grey filth at Tufnell Park crossroads.

Death is a nasty reminder of what might have been. After Davie's funeral, remorse beset me on the dismal midday tube and in the grey rain, regretful sorrow for the threadbare spaces in our friendship which only I could have stitched up. We shared two disabilities, short-sightedness and melancholia, which in a way that now makes me inclined to laugh kept us apart at times when our real need was each other's company.

We were never close friends, but we both liked the Edinburgh Castle, especially its garden in summer, and though I had explored more modern literature than he we had been brought up more or less on the same kind of reading. He taught me a lot about the Old Testament and when he told the stories of Cain and Abel, Jacob and Esau, Ruth, Esther, Absalom and Achitophel, reminding me of all I had forgotten and bringing ancient names to life, his voice slowed down, his Edinburgh accent took on a tinge of Highland because it was from his Highland grandmother that he first heard these stories told.

I have had from childhood visions of the people in the stories, some remembered from picture books but most, and the most vivid, derived from real people who frightened me as, on top of the high garden wall of my grandmother's house at Nairn, I watched them pass. Among them walked the gnome, the giant, the witch, and at night from my bed the dead man howling in the graveyard and the skeleton clanking his chains beneath my window, especially on windy nights when the iron ball scraped the pebbles as he dragged it after him. These characters fitted the Bible and the fairy stories clearly in my mind as a child, just as clearly as David Laing, when I first met him in my middle-age, became the Preacher, Ecclesiastes.

He was eloquent and pessimistic. He was gaunt and he was cold; I cannot remember him without an overcoat even on hot summer days, and in its pocket he always carried a copy of Omar Khayyam. He pulled it out of his overcoat pocket so frequently to read a stanza aloud that the life of one copy was short, but when one fell to pieces, friends replaced it. In the library and in his room at Arlington House he read much else but he carried with him only Omar and when alone in cafés or pubs would read it again and again from beginning to end. It was a tattered copy of this book and my curiosity about it that introduced me to him.

Like anyone else in Camden Town I had so often come face to face with him on the pavement, or stood beside him, waiting to cross the road, that it had seemed unnatural not to speak or at least nod a greeting but, I think from shyness, he did not allow it. The expression on his face when alone was severe; he kept his wide mouth tightly closed and his cheeks were dented as though he sucked them in against his teeth. Like me he wore a cap, and spectacles that hid his eyes. He was tall like a plank with a head on top which leant forward. He walked very slowly, placing each foot deliberately like a giraffe and he always had a walking stick as my father did, not to support a lame leg but because it had been the fashion in his youth. Once, when a young man jeered at him, saying, 'Why do you need that?' he answered, 'I need it for clouting ill-mannered boys with.'

He was always afraid of being mugged and on the lookout, but when he encountered danger he was more courageous than most men. I believe it was his dignity in manner and movement that kept him out of trouble most of the time, for all old-age pensioners are threatened, especially on pension day.

For most of the time too he kept his personality well hidden. He shared with many other lonely people that unhappy pride in 'keeping himself to himself'. But once you gained his confidence he gave you measured pieces of himself, a different measure for each of his few friends, as I discovered only after his death. He was born in Leith and his numerous old relatives had till some years before been sprinkled liberally through Edinburgh, as mine had, but his memories of that beautiful stark city were warmer than mine, far removed from icy respectability, and after the image I had formed of his almost ministerial severity it was a relief to share his enjoyment of scandalous gossip, the part of which I remember best was about Sir Roderick Ross, the legendary chief of police, by whose name the Madame of the Cosmo 'Whorehouse' in Swinton Road behind the Catholic cathedral, defended her establishment against police raids. She had only to say, 'Sir Roderick's upstairs,' and they would leave. He was, they said, an illegitimate son of Edward VII, and David had watched him in 1920, leading a procession on a white horse up the Royal Mile, trimming his manner and having trimmed his beard into an image of the late King. David was sixteen at the time and just about to leave George Heriot's School, full of confidence and lightness. Storytelling was a gift he had retained when I first knew him, and he told this one and others with a descriptive power that revived adolescent arrogance, optimism and ribaldry. He seemed so absorbed in those young days and his schoolfriends that I was startled when once he stopped, looked at me grimly and said, 'It's as though I am speaking of somebody else. I know it was me, but it's not me; it's as though it is someone I've read about.'

It was not that he disowned his former self or disapproved.

After nearly a year of casual meetings during which our talk was light, he appeared one evening to be in the deepest gloom which someone made worse by clapping him on the shoulder and saying, 'Come on, old chap, it's not so bad as all that.'

He left his beer on the bar and walked out. Next day and on several occasions later, in the dairy and the street, he shunned me and he stopped coming to the Edinburgh Castle. I saw him by chance in a dark corner of another pub and, distrusting myself for breaking his chosen solitude, I went to speak. I need not have been doubtful. He was pleased and said I was the only person he could talk to and yet he had not wanted me to see him as he was. He had been avoiding all the places and the people that he knew. He had reached a stage of depression which makes me think of walking on the Cairngorm moors in early winter on the heather, before the snow but after the flower has withered into dead paper, when the leaves can no longer be described as brown, grey or green but as a dull mist with no end to it. You do not know which way to take on the moors; they lie in ridges before you and as you climb each ridge you expect a view from the top. You know there is a warm and lively village very near in the green Spey valley and that the snowy mountains are not far away, but when you reach the top of each ridge all you see before you is another one, the dreary same. In your agitation you reach a pitch that even to feel calm is an achievement enough in itself without mental or physical activity.

Whenever he reached this stage David Laing sought a cause for it outside himself and although the real cause probably lay within, for the circumstances in which he lived remained the same as they had been while he was happy, there were causes enough to choose from – the main one being life in Arlington House which he regarded as no better than a prison from which he was sent out on compulsory parole each day from nine o'clock in the morning till four in the afternoon. While he was depressed he made no plans for escape and, during the years of our friendship, each recovery led to hope for somewhere else to live. That first year his recovery began with thoughts of Leith and Edinburgh, with anecdotes of youth and childhood, and before long he had made up his mind to end his days where they began. He had no surviving relatives there, but one friend, in his early seventies like him, with whom he sometimes corresponded. This friend, whose name was Alick, would find him pleasant lodgings much cheaper than Arlington House. At Leith he would be near the sea and healthier than in London. He gave every kind of physical reason for the decision but privately built a dream of contentment.

Jack Winocour and I helped him with the fare, a single fare. I remember suggesting a return, but he would not have it; he would, he said, be able to afford a weekend ticket now and then or use a football excursion to see his old friends in London and when he did, the very first place he would visit would be the Edinburgh Castle. And so it was. But not on a weekend ticket. On an October evening about six weeks after his departure he walked into the bar looking pale and even thinner than before and choked off every question about Edinburgh with a shake of his head or a monosyllable. He had come back for good and was ashamed as anyone might be who has set out for paradise only to find a desert. The cafés and pubs that had been high-lit in his nostalgic dream were sordid and filled with strangers, mostly young 'yobbos' who were rude to him; the streets were unswept, the people walking in them hostile, not like Leith or Edinburgh folk at all; his lodgings smelt of rancid bacon day and night. Even the sea was full of polythene bags and plastic cups. And Alick, his one surviving friend, was in such an advanced state of alcoholism that he could not afford to drink with him. Alick alone remained kind and witty, but you had either to avoid his company or spend rent money on drink.

Davie, as he often did in difficult situations, found a text in

Omar that fitted this abortive expedition. He sorted the loose
leaves of his torn copy and took this page out to read aloud:

> The Worldly Hope men set their Hearts upon
> Turns Ashes – or it prospers; and anon,
> Like Snow upon the Desert's dusty Face
> Lighting a little Hour or two – is gone.

He said that Edinburgh seemed to him a ghost town and that
Leith was dead – 'quite dead' – and I knew it was his own
youth he was lamenting as I unconsciously had lamented mine
on every visit to Oxford where places were familiar but the
people in them strange.

Davie had always dressed with care, wearing clean shirts and
ties and preserving his few clothes from stains and tears in a
way that no one else living solely on an old-age pension could
manage. His clothes went down with him in Scotland; both
cuffs of his jacket were frayed and the right elbow of his shirt
showed through; the knees of his trousers were shiny and thin
and his boots leaked; all of which increased his shame. My
clothes have often been like that, not from poverty but because
I didn't bother about them, and I wouldn't have noticed his
had he not apologized for them and shown the defects to me
one by one. Neither he nor any of us knew that he was entitled
to a social security clothing allowance.

But during that time he made the only friend he ever was to
make among the thousand inhabitants of Arlington House – a
fellow Scot named Peter Cochrane. It was Peter who introduced
him to that ancient charity the Royal Scottish Corporation,
whose purpose is to relieve 'persons resident or found within a
radius of 35 miles of Charing Cross who are in conditions of
need, hardship or distress, being persons who were born in
Scotland . . .' At the premises of this charity, a beautiful Queen
Anne house in Covent Garden, you can still see the brass-bound
kist, now known as the Scots Box, into which its founders put
coins for the poor. They were the better-off members of the
Scottish colony which began in London when James VI moved
his court from Holyrood on his accession to the English throne,
bringing with him thousands of followers, many of whom were
driven to destitution by racial and religious discrimination, and

by the difficulty they had with the English language. Later in the seventeenth century the charity received royal favour and became the Scottish Hospital of the Foundation of Charles II.

It is managed in a very personal way. Everyone it helps is put under the care of a so-called welfare visitor who keeps in touch with him so long as his poverty lasts. David Laing's welfare visitor was Margaret Watters, the pretty girl who came to his funeral years later. They met on 13 January 1977, three days after his seventy-third birthday. She was in her early twenties. He fell in love with her immediately. In her report of their first meeting she wrote 'very clean and tidy man, doesn't like to receive visits at lodgings, will meet elsewhere. Recommendation: Assistance with clothing'. She went out with him to buy shoes at once and then applied to the social security for a 'special needs allowance', which was granted not only that year but eighteen months later and again in the autumn of 1980, six weeks before his death. When I saw the form that came with one of his grants I at once remembered the ominous days before I was first sent to boarding school, at the age of eight, when a list of 'required clothing' lay on the writing table at home. In proposing to dress me that compulsory list seemed to undress me. Underclothes are private, only to be seen by the intimate, and all clothes are personal, to be chosen privately, or with someone you love. Later in life there was a list of things to take to hospital, including pyjamas, which I never wear. It seemed to me as a boy that hostile strangers would strip me of my own clothes and force me into things belonging to someone else. It was indecent. I don't think David Laing felt that but he did accept all grants and gifts with resentment. There is always the hateful feeling – 'other people depend on themselves, as I used to' and he probably read the list with the same mixture of resentment and amusement as I did.

Raincoat £17, 1 pair of shoes £7.50, 2 vests £3.20, 2 pairs of pants £2.30, 1 jacket £20, 1 pair of trousers £7.50.

No socks, I noticed.

My mother tempered my list to some extent by taking me with her to buy the things. Margaret Watters went with Davie to Kemp's second-hand shop in Camden Town and the advice she gave him, and her very presence, transformed the occasion which he dreaded, for he hated going into clothes shops, into a delight. She laughed at some of the things he would have chosen but took him seriously and guided him towards what suited him. For him it was a holiday outing away from the day's routine of passing the time. The prices on his list were meant for new clothes of the cheapest make but if you don't mind wearing dead men's things or living castaways you can find much better cloth and cut second hand for less. The worst part of it is the smell, for most old clothes shops are rancid, their goods reek of urine and stale sweat in dingy chambers where you cannot see to choose. But Alfred Kemp's is spacious, well aired and lit, and smells when it smells at all of floor polish. All the clothes that I have ever handled in it are spotless, revived and freshened by the cleaner.

Most London clothes shops have wheelbarrows and cart-wheels in their windows: anything but clothes. Kemp's has suits, jackets, trousers, shirts and shoes, hung one above the other and all along, filling all the window space. You can get a good look at them from outside the shop before you summon up the courage to go in, and by the cash desk on your left when you do go in, instead of the supermarket notices 'Thieves will be prosecuted', you see to your left beside the cash desk, a narrow sentry box which Mr Kemp inhabits when he is not buying or selling. On it there is a card in red and black to threaten you with the police. By a secret as sure and hidden as an invisible ray, they and every trader in Camden High Street are roused whenever you attempt to steal one of Mr Kemp's garments. He is superior in height to me, to his shop assistants and almost all his customers, though I guess Davie Laing may have outdone him by half an inch. His verbal politeness towards customers is superior too in the old-fashioned 'take it or leave it' manner of the most exclusive firms. He told me that in his father's time there were more than five hundred shops of this kind within two miles of here – he and Moss Bros. are the only survivors. Moss Bros. started at just the same time as Kemps.

He was interrupted by a man who pushed open the door with a stack of suits which he held before him as though supporting a spare belly. His real one was large and his arms and face a deadly white. He was about sixty. He laid the stack on the table and gave Mr Kemp an expressive look which I can't interpret; perhaps he was merely trying to guess what luck he would find behind the inexpressive leather shield, pierced by blue eyes, which was moving slowly towards him.

Mr Kemp picked up each neatly folded garment in the fingers of one hand without glancing down at the table and raised it to the level of his eyes as though to sniff at it but really to give it a penetrating look; then he felt it with a light touch and a short pull in chosen places – jackets at the seams of the armpits, trousers at the crutch – and let it drop onto the table as a boy undressing lets his clothes drop to the floor. The would-be seller and I stood watching as the untidy heap on the left grew rapidly higher than the stack. I had never seen clothes handled in that way, rhythmically, exactly, and was fascinated by the knowing expertise. I saw no emotion on the seller's face but knew that his hopes were falling as one after another of the garments fell. No one spoke at all, even when the last suit had gone from the stack into disarray. For a moment no one moved. Then Mr Kemp performed what seemed a miracle to me by remaking the stack symmetrically within a few seconds, taking up each fallen garment and folding it quickly and gently with invisible skill. As he replaced the last jacket he picked up the stack and placed it on its owner's ready forearms, advising him to try such and such a firm. When he had gone, he turned to me and said, 'You saw that? Quite unsaleable. Some people have no idea.'

I asked whether they were out of date in style, in bad condition or what, but all he would say was, 'I couldn't sell them.'

Davie's new friendship and the newly bought clothes took away the black dog from his shoulder and for several months he was happy and calmer than I had ever known him. In March 1977, when the RSC granted him one of their very small pensions – less than £10 a month – he wrote:

Dear Margaret,
    I really don't know how to thank you. I had not expected such good fortune to come so soon and, believe me, I've been very 'down' recently – life seems pointless – but not now, at least not so much. You see I'm in this Hill Wood Centre [the club for old people where he had lunch every day] but as the younger generation

would say, 'it's not my scene'. Now I'll be able to get a real meal outside. I had hoped to see you and have a wee chat and maybe you'll let me know any time you're up in Camden.

Yours in gratitude and if an old chap like me may say so – with affection –

David Laing

His letters grew more and more affectionate and anxious. She had noted down at the beginning that he did not want to be visited at Arlington House where the public rooms are bleak and crowded with inquisitive ears, so they met at Euston Station in the buffet or in summer at Lincoln's Inn Fields, which had long been his favourite place in good weather. But sometimes, when other work prevented her from turning up and there was no way of warning him, he would wait in vain, in terrible distress. That often happens between friends when one has too much to do and the other too little. It often happened between me and him as well, and although I never purposely 'stood him up' his letters to me like the ones to Margaret are filled with disappointments.

Today, Monday, I was up at the York and Albany from 1–2.30 hoping that you might turn up. I remember you said perhaps at 1.30 but then again I know you didn't promise . . . Well, David if you are free this coming week could you possibly ring Hill Wood? Between 1 and 2 if possible. There are many things that I should like to discuss with you as you are my only friend (excepting my dear Margaret Watters).
Cheerio for now – Yours Davie.

Saturday – It's been such a very long time since I had the pleasure of your company . . . I was in the Spread Eagle and also the Edinburgh Castle but knew that I was wasting my time. Anyhow, I'm putting this through your letter-box in the fervent hope that I may see you tomorrow . . . I am very lonely David, very depressed, but if fate is lucky for me (for once) we'll meet again . . .

Saturday – Dear David, could I hope to see you tomorrow? . . . I am indeed very desolate and wish with all my heart just to have a friend to talk to . . . I was in the Spread Eagle hoping to see you but you must have been elsewhere.

It was a relief sometimes when I tried in vain to find him.

> Dear David, I am indeed very sorry that I was elsewhere when you called at Hill Wood. You see what happened was this – by sheer accident I ran into a chap who was with me in the Army – one Jack Cocks, a Cornishman and a good fellow: he and I had good times together when we were both at Catterick. Our main rendezvous was the quaint old city of Richmond (York), where we made as much whoopee as Army pay would allow. Well, David, he wouldn't let me put my hand in my pocket and bought me whisky after whisky and the Christmas cash I had (by courtesy of the Scots Corporation) vanished like 'snow off a dyke' because I just can't accept hospitality of this sort without some return . . .

There follows a list of possible times and places at which he would wait for me hoping, and then:

> I do wish I'd seen you when you called at Hill Wood – it would have been just dandy but, of course, I had no premonition that you would call. Two Sundays ago I spent an entirely miserable hour at the York and Albany, hoping that you would turn up but I quite realise that you have other calls on your time.

As I reread his letters after his death I knew that I had wronged him many times when I wished to be alone, not blatantly by missing an appointment, but by avoiding the places where I knew he would be. Yet there have been long periods in my life, as in most people's, when loneliness and lack of purpose made solitude a spectre, as it was to him, a dark misty figure that cramps the mind, creeping in to empty it and leave a dark vault, when it was a relief to be stopped on the pavement by a stranger who wanted to know the way to the tube station.
In April 1977:

> Well, it looks like another day of sunshine and showers: I'll have a turn on the bus somewhere – Croydon maybe or Putney. Believe me Margaret it's hard work just passing the time.

But when deep depression had lifted – it came in bouts – he was able to make the empty days sound full.

> Dear Margaret, Remembering that I had promised to write, so

here it is, not mind you that I have anything to write about except to say I am glad to write to you – my Guardian Angel. My day has followed the pattern of all my Sundays, in other words, merely putting in the time, first of all poached egg on toast in the only café that opens on Sundays around here – then to the bus stop and away to Putney – a wee walk along the river and then back on the bus to Camden and my usual Sunday refreshment – two pints of Guinness – buying on my way back some bread and a tin of sardines which is my lunch and supper combined. Now I'll turn on my radio (disturbing no one because I have an earphone) and I have the Sunday Post to read. I know full well, Margaret, that life has passed me by. I live like a monk in his cell or like a hermit – only by God's grace I've got the mental ability to overcome it. But enough about myself or you'll be accusing me of self-pity which just is not true, although everybody nowadays seems to suffer from the prevalent London malady – the 'hump', especially at the Hill Wood! I am indebted to you for many reasons my dear, one of them being your vitality and the sunshine of your smile. I think of happy summer days in Lincoln's Inn Fields and hope very much we will meet there again this summer. I would like to have a look at the Barnet flats. Maybe you could manage to take me one day.

The Barnet flats like his Edinburgh hope raised him up for some months and let him drop even deeper than before. The flats had been acquired and renovated by the Royal Scottish Corporation as a provision for the homeless, and from the day he heard he had a chance of getting one, of starting life on his own again, without restrictive rules away from his thousand housemates, he started daydreaming again, describing to me with renewed enthusiasm whenever we met, which was more often then, the new and independent life he saw before him. He said that instead of using his free bus pass for lonely trips to Putney, he would come in to Camden Town several times a week to see his friends. His daydreams included a woman, who would be his companion at Barnet, help him to arrange the flat and perhaps even stay in it. All this and more he frequently told me, and the nearer the time came to leave it the more he reviled Rowton House. But as soon as the Barnet papers were ready to sign and a date fixed for the move he lost both faith and courage – for it did need all the courage he had summoned up in contemplation. His reasons seemed somewhat confused as he gave them to me, but on paper to the Scottish Corporation he had wanted

> . . . to say this clearly – I see no prospect of taking up residence there: I know that, as you say, the security people will pay my rent but . . . I can't see how I can pay my electricity bills . . . I've become habituated to this place, it has its merits. Heat and light included in my £7.60 rent, clean sheets and towel weekly, my room swept by a porter – even occasionally washed – so for many in my position and at my age, it's better than being in a flat. Another point is the Hillwood of course, dinner at 15p is not to be given up lightly. I couldn't cook the same for 15p! not to mention messing about with pots and pans . . .

When he told me it had taken several nights of anxiety to come to that decision, he looked calmly at me and I believed the decision had calmed him. But it was not so for long. He hid from his few friends again and wandered about London in private hopeless gloom.

One morning some weeks later, catching sight of him from the front window as he was pushing something through our letterbox, I ran to ask him in. He was trembling. His face had a hunted look and he was short of breath as he protested, 'I never intrude. It is all in the letter.'

He came in through the hall and into my room with his head bowed, as though ashamed to look about him, and as soon as he sat back in the big armchair, he stared at the ceiling instead of the carpet, making me as embarrassed as he was. But luckily there was some whisky in the bottle which soon eased us both.

It was a Friday morning, rent day at Arlington House. He had collected his pension at the post office on the Thursday and after a few drinks by himself in the evening had gone to a café for a snack. He sat down opposite a stranger 'but a Scotsman and a decent enough fellow', and found much to talk about – places and people they had both known. The stranger had half a bottle of whisky in his pocket and offered to pour some into Davie's tea, but Davie said. 'No. Not in the café. It wouldn't do.'

They went to the park to drink it. It was a beautiful, warm evening and they sat on a secluded bench to drink it behind the children's playground near Gloucester Gate. David swore he did not drink much. There must have been something put in it – but the next thing he remembered was waking up just as darkness fell, lying on the grass on his back looking up at the sky. His wallet and all his money had gone. The clouds were tinged with red when he woke up. He watched them moving. They were part of a dream about blood which he tried to remember but could not. I searched his face for signs of a fight but saw none.

'At Arlington House,' he told me, 'if you don't pay your rent on the proper day your belongings are taken out of your room next morning and the room locked against you.' I had enough money for the rent in my pocket and gave it to him with a little bit more, but he didn't wish to leave; it was as though he dared not, as though he had rediscovered physical comfort together with companionship and had to hold on to them until I tore them from him. Only I could shelter him or tear the shelter away. I was conscious of that at the time and much distracted by the knowledge of it, because I was correcting proofs that morning and was very near a deadline. I had dropped the typescript and was restoring its loose pages to order by arranging them in little piles all over the floor. Davie had reached his chair carefully via stepping stones of carpet and now sat clasping his stick and cap between his knees with both hands. When I told him I had to finish the proofs before the last post that evening, he kept quiet for a while but none of the books I seized from the shelves, not even Jamieson's 'Muckle Buik' (*The Dictionary of the Scottish Language*) could keep him quiet for more than five minutes. Memories roused by everything he looked at came out in little bursts of speech – the spacious room, the books in it and the old-fashioned armchair in which he sat were like his grandmother's; on the farm where he worked when he was young, a man got his foot caught in the threshing drum and instead of stopping the machinery, the crew ran away in a panic and the man's foot was crushed; the best speakeasy in Boston during prohibition when he was twenty-three; a cat he once had; the incredible size of the rats by the Charles River, Boston; the parrots that walked free about the bar of the Volunteer, a Baker Street pub, only half an hour's walk across Regent's Park from where we were sitting. Then suddenly he stood up and said, 'Thank you, Davie. I never felt more like doing away with myself than I did this morning.'

That was the only time he spoke of suicide to me. I suppose I protested against his thought of it, but I was not alarmed because the causes were real – remorse after drinking too much and fear of being turned out on to the streets that night. The days of his heebie-jeebies, when despair had no outward or actual cause, had been and were to be more dangerous.

Long before the Hillwood Day Centre gave him an alternative, David Laing learned to hide the shame of his address by heading his letters 220 Arlington Road without the name of the building. The only people I've met who are not ashamed to name it are those who have lived in it all their lives like Tommy Sweet, now about seventy-eight, who moved in at the age of sixteen, a week after his father died, and those like Bob Marriott who had lived in the worst of lodging houses and considered it a privilege to be admitted to a superior one.

People love nicknames anyway, but I think Rowton House has more than most places because of shame. Its inmates speak of it as the House, the Big House, the Mickey, or the Mickey Mouse which is their rhyming slang for house, as San Quentin or Dracula's Castle or Dracula's or the Castle. Its owners, Rowton Houses Ltd, who run it as a commercial concern, tried to cloak this sense of shame some years ago by renaming it Arlington House and changing their own name to Rowton Hotels. But euphemisms soon wear out and you have to find another one. It was no use changing shit-house to latrine and then to lavatory, both of which mean washing places, because as the years went by you had to say cloakroom, toilet, comfort station, little girls' room, dukes, necessary house and the rest.

But Rowton is a real name and an honourable one. I wish it had been kept as the last memorial to the wise and benevolent man who founded Rowton Houses, Montague Corry, Disraeli's private secretary and confidant from 1866 until his death in 1881, friend and occasional adviser to Queen Victoria until her death. She, on Disraeli's recommendation, made him a peer in 1880 and he chose the title Lord Rowton from his aunt's home in Shropshire, Rowton Castle. He was born in 1838, the first year of Victoria's reign. His mother was a sister of the great Lord Shaftesbury who had made enemies among the aristocracy and endangered his political career by devoting a long life to social reform, reform of the lunacy laws, poor law, amendment of the Factory Acts, initiation of state aid to ragged schools, expansion of state regulation of industry, abolishment of apprenticeship in mines and other private concerns. He is probably best remembered for the Ten-Hours' Act, the first effective law to protect children, young persons and women from their employer, which he pushed through Parliament against heavy opposition in 1847, but another of his works, now almost forgotten, was the Lodging House Act of 1851 and it was this that aroused his nephew's interest in the loathsome places in which thousands of workmen had to live.

The 'common lodging-houses' of the first half of the nineteenth century were worse than any public dwelling places before or since and they were not cheap. Dozens of lodgers were crammed into one kitchen or dormitory so tightly sometimes that there was no room to lie down. Ropes were stretched from wall to wall for them to rest their elbows on as they slept standing in rows. Ventilation was bad; sanitation did not exist; cholera, typhus and smallpox flourished and spread to work places and eating houses outside. Lord Shaftesbury's Act enforced some improvements, some state supervision, and required all lodging-house keepers to admit government inspectors into their premises. Dickens, who was then writing *Bleak House*, called it the best piece of legislation that ever issued from Parliament. One of its clauses gave local authorities the power to build lodging houses of their own. Very few did so. And that strengthened Lord Rowton's resolve to act privately – not on model lodging houses but on an alternative which he first thought of as the poor man's hotel and then, to remove contempt, the working man's hotel. Every man was to have his own cubicle and his own key to it. Each cubicle would have a window which only he could open or shut. In the end the first one which he built in Bond Street, Vauxhall, was named Rowton House. The five others built between 1892 and 1905 were all called that.

His cousin Cecil Ashley, one of Shaftesbury's sons, and a

friend, Sir Richard Farrant, had long been energetic directors of the Artizans Dwelling Company which built or renovated dwellings for families and let them at low rents. He himself had for ten years been chief administrator of the Guinness Trust which had the same aims and similar successes in Dublin and London. So he knew a great deal about the practical work involved.

With Sir Edward Guinness and a plain-clothes policeman who acted as guide and guard – both were essential for strangers in the dark tangled alleyways, roofwalks and rotten stairs of the Rookeries – he explored day and night for weeks every part of London where the poor lived. In all that ghastly tour, having seen unburied corpses lying in rooms where ten or twelve people ate and slept, it was the 'common lodging-houses' that shocked him most of all. Families were gradually, far too slowly, being rehoused. No one had yet paid any attention to the plight of homeless men.

Lord Rowton was rich but, like the founders of the Artizans Dwelling Company, knew that no enterprise requiring large capital investment could last unless it was made to pay. And besides, he thought charity degrading; religious services, missionaries and goodwill visitors were to be forbidden in the working men's hotel. Having no experience of company finance, he asked Farrant to help him. Farrant dismissed the project utterly, saying that the public could not be asked to invest in an experiment never tried before. All building costs were high at the time, and Rowton's hotel would be so constructed that if it failed it would be useless for any purpose. Conversion into a factory or workhouse would be impossible; the cheapness of the site, the smallness of the rooms, both essential if sixpence a night was the maximum charge, would make it worthless as an ordinary hotel. Farrant estimated the building costs at £30,000 which now, in the 1980s, means at least half a million.

Lord Rowton was despondent, Farrant says, but kept on talking about it during the next few weeks and one day came to say he would pay the whole cost himself. Farrant warned him that he would probably lose it all. At last, when Rowton insisted, he offered to organize the work.

It was Rowton himself who looked after details. He ordered

beds to be delivered at his house in Berkeley Square and slept a night on each before making a choice. He chose sheets and blankets with Lady Farrant's help and summoned in turn other women he knew to advise him on the furniture. Having seen cold water tubs shared by all in the better lodging houses – those that had any washing arrangements at all – he decided to have large lavatories with hot and cold water to each basin and, to find out how far apart the basins should be set, he got Ashley, Guinness and Farrant to face the bare wall side by side with him pretending to wash their arms and necks. If their elbows touched he widened the space. But where, someone asked, would they put their coats while they were washing? There was room for a row of pegs on the opposite wall behind them, but Lord Rowton was against that. Hat-and-coat rails were fixed above each basin so that everyone could be sure that nothing was taken from his pockets.

> We fitted up a laundry with hot and cold water to each washing-tray, and in this laundry we put a large stove of special make with fixed drying horses round it, so that a man who had only one shirt could wash and dry it whilst waiting.[21]

I was specially interested to read that because nowadays, exactly ninety years later, I often see men from our Rowton House club together, take their shirts off in the launderette and wait in their jackets till washing and drying is done.

'The sixth house', wrote Farrant in 1905, 'which is now in course of erection at Arlington Road, Park Street, Camden Town, near the well-known Britannia public house, will contain about 1,150 cubicles. One of the last acts of Lord Rowton's life was to attend a meeting of the directors at which the plans of this house were approved.' These plans, which led to the forbidding building now known as Arlington House, were made by H. B. Measures, a military architect who did not see the work through because he got a War Office job as director of barrack construction soon after it began.

It was the last, the largest, and is now the only survivor. Perhaps by the time this book is published it will have gone for it is outdated and subject to official criticism. But in its early years nothing in Europe or America came near it for comfort at a low price. Official delegations came to study Rowton houses from Budapest, Milan, Paris and New York. The Albergo Populare in Milan, L'Hôtel pour les Hommes in Paris, the Mannheim in Vienna and the Mills Hotels in New York were all modelled on Lord Rowton's idea. Sir Edward Guinness opened the Iveagh Hostel in Dublin in 1901.

The first Rowton House filled up so quickly during 1892 and 1893 that there was soon a waiting list. Men walked miles to and from their work for the privilege of staying in it. This gave Farrant confidence enough to allow Rowton to form a joint stock company, which because it paid sufficient dividends enabled them to build the others. It was an ideal fulfilled long before Lord Rowton's death and a gigantic relief to the poor which, *faute de mieux*, Arlington House still is.

But all the idealism passed away long before David Laing's time. Lord Rowton himself abandoned several generous schemes in his last years. The open shelves in the libraries of the early houses were soon emptied; new books and glass-fronted bookcases were bought, which needed a librarian with a key. That became unmanageable. Libraries and librarians ceased. Free soap in the lavatories and laundries disappeared on the day it appeared. Men were told to buy their own and keep it in their lockers.

Only one form of theft led to an improvement. Fishing with hook and line over cubicle partitions for your sleeping neighbour's possessions led to the raising of bedroom walls. In Arlington House all reach the ceiling. McL., who prefers prison to any other communal living place, says that fishing still goes on in lodging houses that have cubicles. You have to put everything under the bed before you go to sleep.

Ben Dollard's voice baritone. Doing his level best to say it . . . Now in the Iveagh home. Cubicle number so and so . . . Ruin them. Wreck their lives. Then build them cubicles to end their days in. Hushaby. Lullaby. Die, dog. Little dog, die.[22]

November 22nd, Saturday

The deaf and dumb road sweeper who works in the terrace instead of Mr Corp has for years been cut off from me – but this year for some weeks he has been every day, instead of Sats. only, to sweep up the leaves and make daily bonfires. And now we can converse in sign language.

He points to the sky. He spreads his arms wide, clasps them round his body, shivers, shudders with cold, takes off his hat to show his bald head – laughs. I don't know what my antics look like – I am not so good at mime.

It was on Oct. 20th, I think, that I had a shouting match with the manager of the Inverness St supermarket – an Indian. I had bought a mouldy 'Long Tom', Mother's Pride loaf, on Sunday, the day before. I didn't want another in exchange. He refused to give the money back. 37½p and at first he refused a credit note, saying

– How do I know you bought this here? You may have bought it in another store and you come to me for the money!

I suppose the stupidity of that idea was what made me shout and snatch the wrapping paper out of his hand – I had given him the mouldy loaf in its paper with the guarantee

– What d'you want that for?

– I want to write to the makers.

– Then I won't give you the credit note, but I snatched that from his hand too. I was enraged and trembling. I nearly hit him. And Martina invented headlines when I told her; 'Racist Camden Town Writer Attacks Indian Shopkeeper'.

She has been in a similar situation at Gt Portland St where the Indian ticket collector tried to take her return ticket away and charge her more – she snatched it from him and walked off and he held up a finger to his inspector to show how her scratch had drawn blood.

November 27th, Thursday

In the Edinburgh a boy was angry with his girl for being late

– The trouble with you is everybody's in love with you. I'm not. Let's get that straight.

Most people avoid open quarrels – as I do. Once when I was

reading on a stool in the Spread a man stood between me and the window and I remembered how we used to say to each other as children, 'You're in my light' – polite version – or 'Get out of my light.' I said nothing. (Ancient lights, like rights of way – the notice on the old heathside houses opposite the Bull & Bush.)

Almost everybody avoids quarrelling about chairs, as I would. In the summer, outside, one of two men at a table went in to get drinks. Someone else took his chair. His friend, instead of protesting, fetched another one. But once in the Spread, when I asked a young man if he wanted the stool his coat was occupying, he said yes. No one sat on it all the time I was there. Sometimes I feel ashamed of avoiding rows in that way.

Pub chairs, outside, are often occupied when the pubs are shut. Wherever a low wall is built, as at Henlys garage or by the Edinburgh Castle 53 bus stop, you'll find people sitting on it – and this makes me remember that one of the most tiring things in any strange city is having nowhere to sit down. Davie Laing and many old men in Rowton House have only the public library. There ought to be lots of street chairs and seats – tables too, I think, to encourage businessmen and writers to stop and make notes on their way to the tube.

In one of the white metal armchairs outside the Dublin Castle last summer a young man sat playing the viola. I thought it an unusual instrument for a street musician but, guided by the superstition that makes me throw money to the gods, I tried to put 10p on the table in front of him. He said

– I'm not playing for money. If you want to give it away, find someone who needs it.

December 6th, Saturday

The upright part of our ash, the trunk that is not weeping, shows now that its leaves have fallen, slight branches sloping upwards, with fingery twigs at their ends curling towards the sky, but not like open hands, which I first thought of, because there is no palm to them and their fingers are so wide apart that nothing except an old cloth thrown down from above could be caught by them. The weeping ash part weeps straight, its long thin twigs pointing to the pavement, the roadway and the grass.

I think it was Charles Causley who taught me to love the beauty of trees in winter. I remember our meeting when I was in exile in Siberia – Plymouth – and he was the first friend I made there though he lived too far away to be a constant one, and how he gave me his first book of poems – I think his first – a small book bound in yellow paper. He inscribed it affectionately to me. I looked for it just now, but can't find it. I can't remember what we usually talked about when we met. I seldom can with anyone I know well and like. But I do remember how he told me about the poverty of his family when he was a boy – they lived in a tiny cottage in the village where I went to see him – and how his father suddenly got enough money to have running water laid on.

He boasted at school that they were going to have a lavatory inside the house – and his friends said, 'How disgusting.'

December 8th, Monday

We must make a comic pair when we sit near each other with our newspapers – the short man with the moustache and me. We both have thick spectacles and look closely when we read. He usually sits with his back to the bar and the people, facing the door of the smaller Parkway bar, and is always looking over his shoulder. When he has finished reading he folds the paper and uses it as a fan; his face grows very flushed at times and he gets restless. I think he is asthmatic or has bronchial trouble. On Sat. when the pub was very smoky and crowded, he went to the door several times, held it open and breathed the cold air. But no amount of smoky discomfort will drive him out on to the pavement, or even to a less crowded pub.

A tall pale man whose name I have never known, but we used often to talk in the old days, greeted me in the Mixer as he came past.

– You never come in to the Windsor these days – well, it's too crowded, isn't it?

I asked the conventional

– How are you keeping?
– All right. I'm 74. I'm getting married next week.
– To a 14-year-old girl, I suppose?
– I think it's a boy.

December 19th, Friday

The long leafy branches of the privet hedge outside my
window, untrimmed for a year or even two, gave an effect of
a large puff of smoke as the wind raised them, showing the
white wall on the other side of Oval Road.

December 22nd, Monday

Behind the cinema the winos, who've been absent for weeks,
shouted 'Davy' across the road, which is both a friendly
greeting and a begging. M. thinks she saw Davy Sloan among
them. A fortnight ago Mary said he'd 'gone a-missing' and
some time before that I met him perfectly dressed, in new but
gipsylike clothes, declaring proudly that he hadn't had a drink
for 3 days because a doctor – he liked one for once – had
persuaded him. He said he had agreed to go into the Royal
Free next day and when I wouldn't believe him swore he would
– perfectly sincerely as he is when he believes in what he'll
do tomorrow.

December 23rd, Tuesday

On the way with M. to the 31 bus, they were all there again
on the corner of Arlington Road and the market.
    – There's the whole arrangement, she said, but for once they
didn't see me.
    It's a mild cloudy day with little gleams of pale sun. When
I drew the curtains this morning and M. saw the sky from
the bed she said how beautiful it was. I hadn't noticed till then
the white stripes, curving and straight, between the grey
clouds.

Boxing Day, 1980

Christmas Day was mild and sunny and in the evening at about eight a large moon at the lower end of Jamestown Road, so low that it looked like one of the street lamps (but they are orange–yellow). The day began with dread for M. and me and on Christmas Eve, decorating the Christmas tree alone together, she said
    – It's sad doing this, and I said
    – And it's sad if you don't do it, as well.
    But it was worth it and lunch with everyone was very nice when it happened; but I dropped a new Campari bottle on the floor and smashed it. It looked like blood, floods of it streaming from a pool on the light floorboards. Ben mopped it up carefully and neatly and conscious of my shame.

January 19th (1981), Monday

I have never seen so many destitute people sitting for warmth in Cam. Tn tube station as this year – not the usual drunks and winos. Last Monday on my way to meet M. at St Pancras there was one large man in brown tatters on the platform bench with his head bowed between his knees, motionless. And on another bench an agitated tatterdemalion who was asking a strolling passenger for the price of a cup of tea as I passed. He got some money. We waited a long time for the train and I found it impossible to stop watching him, his movements were so nervous – feet tapping or jerking, head up, down and to one side, and all the time he kept wiping his skin, as much of it as he could reach, with a neatly folded handkerchief – an unrumpled ironed square which except for its blackish grime could have come straight from the laundry. With this in the palm of his right hand, he rubbed his forehead and cheeks, then his neck, shoulder and chest, reaching as far as he could underneath his clothes. Then he changed hands and without unfolding the handkerchief or even turning it over, so far as I could see, did the same to his other side.
    I went to give him 15p and felt pretty mean because I had a 10 bob bit in my pocket not to speak of pound notes in the

other, and I sat down beside him hoping we would talk, but all he said was 'thank you' and, when I said
 – How are you, he answered
 – Not too bad.
He was thinly dressed, so he can't have been sweating unless from a nervous habit. The bowed-down man had a heavy overcoat.

January 20th, Tuesday

About ten years ago an article in one of the colour supplements astonished me by showing the destitute of New York in clean and expensive-looking clothes, women in fur coats, men in sleek overcoats, every one of them in shoes that appeared to be without splits between uppers and sole. This has now become usual in London – there are now so many clothing charities that even the winos who grudge every penny not spent on drink are much better dressed than many of the people you see in the supermarket and the Cam. Tn streets. Even the Pole who walks all day and stands swaying at the entrance to the tube station acquired a good overcoat this winter – the one he had for years, which eventually hung in ribbons about his shoulders, may still be underneath it, for it's certain he kept it because he loved it, not from poverty.

Jean Graham thinks David Laing died because he lacked the will to live. I asked Dr Haas about it. He knows it can cause death and described one other case. He has known several. It's a sort of 'giving up' which weakens the natural resistance to illness. Tipsy Davy certainly has the will to live, and as to David L.'s notion that happiness, even cheerfulness, is unattainable if you are poor, Davy's very existence belies it. There he is homeless, as he has been most of his adult life, dependent on begging, in physical pain all the time. If he were at all like D.L. in temperament he would envy the room in Arlington House, the absolute security of the old-age pension, just as the other David envied my room, my money.

Sitting in the Spread Eagle yesterday when the lunchtime crowd had gone, Texas Sue, clearing my table, made me feel

I was in hospital with the nurse coming round. Wish I had told her so and got one of her witty replies.

January 22nd, Thursday – 11 a.m.

A blackbird has just perched on the rounded top of the middle post of the iron railing, exactly opposite me, as I was gloomily wondering what on earth to do today, when I feel I cannot write this diary, far less write the book. It cheered me up.

Once, when Ben ran after me in the terrace to borrow a pound or so, knowing he was broke most of the time, I asked how he was managing for money. And he said

– I try not to think about it.

I really do feel sympathetic to him. And I remembered the few times in my life when I have achieved that state – though for the opposite reason – my huge salary at UNESCO, the disregard for money that comes with high moods. This is quite different from winning a lottery – the winner does think about that – thinks how to spend it or how not to – and with large sums that obsession lasts him for years. And then, to achieve Ben's ideal of not thinking about it, you must neither be proud of having it nor bitter about not having it.

January 27th, Tuesday

Luke left his cigarette tobacco here on Sunday and I have just seen it. I wish I had not seen it. The last bit I smoked was from it, shared with Martina alternate puffs the old nice way after lunch on Sunday, and now the sight of it entices me, and I started writing much later this morning. It is now 11 a.m. The Spread is open. The first pint delicious with one newly rolled cigarette. Both are part of a ritual with memories and sentimentalities. What I don't like about the Spread in the mornings is the number of men over 60. Most of them solitary like me.

January 28th, Wednesday

Jack Dillon and I used to collect fragments of overheard talk.
I never wrote mine down, but remember how mysterious they
usually were and some like fragments of a poem. Now that I
am deaf they are even more mysterious. Crossing Primrose
Hill yesterday two men like old-fashioned comedians – a fat
one and a taller, narrow, straightbacked one – came off the
grass onto the path a good way ahead of me. They walked
ambling arm in arm, the fat one dressed in bluish grey and
the thin one in brown and yellow, and they zigzagged arm in
arm from one side of the path to the other. But until I got
close to them it never occurred to me that they were holding
each other up drunk. The fat one had a resonant voice and I
could hear him but not what the other one said in reply. And
all I could hear in that deep voice was numbers, spoken
persuasively, almost emotionally
  – One three nine.
  – Then one three three?
  – Three seven seven.
  I had difficulty in passing them and feared they might stop
me and get me to join in – and I was in a hurry to reach
Maida Vale. They controlled their staggers with linked arms
as though they were learning one of the movements in a
ceremonial dance, and, not wanting to call their attention to
me by circling away from them through the muddy grass, I
waited for one of the slower veerings and passed quickly. All
the way to the gate I heard the numbers, the varied
expressiveness of the deep voice.
  I was the only person to hear it. I've tried interpretations,
all of which anyone not hearing the tone of voice might believe
in, but none works. And it was the friendly relationship that
struck me most, the harmony and ease. Somewhere I read
that every movement has a meaning.
  Last week in that dark alcove in the long public bar that
looks like an altar because of its lights from above, a tall heavy
man sat down beside me, a man I know by sight but have
never spoken to, a gruff man who never has a newspaper or
book, which most solitaries protect themselves with nowadays.
He glanced at me with no expression of recognition such as I

was ready to give him. He drank rapidly and whenever he stood and walked the few steps to the bar he darkened my book, unconsciously forcing my attention on him. His back and limbs were rigid, like a statue in black stone. At the third sitting-down and the third pint – each made the table tremble – Alf on his way to the gents stopped and asked him something. Alf has a soft voice. He went on questioning him, but I only heard the answers. Here are the answers:

– Because my hand was in my pocket.
– I couldn't get it out.
– My hand was in my pocket, see?
– No! I couldn't get my hand out of my pocket.

He repeated this several more times in different ways till Alf, believing him at last, left us. I had been glancing at their faces. Now I looked at the gruff man's hands. The left one was white and fat and resting on his knee. It looked normal, for such a bulky man, until I saw his right hand as he lifted his mug of beer. The right hand was a healthy colour, large and strong but not a bit swollen – the tendons showing.

January 29th, Thursday

Mary came this morning and said Davy had been given a grant to buy boots, etc., but did not buy boots, etc. They've gone on like that about each other ever since I've known them – seeing each other's faults. I think most people do, but not so obviously.

She gets savagely angry and fights like a wildcat I'm told, but when I meet her sober she is gentle. She still always shows me her cuts and scratches – from breaking down boarded-up windows to shelter for the night, from falling in the street, from fighting. Today she had several bad burns on her fingers from smoking cigarettes when drunk, she says, and smiles.

Came back to my room and watched her cross Oval Road to the nuns' house opposite, a dignified scarecrow in some tattered furs she's got hold of. My window is like a film screen almost as wide as the room, three windows in one, a transparent triptych framed on one side by our front door and the long hedge which are at a right-angle to it, and on the other by the tree, the stone curb of the lawn and an old brick pillar which marks the open gateway into Oval Road. The terrace roadway curves as it enters the frame. Everything that moves comes into sight suddenly, then vanishes, except for the people who ring the bell and wait. I can't hear it, and luckily strangers don't connect my window with the door. An electioneer told Martina, pointing at me, how annoyed she was with the man next door just sitting there, refusing to answer. I do look up usually when someone comes and watch them walk away – young people with circulars, usually girls, winos, Jehovahs, that bailiff I had to speak to with his constipated face and fussy gait. Maybe there's a link between a scattered state of mind – I'm thinking of Marion Milner's 'chattering thoughts' – and a fussy gait. The way people move does change with moods; some are jittery, then calm, every ten minutes or so for no exterior reason.

January 31st, Saturday

Her name day but I had forgotten and forgotten the dreadful four horses of Saint Martina's martyrdom.

Last night, I mean the 28th, she was woken by scrambling, like cats climbing over the fence which she often hears, she says. She sleeps very lightly and at about 4 a.m. Ben hadn't yet gone to sleep, perhaps not to bed, and it was police chasing a man from across Glos. Crescent. He had got into the Shaeffs' garden. The policeman caught him there and said

– Right. You're nicked for being on closed premises. What are you? Some kind of pervert?

Both B. and M. heard this, and Luke has confirmed the impression formed a few years ago – that there's now a police tradition of coarse and insinuating nastiness that didn't exist in Sam's time. They then heard the PC say

– All right. If you're so good at climbing you can jump that gate.

(The big blue gate in the place of the old gate of our house's garden is locked at night.)

February 5th, Thursday

Early morning waking is hell, as it might be Davie L.'s; he used always to keep his eyes shut and covered by the blanket, trying to go to sleep again, to think of colours, of waking up in childhood, or of occasions in Canada when he looked forward eagerly to the day.

Sometimes, even out in the sun, he would sit huddled in misery (I suppose), his hands curved over the handle of his walking stick, his chin on his hands. But naturally and almost always when with me or Martina, he was alert and lively. 'Gallant' towards her, she says.

His youth? My youth. One wasn't conscious of it at the time.

February 9th, Monday

About mugging, it never occurred to me till last Monday that a man could be afraid of me in the street – women often are, as when I've tried to ask them the way. But last Monday, as it was growing dark and the street lamps were at the red-hot stage above the wide pavement of Maida Vale, I was walking on the inside near one of the low walls that run beside the endless blocks of flats when a person came towards me on the same track, almost touching the wall as I was. I began to move out. I would have done so anyway, but I thought it was a woman and wanted to let her keep her path. It was a man. He must have started to move out at the same moment, but the farther I stepped towards the road, the farther he stepped as though he was trying to stop me, to confront me. We came very close to each other and I could not understand him, he seemed determined not to let me pass on the outside of him, the road side of him. I was puzzled and only afraid at the very last moment when he could have grasped or hit me. I swerved quickly in again towards the wall and passed him and as I did so he stared into my face, turning his to keep me in sight as I passed.

So much passed between us during these seconds. Neither knew the other's feelings yet our minds were as close as strangers' can be.

I walked on without quickening my pace and without

looking back. He had stared at me so tensely that I thought he might follow me. He did not. Soon I reached the bus stop where many people were.

It did not occur to me that he might have been afraid until I was telling M. about it days later.

February 17th, Tuesday

> What I fear most, I think, is the death of the imagination. When the sky outside is merely pink, and the rooftops merely black: that photographic mind which paradoxically tells the truth, but the worthless truth, about the world.
>
> Sylvia Plath[23]

It's what I fear too, not exactly in her sense. But for any imaginative person, perhaps it's always only temporary as mine is when it happens.

I think she's put pink instead of blue to give herself courage. The worst thing is not to see anything or any colour because it's always there or because your mind is turned off for days at a time. Davie Laing looked down at the pavement all the time when he was walking alone.

Sylvia Plath also said about going to a party after she had been ill and not seen anyone: 'I always feel I turn into a gargoyle when too long alone, and that people will point.' Martina sympathized with this at once, recognized it in herself.

With me the inability to write and the depression that goes with it, which is sometimes cause, sometimes effect – a vicious circle – makes me self-conscious. I know my face shows emptiness or gloom because people often point at it figuratively by saying
   – Don't worry.
   – You're looking worried.
Or even without any introduction
   – It's not so bad as all that.
Also I am very conscious of not being able to talk or even listen. In talk I assume an artificial brightness which I despise or I hear a nervous hasty speech that doesn't belong to me

come out of me. The instinct is to keep to familiar places, streets, cafés, pubs, and yet you want to hide from friends, from places where you are known. And in the past in my worst times this has caused a dreadful state of indecision: hungry or wanting a drink and not having either.

At bad times I imagine my drooping mouth, the deep crevices on each side, and keep covering it with my hand.

March 3rd, Tuesday

Yesterday evening on my way to meet Martina, I saw the Tatterdemalion again. As I got out of the tube on to the platform he was walking in front of me, head bowed, with agitated movements of his hands towards his chest. In the rush-hour crowd at the bottom of the escalator people glanced at him and stepped away from him. A pretty girl looked at him with an expression of fear, disgust or both, and when he came near her on the escalator, on the step behind her, she was forced to walk up to get away from him. No one pushed their way past him for fear of touching him. In the crowd he was like a privileged person.

I left one empty step between him and me and saw how very thin his coat was, long, gaberdine-like and torn in many places, black trouser legs so long that they hid his heels, greyish hair matted and sticking out at one side like two horns. Some punk boys have theirs like that on purpose.

All this time I've been curious to know how such people get in or out of the tube. Is it worth the cheapest ticket for a day's warmth, do they sneak out, or are the officials kind to them? So when we reached the top, I hung about a bit to watch what he would do. He shuffled immediately to the downwards escalator and went down in the crowd. Had he been told to leave one platform, or is it just what he does when he gets bored?

March 9th, Monday

Yesterday after lunch we went to the zoo and M. was at her most imaginative, appreciative artistic. We saw only a few animals all of which were ancient – out of the Bible, Mandeville's *Travels*, or an old bestiary like Topsell's where a leopard with a human head is described as factually as a camel.

The Bactrian camel, with two humps, huge feet on legs too slender for its hugeness, and a great long head, seemed to me the most ancient, timeless, and the thought of meeting it in a desert, never having seen one before, is more alarming than meeting a lion. It's the same as the fear of the supernatural. Then one of the humps usually flops over. We saw two outside in their enclosure, surrounded by a moat – in pale sun, a mild, a springlike afternoon with a strong southish wind. And later, inside the building, we were close to one, it loomed over us enormous and shaggy, with straw in its long hair.

The giraffes were outside walking in a procession past the high arched doors of their house – two families, with young ones, yearlings? – six or seven of them altogether, very light and dignified in the way they move. Their gait is dainty and their heads sway forwards and up, very small on the long broad necks that taper up from shoulder width. Last year I watched them alone for a long time and made up my mind that when they walk the left legs go together, and then the right. Ben, watching them with me some days later, showed me I was wrong. But their paces are unlike other four-footed animals. Yesterday there were two small zebras there to show it. The left hind leg of the giraffe seems to come forward more quickly – as though, M. said, it was kicking the left foreleg on. And so with the right. We could see both clearly because they played follow-my-leader up and down in front of their doors, turning at the ends and walking back again in a formal procession. The little zebras sometimes joined them looking podgy. I think they were all waiting to be let in for food and the night.

Smooth short hair, clean-looking bright clear pattern. M. immediately compared it to a net, and so it is – a white net laid over the reddish brown or fawn. She stays and looks for a long time at every animal she likes.

Above the wild pigs on the Mappin Terraces there was an old polar bear, padding up and down in a fast walk with a mannerism horrible to watch – which we felt sure was a neurosis caused by bereavement or separation from a mate in the next cage. It came down by the wall each time and when it reached the cliff that separates it from the people it turned its nose towards the wall, pointed it to the sky, sat back on its haunches, its yellowy white throat stretched before us, and swung the front of its body round, planting its forefeet in the position for walking back again, without moving its hindquarters. Then back again to the top of its rocky concrete space. Up and down, up and down, and every time this agonized swing of a turn. When we left the terraces twenty minutes later, it was still doing it.

The Barbary sheep above, the flocks of Abraham, most of them lying down chewing the cud, their front legs tucked back beneath them. A huge ram on a flat ledge above the others, restful glances, huge and beautiful horns.

When I used to take David Laing to the zoo on my free ticket we hardly looked at any animals. Perhaps he did when I left him. The main idea was to get him in there, have a drink together and leave him to pass the time, to get through the afternoon in a different way from usual.

At first I could not persuade him to enter the members' bar.

– I'm no' going in there! he'd say at the door.

It was only on one day when there was a long queue at the ordinary bar that I persuaded him. And of course he didn't feel shy once he was inside. His long years of Rowton House life had given him a false opinion of himself. If it was clothes he was shy about – what else could it be? – he was always more formally dressed than me.

Giraffes place their feet gently, deliberately, as people do when they wish to be unobtrusive. I've watched Irishmen come into the Dublin Castle with similar steps.

March 11th, Wednesday

Philip (O'Connor) returned to France yesterday. We both felt sad at only having seen him twice – here at lunch a week ago, on the 4th, and at his Earls Court poetry reading last Friday. I think he was punishing us for not letting him sleep on the red sofa. He always did sleep on it in the old days, but I wrote to say it would make me too nervous now. You have to surrender the whole morning to him. The Poetry Society thing was good, but I had to read the poems afterwards, not only because of the deafness, but because he doesn't look at his audience, keeps his head down and rushes along at high speed. Everyone was watching him fascinated by his long-stretching legs. Only John Heath Stubbs, who can't see, asked him to speak louder.

The 2nd of March was his 4th anniversary of giving up drink. I wish I had asked him more about it in detail because I find it more difficult to limit my drinks than I did to stop altogether. You need a strong inducement to stop. Philip had fear; he says the doctor warned him his liver was so bad he would die.

And then it's not only drink, with me, its restlessness. 'I have discovered that all man's unhappiness derives only from one source – not being able to sit quietly in a room.'[24]

Just as I was about to leave the Spread, in came Mary with a puppy (6 mths?) on a lead. Davy is always catching dogs, partly for company – he likes them. I don't think either of them would have the energy to seek out the owner and a reward, but maybe the owner searches Parkway and the back-of-the-cinema den and is grateful to find it on a lead, safe.

I was reading the paper just about to leave. It was the dog that made me look up by putting its paws on my knees and at first I didn't recognize Mary. She had no headscarf and has dyed her hair blond. She sat down opposite me at the little table in the windowless Parkway bar. Afraid of a scene with the barman like the one I had when she did the same thing two summers ago, I said

– Mary, you mustn't follow me in here – you know they'll throw you out like last time.

And I stood up and left her there, walked swiftly down Albert St in a direction she wouldn't expect me to go.

I'm now ashamed of my treachery. It's to do with the low mood. It was especially hurtful to her who takes so much trouble about her appearance. It was insulting.

Last time, when I defended her, I said truthfully that she had just come out of hospital and sat it out with her till I'd finished my drink while the angry barman stood over us, I was in a good mood. It's something I don't remember when other people insult or welcome me – how much moods govern manners.

March 13th, Friday

Met Mary again this afternoon, all smiles in the rain. But then she has so little memory. She has gone back to her raggedy appearance. The dressing-up bouts don't last.

There was a tall woman, shopping bag in one hand, passing the veg queue outside Downs, holding on to my belt – the half belt of M.'s naval coat – and then the next belt, then a hand on the next shoulder and exclaiming

– Whoever would have thought I'd come to this – my legs won't carry me.

But farther on, where there was nothing to hold on to, they did carry her.

The sunset last night through the first-floor windows opposite – the nuns' house – was like a room on fire. Early this morning in Parkway bursting rubbish bags on pavements, Coca-Cola tins rolling in the wind, bottles from the Trattoria stacked high waiting for the dustmen, the 'best gang in London' Bob tells me. He works in Kentish Town now but used to empty the bins from our house and greet me through my open window. I've never watched another 'gang', but the Parkway one, which also does our house, attacks the rubbish like pirates in a hurry, huge gloves on their hands, red pompoms, blue and yellow tam-o'-shanters on their heads. The driver moves too fast for them and they almost have to run.

Behind me and in front of me Japanese children on their early way to school, at least an hour before most London children have got out of bed, their voices like a happy riot. I saw in some paper that in Japan parents and even the government were alarmed by the long hours and stress the children undergo there. Suicides, etc. And it's astonishing to me to see them in the evening, the little ones about four o'clock and the older ones at five, dawdling down Parkway to the tube, laughing and banging each other with their satchels. They are nearly all beautiful, even most of the boys. When we were looking at pictures of child refugees from Vietnam M. said

– at least they'll start with one advantage in Europe, meaning physical beauty. It's the Japanese teachers who look tired after school when they are released an hour after their pupils and come into the Dublin on their way home.

March 14th, Saturday

The most depressing thing I remember about my depressing relationships with publishers is Kaye Webb's letter asking me to sign copies of the *Danny Foxes* and add an inscription to the children of the future, a hundred years hence or it may have been five hundred. I imagined their deformities after nuclear wars and hoped there would be no children. I put something vague and signed the books. Hundreds of other Puffin authors signed theirs too and Kaye had the whole lot buried in capsules somewhere in Kensington.

It is a little better, but not much, to think of the children of the past. At Oxford I spent far too much time on the history of the Industrial Revolution when I should have been reading other things and, of all its horrors, child labour struck me as the worst. The workhouses too. Camden Town which was so desperately sordid and poor at that time possessed one of the most evil workhouses of all, and that was partly because St Pancras parish was one of those allowed to opt out of the Poor Law Act of 1834, which in itself was evil. I wrote some stuff about that in 1976 or 1975.

Poverty is shaming, especially in communities where the poor are few, but although some individuals despise the poor and the unemployed, neither condition is nowadays a crime. The disgrace is private. It was not always so. Under the statute of the 22nd year of Henry VIII's reign, all able-bodied beggars were to be whipped. In 1536 another Act made legal the whipping of 'a sturdy beggar for his first offence, his right ear to be cropped off for the second', and if convicted on indictment of a third offence, he was to suffer death as a felon and as an enemy of the Commonwealth. In 1547, 'any able-bodied person

144

who did not apply himself to some honest labour or offer to serve – even for meat and drink, if nothing more is to be obtained – shall be taken for a vagabond, branded on the shoulder with the letter "V" and adjudged a slave for two years to any person who shall demand him', and if he ran away during that period he was to be 'branded with the letter "S" and adjudged a slave for life', and if he ran away again he was to 'suffer death as a felon'.

Most of these valiant or sturdy beggars were what we now call 'the unemployed'.

The impotent poor were to some extent looked after in hospitals but it was not until after the Restoration that the sturdy and the valiant received any public care. There were no poor-houses at first, but by the Act of 1601 overseers of the poor were appointed and required by law to provide for the sick and destitute as individuals. No doubt there was favouritism and certainly few obtained the help they needed, but the attitude of the St Pancras authorities was humane, as can be seen from the minutes of the open vestry meetings of the early eighteenth century.

'It is also ordered that at this Vestry Mr. Balls Overseer for the last year shall pay the widow Rydler three guineas for the Care of John Hall's Leg.' The widow was probably 'a wise woman' who made medicine and lotions from herbs. On 10 June of the same year, at the Black Bull in Kentish Town, 'it was agreed that the upper Churchwarden Should Disburse one pound and ten shillings unto John Bliss of Tottenham Court for the relieving of him and his family.' 6 June 1722: 'The vestry likewise allowed of Mr. Bosworth his bill for medicine, to the poor amounting to five lbs 5sh and 5pc.' 31 July 1722: 'Amy Ripper of Highgate shall be paid twenty shillings . . . for nursing and attending of her father, William Banden, in his illness.' And on 4 July, 'It was agreed and ordered that Mrs. Parry widow of Thomas Parry Surgeon at Highgate should be paid . . . the Sum of three Guineas in full for Medicine and Attendance on account of Mrs. Perryman in Kentish Town.' In the same year the upper churchwarden was ordered to bind out a pauper boy as apprentice 'to what Person or Business he shall think most Proper and to make as cheap a Bargain for putting him out as he can.' The fees were to be paid by the parish, which is to say that the overseers acted as any parent with enough money would towards the boy.

Homeless adults born in the parish, orphans and certain children of the very poor were boarded out with or even billeted on families. The children grew up as members of a family, single men ate at the same table as their hosts, and although this led later in the century to the overcrowding of cottages it gave the unfortunate a natural way of living. The overseers were required by law 'to provide stock' – working materials such as flax, wool, leather – to pauper weavers, saddlers, cobblers and other craftsmen, to enable them to start work again in their own dwellings. Until 1801, the vestry was supposed to look after all the bastards of the parish by a method that was often abused. The overseers could settle with the father for a lump sum which freed him from responsibility. In many cases he only had to pay them £10 'by which means the parishioners became saddled with a rich man's offspring for ever'. In 1801, 'A Committee appointed for investigating matters of bastardy were instructed not to accept less than £60 from any person on whom a child might be affiliated, whose station in life was superior to that of a servant or labourer.'

We should remember, if we praise the old Poor Law, that the population of the whole parish of St Pancras was under 600 as late as 1776 and that it is impossible to find out how many people were able to obtain relief or how the overseers defined deserving poverty. Poverty like riches is a relative term. But certainly its administrators were free from the abstract principles which caused so much physical and mental suffering between the Poor Law Amendment Act of 1834 and the establishment in 1945 of the welfare state.

The first reference to a workhouse or poorhouse – the words become synonymous in 1834 – in St Pancras that I can find is in the open vestry minutes of 16 July 1730. This, our first, was built in 'the Kings Road [Pancras Road] at the side of the River Fleet'. It was near the old St Pancras church.

Then on 2 March 1788 the ratepayers took a ninety-six-year lease of a pub called the Mother Black Caps or New Halfway House as a site for another workhouse at Camden Town.[25] General Fitzroy, whose name remains famous only on street labels – Fitzroy Square, Road, Street, and Fitzroy Park Street, all of which were built on his farmlands in St Pancras, which he sold or let on profitable terms to building speculators – gave free of charge to the parish a patch of ground, copyhold land, about 98 by 224 feet, beside the Black Caps, which the overseers of the poor made use of as an adjunct, after humbly thanking the Right Hon. General for 'his great politeness and very obliging kindness in giving to this parish for the use of the poor thereof the piece of ground which is now fenced in with a brick wall adjoining to the present parish workhouse.' It became bit by bit, from that time on, the fate of the poor to be fenced in.

Everyone who has travelled by tube on the Northern Line knows the site of this Camden Town workhouse. Thousands of people cross it every day through the open hallway of the booking office on their way to shops or buses, and thousands more ride up and down the escalators which dive below Lord Fitzroy's generous copyhold gift. Nothing except the buildings on that site has changed. There is to this day a pub called the Halfway House across the road from the tube station; the ancient Mother Red Cap, many times rebuilt, is on its old site opposite. The Black Cap, or an older pub which adopted its name when the overseers took the original Mother Black Caps, is only a few yards southwards nowadays on the main Hampstead Road, in a section now called Camden High Street. The Black Caps and the Red Cap were both known in the eighteenth century as halfway houses because they stood halfway between Highgate and London. Everybody broke the journey there for rest, drink and food. Both had spacious yards and ample stabling. (Some of the Red Cap stables have survived and are used as a store for barrows, fruit and vegetables by the Camden Town costers who still refer to them as stables.) The halfway houses were in open country until the 1790s. Their nearest town was Kentish Town less than a mile away, to the north, on the Highgate or Kentish Town Road, a road that was impassable whenever the river Fleet was in flood. It was at the church of Kentish Town that the vestrymen held most of their meetings. For open vestries they adjourned to the Black Bull across the road where the polytechnic now is.

It is no coincidence that both poorhouses stood near the river Fleet. The Fleet ran through the cheapest land in St Pancras, near the main thoroughfares where damp and undesirable buildings were available; there were several marshes beside it and between Kentish Town and Camden Town and by the New Road, summer and winter, it often overflowed its banks. From its source in Hampstead till it reached Camden Town it was a beautiful stream and a watering place for cattle and then it became a filthy open sewer on its course through London to the Thames. It still flows on the same bed but has been imprisoned underground so long that no one nowadays remembers its existence; few even connect its name with Fleet Road in Hampstead or Fleet Street, the newspaper street, in Westminster.

Damp, filth, overcrowding and a stinking graveyard where corpses were burnt had made the New Road poorhouse uninhabitable, and soon all these horrors except the graveyard seeped into the poorhouse at Camden Town. Thomas Eades was paid the sum of 11s 2d 'for Druggs to Kill Buggs at 4 several times'. 'The wards became so overcrowded that five and six persons slept in one bed, and there was dread of putrid fever breaking out amongst the inmates.' In 1809, after a third workhouse had been established, a report on the articles to be moved to it from Camden Town says: 'On examining the bedsteads, the number is 224, 52 of which are single and 97 double bedsteads, all of which may be fit for use if they be cleaned from vermin.' The remaining seventy-five bedsteads were said to be useless. But I have not seen in any account of the lives of the poor in those days a mention of the fact that families were not split up until the Poor Law Amendment Act of 1834. The 'five and six persons' who shared a filthy bed were sometimes a father and mother with their children. Orphans were kept in separate wards and never allowed out.

'From the age of four years till I had completed my seventh I was supported in St Pancras poorhouse, near London,'[26] said the boy who had no name as he told a friend how he stood every day at an upper window watching barefoot, ragged children of his own age begging from door to door across the Highgate Road and selling matches outside the Mother Red Cap. He, who had boots, warm clothes, fire, lodging, food which later in life he considered good, and 'not at all overdone as regarded work', envied the beggars. It was liberty he wanted. He was 'cooped up in a gloomy though liberal sort of prison house' where the only people he met from the outside world were 'givers destitute of charity, receivers of insult instead of gratitude'. He grew melancholy and when the overseer announced that the master sweeps of the metropolis were coming to select a number of boys as apprentices until the age of twenty-one, he was, he said, the only one who longed to be taken. The rest were frightened. The master sweeps looked them over and told a bunch of them to stand at one end of the room. They examined their chests and felt the muscles of their arms and legs. Boy after boy was taken. He, who was handled and peered at by one sweep after another, was the only one of the bunch to be rejected, left behind.

He had always known he was an oddity, because he had no name. He was the only orphan in the poorhouse without one. He did not believe his parents were dead; he thought they, like the master sweeps, had rejected him because he was known as 'The Parson' which made people laugh. Most of the others had relatives who came to see them at Christmas, some even had a mother or father, and all said they knew where their parents' graves were. He had seen pictures of gravestones in the holy magazines and each had a person's name carved on it.

He tormented the nurses about this and touched their hearts.

'Why are you crying?' said one, an old woman he was especially fond of.

'No one comes to me. No one has ever owned me!'

She said that a woman had called soon after his arrival and given him a penny piece and told him that his mother was dead.

'You were brought into the poorhouse,' the old nurse said, 'because your mother was too ill to look after you.'

He had always worked hard at his lessons and was exceptionally good at learning by heart, but when he was six years old and learning the catechism with the others his voice failed him at the Fifth Commandment, 'Honour thy father and mother . . .' The teacher was surprised to hear him falter and when another boy prompted him in a whisper, he suddenly burst into tears and collapsed trembling in a fit of agitation that alarmed them all.

'What caused that sudden burst of grief?' the old nurse asked him later. 'You cry at God's word?'

'I cry because I cannot obey one of God's commandments. I know not either my father or my mother. I cannot be a good child and honour my parents.'

In 1792 all the seven-year-old children in the poorhouse were promised release if they behaved well and made the best of themselves before new masters, who were travelling all the way from Nottingham to choose those worthy of their favour for a new life in which they would be fed on roast beef and plum pudding, be allowed to ride their masters' horses and have silver watches and plenty of cash in their pockets. It was not the nurses who told them this. It was the parish officers, at an assembly specially arranged. The children were told that none would be forced to go to Nottingham – they were asked later whether they were willing to go – and it was made clear to them that any who did would be assured of a good career; the boys would be instructed in the trade of stocking weaving, the girls in lace making; their apprenticeship was to be for fourteen years; they were promised their indentures at the age of twenty-one. Eighty were chosen. The Parson was one of them.

When at last the day came two wagons drew up in the wide front yard of the Mother Red Cap. Two rows of beadles in uniform, each holding a long stave, lined up facing each other from the poorhouse door to the Red Cap yard leaving a pathway between them along which the children crossed the road. The children were scared at first sight of them but shouted 'Hurrah!' and clapped when they heard they had been given a guard of honour. They climbed into the wagons, each of which was uncomfortably crowded, and were closed in by barred doors such as those used for bears in a travelling circus. No child could escape. But there was plenty of clean straw intended for sleeping on at night which they threw at each other joyfully.

It took four days to get to Nottingham. The muddy ruts and potholes had hardened, the clumsy wagons were unsprung and the children were thrown about by the jolting and severely bruised; most of them were seasick, some became seriously ill, and although they felt warm in the daytime, the nights in the middle of August were cold. After their first night in the wagons, they began to entreat the guards to take them home to the poorhouse and by the time they reached Leicester they set up a wailing clamour that drew crowds. But the guards calmed them by saying they had only to wait till they met their new masters at Nottingham, when any who wished to go back would be allowed to do so. The Parson was one of the few who swore he would never go back.

When they reached Nottingham they were surveyed and counted by 'a stately sort of men', one of whom, who held an invoice in his hand, harangued them about humility, obedience, diligence and care. In 'a severe and dictatorial tone' he threatened the idle or insolent, if there were such among them, which he hoped not, with flogging and disgrace.

Anyone who has learned the slightest bit about the Industrial Revolution will know at once what their fate was to be. They were taken to Messrs Lambert's cotton mill in the village of Lowdham, ten miles from the city. Iron gates in a high brick wall were closed behind them.

The stench of cotton, the gaunt black lodging house and the dimly lit dormitories into which they were locked frightened the children and yet their quarters seemed to the Parson less gloomy than the poorhouse ward. His first shock of disappointment came when they were herded downstairs into an eating room where the smell was worse. He was surprised to see no tablecloth, no plates, nor knives, nor forks, and the long tables at which they sat, boys and girls apart, were sticky and black, streaked everywhere with cotton oil on to which fluffy nap and scraps of rancid food were stuck. Nap was everywhere – in the sleeping bunks, the food, in the hair of the older apprentices who came to eat with them, on faces, arms and bare feet.

For supper they had porridge of 'a very blue complexion'. The bread was black and so soft they could scarcely swallow it; it stuck to their teeth like bird lime. He managed to eat half of his and threw the rest at the wall where it stuck like plaster. He caught the eye of Mary Richards, his favourite girl at Camden Town, who had been making faces like the rest, and she began to throw hers too. The governor – 'a huge raw-boned man' with a 'carbuncle nose' – whose job it was to keep order watched them for a second, then took a horsewhip from its hiding place in a corner of the room and suddenly cracked it.

He marched up and down cracking it near the children's ears, producing a tremendous echo from the walls and stone-flagged floor. High-spirited chatter was at once brought down to silence. Indeed high spirits were reduced to low from that day on in each of them till he or she reached the age of twenty-one; in those who survived the cruel work, the typhoid and cholera that raged through their filthy unventilated prison, the daily accidents caused by unguarded machinery, by tiredness, by childish curiosity and lack of care.

The work they had to do is well known, well documented by parliamentary commissions of inquiry. The little ones had only to pick up cotton from the floor but were at first 'much terrified by the whirling motion and noise of the machinery'. The Parson was half-suffocated by the dust and flue. His back ached from stooping; he felt sick and sat down but the overlooker shouted at him and he picked up cotton until noon, for six and a half hours without a break. The best part of the day was the walk back in the fresh air for dinner at the lodging house during which the St Pancras boys and girls kept together and could talk. Some wept in each other's arms. Some fooled about and played. Then came the afternoon shift of seven and a half hours.

The Parson was soon promoted to the roving winder. He was not tall enough to reach it and was given a block of wood to stand on, but however hard he tried, in terror of a beating, he could not keep pace with the machine. From that day until his release at the age of twenty-one his body and face were covered with bruises. His scars from floggings were permanent. The overseers rightly believed that only their fists and whips could keep the children from resting or falling asleep. Their day was supposed to be fourteen hours but they were often kept at it for fifteen or sixteen. The work was not hard but it required more concentration than any child can give and they were not allowed enough sleep at night for their age; most of the accidents were caused by sleepiness and near starvation; many by absence of mind. Injuries less crippling than a broken leg were dealt with by the factory surgeon on the spot. The injured were not allowed to leave the frame after treatment – that would have encouraged self-inflicted wounds – so they had to work on as best they could. Of all the Parson's childhood memories, his attempt to rescue Mary Richards from a machine was the most ghastly. Everyone else had been allowed to go to supper, the overseer was in another workshop. He and she were working some distance apart at drawing frames which were turned by a horizontal bar a foot from the floor. It caught her long apron and wound her in. He pulled at her, helplessly shouting for someone to stop the machine, saw her body whirled round and round by the shaft until it was drawn tight into the works and jammed the whole apparatus to a halt. Her head was crushed. Her arms and legs all broken and everyone gave her up for dead. But by the skill of the surgeon she recovered. After some weeks she was taken back into the mill and worked on crutches until she was twenty-one.

When she and the Parson were ten years old a revolution happened at the mill which improved the children's lives immensely. Letter writing had always been forbidden, but Mary and Fanny Collier, aged nine and ten, sent one in secret to their mother whose address in Camden Town they remembered, describing the cruel punishments, small meals, short nights in filthy beds, lack of soap, the difficulty they had in breathing at work because of flue, how they felt ill and hungry all the time. Through the kindness of a wagoner the letter reached their mother within a week.

Mrs Collier, a widow, had been too poor to support them ever since her husband's death, but until they were taken away she had come to see them often in the workhouse and never felt worried about them. Since that August day three years ago, she had missed them terribly and had no news, and now that the bad news came she was angry and distressed. She set out by herself to Nottingham. No one knows how she got there – but most carters liked giving women a lift – nor how she managed, being almost a pauper herself, to stay a whole fortnight in the village of Lowdham. But it is known that the village women were shocked by the sight and the screams of the mill children, and probably they sympathized with her as the mother of two little girls and kept her free of charge.

She found a way of getting into the mill and to her daughters' lodgings but wisely said nothing. As soon as she could after coming home to Camden Town she told the churchwarden of her church all she had seen and heard. It was he who organized a visiting committee.

The St Pancras committee 'arrived just as the dinner was being served out in the usual slovenly manner . . . they tasted the viands on the table.' They saw the sallow and sickly appearance of the eighty victims they had sent to Nottingham. They saw Mary Richards on her crutches and learned the reason why. They questioned the children, the Parson amongst others, admonishing them to speak the truth and nothing but the truth. 'So great however was the terror of the stick and strap being applied to their persons, after these great dons should be at a distance, it rendered him, and no doubt the great majority of his fellow sufferers extremely cautious and timid.' The visitors saw their food, dress, bedding, and they caused, in conjunction with the local magistrates, very great alterations to be made.

Tin cans were provided for every apprentice to eat his porridge or soup out of, meals were made cleaner and better. A new lodging house was built with fewer beds in a larger space. Carbuncle Nose was given the sack and several of the crueller overseers went with him.

When Messrs Lambert went bankrupt a year or two later the owners wrote to St Pancras to say they could no longer keep the apprentices and encouraged those who could write to send letters to their next-of-kin asking to be reclaimed. The Parson and others who knew of no relatives wrote to the St Pancras overseers of the poor. His faith in them had never failed, his respect, fear, distant love, were like the feelings many children had for their fathers, and because they had been kind enough to visit the mill, he felt sure they would reclaim him. Neither he nor Messrs Lambert nor his friends had any reply from the vestry.

The apprentices were moved, some would say sold, to a Derbyshire firm belonging to a Mr Ellice Needham of Burton, whose cotton mills were powered by water in the valleys of the Peak District. Litton mill where those who survived lived and worked till they were twenty-one was at the bottom of a dark ravine remote from any other dwelling place, shut off by rocks from the view of anyone who used the lonely road. Their life there was worse than it had been at the reformed Lambert's mill, accidents and punishments more frequent. Suicide by drowning in the mill race was common. Attempted escape was in one case punished by flogging to death. Inquests were held every year on dozens of girls and boys who died of 'mill-fever', malnutrition, overwork or a beating that had gone on a minute or two too long. The verdict was usually 'death from natural causes', but in a few cases 'death from misadventure'. The mill surgeon dined often at Needham's Buxton mansion.

The most famous of the cotton masters, Sir Robert Peel, first baronet, of Bury, Lancashire, had made by the same methods a much greater fortune than Needham's. As early as 1784, and again in 1796, the magistrates had made complaints about conditions in his mills, and he himself said afterwards that through 'having other pursuits' he seldom visited his mills. Whenever he did so he was struck 'with the uniform appearance of bad health and in many cases stunted growth of the children'. He discovered that their long hours of labour were caused by a system of paying overseers according to the quantity of work done. He disagreed with William Pitt's suggestion that children should be put to work at the age of five, and in his middle age began to reform his mills. As an MP he introduced a Bill which became law as the Parish Apprentices Act, restricting hours of work to twelve a day, excluding mealtimes, forbidding night work, insisting that part of the working day should be devoted to lessons in reading, writing and arithmetic and part of Sunday to church service and religious instructions. Every pauper apprentice was to have a new suit every year; boys and girls were to sleep in separate rooms and not more than two to a bed – as at Lowdham but not at Litton – and the justices of the peace were to appoint two visitors unconnected with the manufactures, one a magistrate, the other a clergyman, who would have powers to inspect the mills and enforce the Act. The Act applied only to pauper apprentices, who had always been even worse treated than the so-called 'free' ones. The reform of Lowdham mill began before Peel introduced his bill and the Parson believed that Mrs Collier's complaints had been heard by Peel. Certainly the visit to Lowdham of the St Pancras committee took place while Peel's inquiries into cotton mills not his own were going on.

The Act was ineffectual because it could not be enforced. Too many JPs and magistrates had shares in cotton mills; some were themselves cotton masters; and almost all of their class had opposed the Bill in a huge outburst of public protest, saying that it would mean not only the end of the cotton business but the downfall of England's prosperity, which was threatened already by the war. Apprentices were not told about the Act. The Parson discovered its existence thirteen years later at the age of twenty, when many apprentices of his age were committing crimes in the hope of being transferred to Botany Bay.

He and his fellow apprentices had often seen the magistrates at the mill. They had seen the worst of the cripples being hidden away, the attempts at cleaning, the softening for an hour or two of overseers' manners. But none of the apprentices knew at the time that the visitors were supposed to redress wrongs. 'The magistrates *could never find out* anything wrong, nor hear of a single individual who had any complaint to make!'

On his twenty-first birthday the Parson saw his name for the first time, or at least a name which was to be his from then on. His indentures stated that 'Robert Blincoe' has served fourteen years' apprenticeship in stocking weaving and was now qualified to earn his living at that trade. He had never seen a stocking weaver in his life or watched anything resembling that type of work. The girls who were released at the same time knew nothing of lace knitting. The indentures meant no more than prison discharge sheets. It was thus that the St Pancras overseers of the poor abused their power of binding paupers to apprenticeship and thus that the cotton masters broke their promise to teach the children a trade.

There was no need for it all. The most prosperous years for nineteenth-century industry came long after free labour was abolished. The age at which children were allowed to be employed was raised, their hours of work reduced, their wages increased. In spite of these reforms, so much feared by employers, or perhaps because of them for they brought efficiency with them, commerce and industry thrived more than ever before.

Saint Patrick's Day, Tuesday

Cold and showery between sleet and rain, and this morning
with M. on the way to her bus, the clouds looked snowy.
Yesterday afternoon, crossing the lower end of Primrose Hill,
the sky was bright on my left, southwestward and ahead, and
on my right behind the hill a huge dark cloud, purple and
black. I only saw one flash of lightning, but there was distant
thunder repeatedly.

As it changed colour the cloud rose higher in the sky, but
didn't cover the whole of it, and the light from the south made
the grass a brighter green and the clothes of people walking
distinct and brilliant, especially reds and white.

As I crossed St John's Wood High Street there was a great
flash and a near clap of thunder that made everyone look up
at the sky, then hail and white sleet blowing hard from the
southwest onto my cheek and ear. It's annoying if you're
waiting at traffic lights, and worse when you want to cross
where there are no lights, to be stopped by people sitting dry
and warm in their cars.

March 19th, Thursday

Last Saturday morning on the pavement by the old lemon man
and both my hands laden with vegetables in a seething crowd,
Davy Sloan called me and held me like the ancient mariner,
although I tried to pass him with a mere greeting. He looked
ill, thinner than ever if that can be, bloodshot eyes, alert as
ever, unshaven stubble going grey, unkempt all over and
leaning on a stick with a rubber ferrule.

– You see this, Davy, he said holding it up, I'll have to walk
with this all my life now.

His leg is worse and on the previous evening, Friday, he
had fallen down drunk and been taken to hospital.

– You know what the spine is?

He touched my back with his left hand. He had hurt his
spine, as well as all the rest.

They wanted to keep him in hospital and treat both leg and
spine. He would not stay even one night, in spite of fearful
warnings from the doctors. I said

– You've got great spirit but you're wrong – you should let them treat your leg.

And he only heard the 'great spirit' part which delighted him.

March 20th, Friday

Kept my 10 a.m. appointment with Brenda Rivett at the Hillwood House, 1 Polygon Road. It is in Somers Town. I heard a lot about David Laing that I did not know, most of it sad.

I walked there via Mornington Crescent down Eversholt St, a desolate street in which people wait at bus stops for a 68 which never comes. The houses on the left as you walk towards Euston become more and more dilapidated. Near Polygon Road – beautiful Regency houses falling to bits, scabby stucco, a broken window with a curtain flapping out, another mended with cardboard which had come loose, some doors and ground-floor windows sealed with corrugated iron. I was too early and stood for a while in the porch of a large black church – the Church of St Mary the Virgin, C. of E., but obviously high because it advertised 'Mass' on a noticeboard. Double doors with glass panels leading into the church were locked. There was a large poster in the porch, a somewhat abstract picture of people in black and white with these words underneath it. I copied them because I knew I wouldn't believe my memory. 'God is the unrest in us that does not allow us to be happy and content. – Jean Luis Segundo.'

Then I saw, above the picture, printed on a slant, the beginning of that statement, which makes it slightly less improbable. 'God is a continuing summons to a never-ending search for authentic solutions.'

But even when you read the two sentences in the right order they are negative – a negation of the usual optimism expressed by priests – the 'peace that passeth all understanding' is peace of mind and soul said to be attainable through many religions. But in Tripp's *Quotations* I see a line from the Bhagavad-Gita which seems to me to say that Peace *is* the negation of Life: 'He knows peace who has forgotten desire.'

The entrance to Polygon Road is an archway beneath some flats with windows opening above it on to Eversholt Street. It is part of a modern brick building – 1930s or 50s – which extends for about 200 yards on either side of the little road and is divided into small council houses or flats – several green front doors opening onto Polygon Road. Joined to the building on the right an old Regency pub has survived. It is only about a minute's walk from the Hillwood Centre – two minutes perhaps for David L.

A long room with long formica-covered tables, metal chairs and metal windows looking on to Eversholt Street. To your left as you come in a serving counter, with sinks and gleaming cookers behind it – but the meals are not cooked there. They are sent by van, ready-made. It is all a bit like a laboratory, everything shining and clean, but it seemed a cheerful room to me and I can see how D.L. liked it after the gloom of Rowton House.

Brenda was working behind the counter. There was no one else in the room. She had forgotten I was coming and said, going on with her work,

– Well, what can I do for you?

She said it kindly, yet it was a reproof because the place doesn't open till 10.30. She had asked me to come at 10. When I said who I was, she laughed at herself and apologized, and took me into the tiny room which is her office.

I told her about the Camden Tn book and how D.L. knew I was going to write about him, and soon she spoke about him in a realistic way, uncritical of his faults, affectionate and admiring, but matter of fact. I liked her at once and think she must be the perfect woman for the job, handsome too, tallish and slim with hair beginning to go grey.

She knew D.L. from 1978 until October 24th 1980 when he 'disappeared'.

– He was regular from 10 in the morning to 3 every day except when he was on a drinking bout.

The drinking bouts were my first surprise.

He would come in every day half an hour before the proper opening time and read the paper. He laid all the tables, every day and served at one of them, but if he had the money he always went out for a drink before lunch. In the afternoon,

and sometimes in the morning he liked to listen to music –
'popular opera and classical music' – and she brought in
records specially for him.

She spoke of his perfect manners, but if he asked for
anything and she didn't bring it or do it at once, he would be
cross. She'd say

– You want it done yesterday!

The only time he was really angry was when she refused to
keep his money for him. She said

– You must be responsible, and he raged at her. She does
not think it right to relieve old people from any of the
responsibilities they have had all their lives,

– And anyway he would only have asked for it back next
day. The council sends young volunteers to do old people's
shopping. That takes away their independence.

She said

– Something happened to David when Margaret Watters left
this area in 1979. She was still in the Royal Scottish
Corporation then, but he no longer came under her care. He
seemed to lose heart. Everyone at the Hillwood remarked on
it.

Brenda made him a case for special care soon after that but
in 1980 she saw him decline further in spirits, in health, in
taking care of his appearance. She had difficulty in persuading
him to see a doctor, and as for a doctor visiting him, 'as soon
as you mention Arlington House no one wants to know – not
even the doctor.' When she grew seriously worried, she asked
the doctor to visit him at the Hillwood. She tried to persuade
him to go again to an optician, but he was afraid of having
his eyes looked at in case they advised a cataract operation.

There was a day when to my embarrassment he pretended
not to see me in the Spread Eagle; then, when I greeted him,
made excuses for being caught drinking on a weekday – he had
always told me he could only afford a pint or two at weekends.
I hated that feeling of his, that I would criticize him for
drinking. In every other way he treated me as an equal. But
he was very depressed on that day and worried about his health.
He pulled up his trouserleg to show me a large inflamed patch
of skin from the calf of his leg to the shin. I suppose it was
eczema. I hated looking at it, and impolitely only glanced,

making absurdly strong protests in my mind – that he need not have subjected me to that revolting sight; but aloud I advised him to go to his doctor or to the Kentish Town clinic.

I remembered this incident when Brenda startled me by speaking of his 'drinking bouts', and I wondered whether I would give his sprees that name. She said that when he had money he would disappear for days, then turn up – unshaven and dirty, his clothes all in a mess. I could hardly believe it and said I'd never seen him like that.

– He wouldn't let you see him like that. Early in October he won money on the horses and went drinking. People always imposed upon him when he had money – they weren't friends, they'd have nothing to do with him when he was broke. Well he'd start off with beer but soon go on to the hard stuff.

– Did he tell you this himself?

– He'd always tell me all about it.

She saw him regularly after that last bout until October 24th when 'he went missing'. The next thing she heard was that he was dead. He had caught flu, then pneumonia. I forgot to ask how she knew about the flu.

She said

– He spoke very little about his past. The only thing I know is that he was a chef.

He had never told me that he had been a chef, and now I suspect that there was a greater distance between us than I thought, that he so misunderstood me as to think I would despise him for being a chef. The more I write about him, the more I regret the many times I had the opportunity, and lost it, of getting him to talk about his life. I felt the same about my father when he died thirty years ago.

March 25th, Wednesday

A white gauze curtain in the window opposite, billowing out above the front door.

March 26th, Thursday

On Monday, 23rd, on my way to the dairy, I was hailed by
Davy Sloan again, hobbling on his stick and trying to cross
the market to me from the back door shelter of the cinema,
where Mary was sitting on a milk crate, to the Mixer. He
could hardly walk and he had a black eye some days' old.
When I asked him if he'd been fighting he said
    – It's no' my eye I'm worried about, it's my leg.
    He is horribly thin and yellow-skinned, dishevelled. Gave
him 50p and when he asked for more said
    – That's all I'm giving you, in a good schoolmaster's voice.

March 27th, Friday

Davy trapped me in the same place next day on the Tuesday.
I suppose he must grow more persistent, now that he can't
walk quickly, with the few people he can trap. Usually he's
the only one of that whole crowd that I like talking to but
that day I'd have silenced him if words could, if anything but
a hand clapped over his mouth could. And then he'd bite. It
was by the Mixer again as I came back from the dairy. With
his perfect eyesight he foresees my movements and crossing
the road he reached the pavement in time to intercept me,
calling out to a man leaning against the Mixer wall behind me
    – Here he is – this is the author! This is the man I was
talking about.
    Confused with shame I protested and he said
    – No back doors. There are no back doors.
    I suppose that means 'You can't back out of it now!' When
he asked me for money, I refused, saying I couldn't give it
every day.
    There is no justice in my decisions to give or not to. I am
governed by my moods or by likes or dislikes for the beggar.
Last night about 6 o'clock in daylight a man with dark glasses
and a clean whitish mac rang the bell. I had seen him through
the window and, mistaking his age, thought he was one of
Ben's friends. As soon as I opened the door he shot his right
hand out for me to shake.
    This man was only about 40 but a real old-style beggar,

leading off with 'I'm an ex-service man' and ending with 'I'm going blind.' And I hated him. I hated his face but I might not have seen treacherous weakness in it if he hadn't asked me to pity him. Except for his mouth, which was sloppy, he was good-looking according to convention – that is to say his chin looked firm, his nose the right size and straight, his forehead broad and even and his cheeks matched each other, though they were too flat for my liking and pink. He had a neat black moustache. Before he asked for anything, I told him I wouldn't give him anything. It was then that he said

– I'm blind, or
– I'm going blind.
Maybe he said
– In one eye, and I didn't hear.
Then
– Look at this. I'm sure you've never seen anything like this, and took off his dark glasses.

His right eye was brown and normal, his left eye crumpled and almost closed.

He went on talking and I repeated my refusal and as I tried to close the door, he pushed it against me, till I pushed harder and he gave up. Later from the window, I saw him accosting a man and girl in Oval Road. He, like Davy, was a bit drunk, yet nothing he said would move me to give him a penny.

How do I know what that man was feeling when he rang our bell? Perhaps desperately needing company or money. One ought to be able almost to be another person, as painters are said to be the object they are painting. I can almost with people I know intimately. With strangers, I doubt my instinctive interpretation of their feelings.

March 31st, Tuesday

March is going out like a lamb, a wet lamb yesterday and today with misty mornings, but on Saturday, when we went to the Hopper Exhibition at the Hayward, it was warm and the whole of London and the people's dress and way of walking were suddenly transformed. We had drinks in a pub called the Sherlock Holmes, near Charing X station, by an open sunny door. I've been on lemonade and dry ginger ale for nearly a fortnight except for 1 or 2 glasses of wine in the evening on some days. It is because I'm having Tofranil or Tryptizol. I hate the pills but giving up drink doesn't make much difference. Perhaps the pills stop the hankering? After a fortnight on pills I feel much better when I wake at night or at getting-up time, but most days I have to 'fight' against depression all morning, and usually the side-effects last till 3 or 4 p.m., after which I feel normal and even cheerful again. The side-effects are all hateful, but the worst is the blurring of eyesight. Dr Benaim swears it's temporary, but this morning I was afraid I was losing the sight of my right eye, and it aches very often.

I haven't gone back to Lithium yet because I think the pills may have a quicker effect without it. Evan Benaim now admits that it is useless against depression. I believe it increases depression. He has said from the beginning that commercial travellers should not take it. It softens their punch. I told him that the same applies to writers and artists.

April 2nd, Thursday

Met Bert Thevenet in the Spread tonight as full of his book as ever. He writes it and rewrites and rewrites it and doesn't want it to be published. He lent me one thick typewritten volume a year ago and when I asked him today for the rest promised another but not the whole. People might steal it and get it published under their own name. Bits came out in the *Ham & High* with a picture of him with his alert, thin face, a French face, or perhaps I only think that because I know that he is of French descent on both sides of his family. His intellect is un-English, quick and without deviation. Today he spoke about climbing into the zoo as a boy through a secret gap just as our children did and about swimming in the canal opposite the Jamestown Street brewery where an outflow made the water warm. He spoke of his grandfather, or great-grandfather perhaps, who came to Camden Town in 1870 as a refugee from the Paris Commune in the days when England was famous throughout Europe for hospitality towards the unfortunate.

This man was a cabinet maker and must have known that Camden Town was the best place to settle in, in order to pursue his skill. That and the many piano factories, some of which have survived, began here soon after the canal was completed. Teak, mahogany and other hardwoods imported from Africa and the Orient were brought from the docks to the timber yards of Camden Town. Camden Town and Somers Town had a large community of furniture makers, French polishers and such, most of whom were French and some Italian.

Some of their names can be deciphered on old tombstones among those of an earlier generation of émigrés – the nobility who fled here during the French Revolution. W. E. Brown, chief clerk, cemetery department, who wrote several interesting books about the history of the Parish of St Pancras, made a list of 124 people buried in the old graveyard between 1790 and 1820. Of these forty-eight are French counts, marquises and bishops.

By far the largest immigrant group here now is Irish. It too began in the 1790s, grew with the building of the canal which when it was finished offered resident jobs to some of the navvies; again with the completion of the railway to Euston where more workers were needed than London could supply; and again with the Irish Famine. But most of those I know came after the Second World War. Thousands of volunteers from the Six Counties and the Republic found work in London when they were demobilized and thousands more were needed for the long-drawnout rebuilding schemes of the succeeding years. As all immigrants do if they can, they made for the district where their relatives and friends lived. Michael Higgins was the first of them that we knew well.

Martina met him as Thisbe met Pyramus and for several days conversed with him without seeing him through the wall of her bonfire garden. 'Thou wall, O wall, O sweet and lovely wall, Show me thy chink to blink through with mine eyes.' Our wall is too high to see over unless you stand on a log and he is a short man, broad-shouldered and strong. He was working in that house in Oval Road whose back garden stretches at a right-angle by ours. It had just been sold and the builders were gutting it; gentrification was progressing rapidly in the hands and arms of Michael and his comrades, who rested beams and floorboards daily against the wall. Martina was trying to pull one over for firewood when Michael heard her and pushed from his side. After that he threw all the best burning wood into our garden and they spoke to each other, screened like the Japanese lovers who were in the *Tale of Genji* not allowed to touch or look. He changed his job several times after that and for several years after Michael Donovan's death he practically ran the Edinburgh Castle for Norma who had young children to look after. It was during those years that our friendship developed.

He arrived at Euston at seven one morning after a journey of twenty-four hours from his parents' little farm in County Donegal. He was twenty-six and had learned enough English by then to manage all right over here. His brother-in-law and sister had written to tell him to wait on the platform where they would meet him. They were late. All the people had gone from the platform, the empty train went out; he felt afraid that he might be asked questions – 'What was he doing there?' He searched the whole station and the crowds grew. His sister was wandering about looking for him. They spent two hours without finding each other.

He had their address in Edmonton which is, I think, under two hours' walk from Euston but he lost his way and did not reach it until midnight with his little suitcase in one hand. The London public lavatories close at midnight just when they are most needed by people thrown out of closing pubs. Knowing no life except country life where you choose any discreet place by a hedge, he went behind some buildings into the dark. A heavy hand gripped his shoulder and held him. It was a policeman who watched him closely all the time he was peeing, waited for the last dribble and said

– This is a respectable area. Residents do not like the smell of urine.

Michael had never heard that word but guessed its meaning. He gave his name as Rodney and invented an address.

– Have you any letter to identify that?

He had nothing on him but a packet of cigarettes. The policeman refused to accept one.

In his sister's council flat he shared a tiny bedroom with his small nephew but when that was discovered by a health inspector he had to go. He came to one of the many Irish rooming houses in Camden Town near the building site where he had found work. The lodgers, all men, shared rooms and some of them shared beds. They had to take off their boots at the front door when they came in and the landlady issued them with bed caps and bedsocks for the night – the bed caps anti-Brylcreem and the socks anti-dirty feet. If she found dirty pillows or sheets when she made the beds in the mornings she gave the offender a week's notice and many had to leave, especially in summer when the outfit was too hot. Michael obeyed the rules and grew to like her. When he moved some years later to a house without a resident landlord he saw the need for the strict discipline which she also enforced, even during meals, because the second house, in Camden Road, was dangerous to live in: men fighting, women screaming all night every weekend. After two men burst into his bedroom and tried to beat him up he bought a six by six block of wood to bar his door with.

Michael did have difficulties with English to begin with but to his surprise he liked the English people of whom, like most Irishmen, he had been suspicious and afraid. He worked in a factory at one time where all the others were English and there he met a girl who liked him and he her. She said that if he ever had intercourse he must wear 'julies'. I wouldn't have known what that meant, either, but he says it means French letters.

When I think of his trouble with certain words I think of the canal navvies most of whom knew no English at all. 'They use only the Gaelic tongue', wrote one of the engineers, 'and it is by sign we direct them and thus they have little traffic with the English and keep together apart.' But by the time of the railways a lot of them could speak English, as was shown at the famous trial of the Round House rioters in 1846, for the completion of the line to Euston six years earlier had not freed Camden Town from the navvies' reign of terror.

It was really a battle not a riot, though riot was the legal term for it, a battle between the English and the Irish which began with a trivial incident at the Round House gates, developed quickly and lasted three hours, paralysing three police forces. It was vicious and bloody; many men were maimed and three crippled for life, but no one was killed. It seemed at the time to be a unique disaster. Nothing like it had happened near London. But the navigators' battles in the Lowlands of Scotland and on the English side of the border were worse not only for deaths and injuries, but because they were not isolated incidents; they led to revenge and counter-revenge in blood feuds that went on for years. These and their immediate causes are well described by Terry Coleman in *The Railway Navvies*.[27] He shows how the Irish were hated in the Lowlands for their religion, foreign customs and for living on cheap food. They accepted lower wages than the Scots. Scottish navvies were hated in England for their humbler needs. He shows too that the great battles in the north were started by the Scots and English. The Irish camped, according to the *Scottish Herald*, 'with their women and children in the most secluded glades', but were frequently sought out and attacked. Near Dumfermline, in 1845, the Scots threatened to drive the Irish out 'by the strength of our armes and a good pick shaft'. In Penrith, in February 1846, the English drove them off the works and when they had fled to the hills, defeated in battle, their camp was wrecked, their huts burned down and their women and children driven away, deprived of food and shelter.

But to me it is clear, from similar incidents in other trades, that a deeper cause lay, far below the surface of the mind, in an innate love of fighting and in fear of foreigners. The Lowland Scots hated the Highlanders as much as they hated the Irish, for their unco' claes, their gaberlunyie ways and the gibberish they spoke. We know that from *Kidnapped*, *Catrîona*, Dean Ramsay's *Reminiscences* and Scott's novels.

It was not by chance that the greatest battles – the one on the Holyhead–Chester line which took the army three days to quench and the one in Camden Town, which the police could not manage at all – took place in the first serious year of the Great Famine – 1846. The Round House is now a theatre but its structure inside and out has been so well preserved that anyone can imagine the vast amount of manual labour used in building it. It covers almost half an acre. Its high circular wall is entirely of brick, its domelike roof of iron is supported by twenty-four slender cast-iron pillars between which, through arches in the outer wall, ran engine tracks like the spokes of a great wheel to join a turntable – a lesser wheel within.

The Irish started the Camden Town battle; an injured policeman's credible evidence given at the Marylebone magistrates' court next day proves it; but why they started it, why their leaders – John Duggan and Joseph Glory – were bold enough to fight this policeman at the building-site gates, how much provocation they had had from the English before that afternoon, or whether they intended to force their way in to ask the contractor's ganger for work can never be known because the Marylebone magistrate, having decided to commit them for trial by jury, would not allow any extenuation pleas to be made in his court. They were all charged with starting a riot with felonious intent.

John Cooper said, 'How can they make it a felony? I have not stole anything; the fact is, your worship, the English have been abusing us for a long time past and have continually called us Irish ——. They have used other bad language which I can't recollect.'[28]

No one knows how he wanted to go on because the magistrate cut him short and told him and others, who had spoken earlier, that 'when before the jury at the Old Bailey you can make whatever defence you think proper'. Long before the Old Bailey trial the police, in their usual way, had persuaded all but one of the twenty accused to plead guilty. It saves the police time and bother. No detailed evidence was printed at that time of not-guilty pleas, and I cannot find a manuscript record.

Anyone passing along that half-mile of the old Hampstead Road which is now called Chalk Farm Road can see the scene of the riot. It is a gloomy place to this day and frightening to walk on alone. If you keep to the left all the way from the canal you are overshadowed by a thick and sombre wall which was built before the Round House to protect the railway company's property. It seems to me higher and blacker than the wall of Manchester's gaol and, whichever way the sun is shining, it makes the pavement dark and damp. Few people choose to walk below it; you cross instinctively to the bright side of the road which is lined with small houses whose windows open to the south. These too were built by the railway company, for their skilled workmen – engine drivers, superior linesmen and such. The black brick wall soon blocked their view of Primrose Hill beyond the railway.

There are two wide gaps in the wall. One, near the canal, led to warehouses and stables and still has heavy gates, now seldom closed. The other was, in 1846, the entrance to the Round House building site and could be closed by a bar let down by the policeman on guard.

On Monday, 9 August, at about two o'clock in the afternoon Railway Constable No. 175 saw a large assembly of Irish navvies across the road by the houses. There were three or four others beside him, a little way off, near the wall. 'Inside the gate' were hundreds of English engaged on bricklaying and carrying, and a long way off towards the station hundreds of Irish at work. (The contractors, Messrs Bransom and Gwyther, employed equal numbers of each nationality.) Constable Carter was aware of the danger because small controllable affrays had happened now and then for months. When Thomas Duggan, one of the three or four, came up to him and asked to go through the gateway, Carter said he had orders not to admit anyone into the ground except those who were working on it. Duggan went back a little way, and afterwards again attempted to come in, at the same time beckoning to 'some of his companions to do so too'. Joseph Glory, the boldest of them, tried to force his way in alone. The constable, seizing hold of him, was immediately knocked down and kicked on the head and body by a dozen of Glory's friends. He cried out for help. A few English labourers, at work inside the gate, ran to see what was the matter. They were felled to the ground by the Irish who had by then in large numbers crossed the road. They were beaten with shovels and pickstaffs. But Carter managed to get on his feet, took hold of Glory again and dragged him away, upon which John Cumming and four others came up with brickbats threatening to knock his brains out if he did not let Glory go. No help from other policemen came and Carter, surrounded by a hostile crowd, in fear of his life, let Glory go. He was badly injured, but went back on duty at the gate. He remembered Glory's face and name.

By then the fighting between the English inside and the Irish who had broken in while he lay on the ground had become impossible to control. Carter went off to summon forces from his section at Holmes Road, Kentish Town, but by the time they reached the Round House the Irish who had been working near the station had come up to attack the English from the rear. The English were now surrounded. They defended themselves and were assaulted not only with the usual weapons – navvies' tools – but with bricks, of which there were stacks on the site, and, worse, with brickbats: portions of bricks, which are handier to throw. The English fought bravely but were outnumbered.

Mary Randall, hearing clamour through her open window across the road, looked out and saw men lying in their blood. She heard screams and people shouting 'Murder!', and ran downstairs and over to the Round House, afraid that something might have happened to her husband who was working there; could not find him but saw another Englishman 'lying upon the ground, while five other men were kicking him most brutally crying with an oath, "Kill the —— Protestant." ' She knew the man. He was Charles Keen who had merely gone, like many other local people, to see what the disturbance was. Ellis, her husband's foreman, lay dead nearby, she thought. Next day's newspapers said he was dead. He and one other who was thought to be dead and several of the seriously injured Englishmen were carried one by one on litters to the North London Hospital in Gower Street, a mile and a bit away. Meanwhile the battle spread all over the Camden Town railway land.

After fighting both English and Irish for an hour, the Kentish Town section of police, many of whom were wounded, withdrew and sent an express – a man on a horse – to the headquarters in Albany Street from which a larger force of constables, with inspectors, came in vans at the gallop and others on foot at quick march. The streets were blocked by spectators. Oval Road, on one side of which Regent's Park Terrace was half-built, and the entrance to Camden Town station at the end of it were completely blocked. The approach to the Round House was crowded. The railway ground was wide and open. Groups of men scattered before the police and joined again to fight far off. A thousand police could not have contained them. The headquarters force acknowledged their defeat and sent an express to their Somers Town section. The express rode back to tell the superintendent that the whole of the Somers Town force had gone to the funeral of a comrade who had died two days before. He was sent off at once to fetch them from the funeral and the man was buried without a guard of honour, with only a few friends and relatives at his graveside. But even this large reinforcement, the whole of the Somers Town force, was ineffectual. The police were utterly defeated. The battle ended only when everybody was exhausted. And as so often happens in such confusion arrests were made haphazardly. During a riot police have to grab the nearest offenders. No Englishmen were arrested.

Twenty Irishmen were carried to Albany Street police station that night, but 'so desperately did they fight that it took seven constables to carry one of them, who, it was stated, had struck an antagonist on the head with a pick-axe, to the Albany Street station house.'[29]

Next day, the main entrance to the magistrates' court in Paradise Street, St Marylebone, where the case was to be heard, was surrounded by Irish navvies. Police had to drive them back to make way for the prisoners and witnesses. The court itself was crowded with reporters, spectators, and amateur ushers who had been summoned to help Mr Franklin, the court usher, who foresaw trouble. There was room at the bar for only five of the twenty accused. The others stood around it with constables to guard them.

The prosecution hurriedly dropped their first charge when Ellis, the foreman supposed to be dead, appeared as a witness to his own murder. His face was shockingly damaged but his voice showed volubly that he was alive. The other murder charge was dropped when news came from the hospital that its subject was recovering from his wounds. Four of his ribs were broken.

The newspapers did not mention even a black eye on any of the prisoners, but all the male witnesses, except a surgeon who had cared for some of the wounded on both sides of the fight, had visible cuts and bruises. Railway Constable Carter, the first of them, was 'much cut and bruised about the face'. Charles

Keen had difficulty in standing up to give evidence; 'he was shockingly bruised and his eyes were much swollen'.

The Times said that 'from some cause at present unexplained an ill-feeling had been generated among the navvies', but neither Mr Rawlinson, the magistrate, nor any newspaper sought out the cause. Two of the accused were discharged because Mr Rawlinson did not believe they had been properly identified. The others were locked up, after being offered bail at the impossible sum of £50, the equivalent nowadays of nearly £1000.

The witnesses who had been booed and jostled on their way in now found the way out blocked by a greater crowd of Irishmen who stoned them and set about them with their fists. The police drew their truncheons, cleared Paradise Street and hustled two more Irishmen into the court where one was ordered to find bail and the other fined ten shillings.

No police force in Great Britain had been able to defeat a mass of navvies united by anger, and it was only by a trick that the Metropolitan force stopped the Irish from rescuing the eighteen prisoners after the second hearing. The crowd in Paradise Street had begun to assemble early that morning, long before the court sat, and during the sitting it filled the adjoining streets as well. For hours people dared not leave their houses. When the witnesses were escorted into the court by a column of policemen, the hooting jeers of the Irish navvies rose in a crescendo, which may now be imagined in its fearful brutality by anyone who has heard an angry crowd of football fans. It is like a storm at sea, a broken dam, a river in spate; you hide from it if you can.

When this second hearing was almost at an end, while the magistrate paused to consider his judgment, the navvies allowed the witnesses to leave the court with their escorts, each of whom had drawn his truncheon. No stones were thrown at them this time. But when word came that the prisoners were charged not only with misdemeanour, but with felony, and that they were to be carried to Newgate to await trial at the Old Bailey, the whole crowd rushed at the door of the court with an appalling shout. The chief usher, Mr Franklin, and the assistants whom he had called in that day, were only just able to close the main entrance and lock them out. The navvies stayed close to the door. They knew that prisoners for Newgate were always brought out through it.

An express had been sent to Albany Street for the Black Maria and it was already on its way. It seemed certain that the navvies would stop it at the main entrance and take the horses out, so a policeman waited in Marylebone High Street, well out of their sight, to divert it. It was turned, and the horses backed it up against a small private door at the side of the court, which was used only by magistrates and court officials. The eighteen prisoners were pushed into it one by one, without attracting attention, and driven off to Newgate.

The timing of cases was more humane in those days than it is now and the accused had to spend only a fortnight in Newgate until they appeared before Mr Baron Platt at the Central Criminal Court. Only one of them, John Sheehan, twenty-four, pleaded not guilty. His counsel's plea that he had not been clearly identified was accepted and he was released. Mr Clarkson, for the prosecution, said that because the others had decided to plead guilty, he would drop the indictments for felony and hold only to the misdemeanour of assaulting the parties named, and creating a riot, without a felonious attempt. Mr O'Brien and 'other learned counsel' who appeared for the prisoners examined a great many witnesses who 'spoke favourably of their general good character for quietness, sobriety and good behaviour'.

All except two of the accused were under thirty-two. John Donaghue, the youngest of them, aged nineteen, got the longest sentence – nine months' imprisonment; his father Jeremiah, who was forty, and John Duggan, twenty-nine, six months each, seven others four months, and seven including the oldest man, Thomas O'Donnell, were sentenced to three months with hard labour, the labour being by contemporary accounts no harder than that they were accustomed to in daily life.

The navvies had acquired a unique reputation for brawls and riots only because in their large numbers they were more noticeable than the other groups of 'roughs' who lived beyond the bounds of respectable society. The people of the London Rookeries, the quarrymen of Headington near Oxford, the Forest of Dean miners and men belonging to outlying communities such as Breckland had always repudiated the law and been ignored by the police who dared not go amongst them. They kept to their own customs, one of which was settling any great dispute by battle. The Oxford police and all the residents of Headington were afraid to enter the quarrymen's settlement. The Rookeries remained throughout the nineteenth century almost immune from the police. And, even among shepherds and farm labourers, fighting as a sport remained popular well into the twentieth century. James Copper, a farm labourer of Rottingdean in Sussex, told me how he and all the young men of his village would set out every Sunday armed with sticks and stones to attack the men from the next village, with whom they had no quarrel. Several, on both sides, were seriously injured every Sunday. The police did not interfere. In the Breckland public houses, until about 1950, it was the custom to offer any stranger a drink out of your mug. If he refused, which many American airmen did, he was forced outside to redeem the insult in a fight. I was warned of this on my way there in 1947. But no one offered me a drink of any kind.

We know several families of Irish descent who have lived in Camden Town since the Famine times and of course they have been Londoners for so many generations that they can only be distinguished by their surnames. Some are even ashamed of their origins. Molly certainly is. The only thing she can't disguise is her face, hair and eyes. I thought she came from the Gaeltacht as soon as I saw her in the bakery and was surprised when I first heard her speak. I once met her at the bus stop and while we were waiting, talking, waiting, I asked what her surname was.

'Gallagger.'

'Isn't that Gallagher?'

'That's too Irish. My father says Gallagher. I don't like it.'

May Day

The dairy and the baker's both have pretty girls. They change from time to time but they are nearly all lovely. It depends on the boss, I suppose – two excellent casting directors, the dairyman and baker. I first met Molly Gallagher in the baker's, handling loaves with floury fingers. You'd never see anyone like her serving in the dairy, and that's a remarkable thing in two shops so near each other employing Camden Town girls between eighteen and twenty-five-ish so different in character that you would think they came from places miles apart and were separated by periods of history, even.

The bakery ones look countryfied, which they are not, and even now when lipstick is in fashion again they don't use it. You can't see their clothes because they all wear uniforms, but Molly dresses simply when her working day is done, with a good sense of colour, without show. She'd hate it if I called her homely but that, in the best of its old meanings, is how I would describe the bakery girls.

The dairy is more cityfied in its enchantments; the servers of milk and butter are robust, forthcoming, open-eyed and dressy, disco-going but not a bit punkish. Sometimes, I guess, one or two go skiing – summer suntan seems to last so long. People go on about 'the young' as though they were a bunch of identical nuts and bolts.

I've found a way to make whoever's serving me say 'Lovely!' You don't have to in France because almost everything a French girl says gives a beautiful movement to the lips. In English 'beautiful' is the best single word, but you can't force anyone to say it. For 'lovely' all you have to do is to have the 'right money' ready. Put it into her hand and she'll glance down at it, then look straight at you and say 'Lovely!'

If you say 'nasty' you bare your teeth in a snarl. I can't make it out.

Told Martina some of this at breakfast. She said
– You don't have such a bad time shopping after all.

May 4th, Monday

A Bank Holiday that feels like another Sunday. Yesterday we went for a short walk in the wind and cold rain and outside the convent (the Japanese school) saw the pavement sprinkled with cherry blossom and drifts of cherry blossom in the gutter. On Saturday afternoon, the day before, there had been crowds of Japanese children and parents outside the school, as though coming away from a celebration. I said

– It must have been a cherry-blossom ceremony.

There were I thought no cherry trees nearby. Martina believed me. In Prince Albert Road we saw more blossom and by the smoke school more, and in the evening in Patshull Road it was everywhere, lying on the pavements in the rain and gathered in small snowdrifts against the curb, dulled and dirty as London snow is. It had flown and fallen in places far from the trees.

Yet I had made myself and Martina believe for several minutes that the Japanese children had gathered and thrown the blossom as part of a beautiful spring ceremony. It reminds me of a series of articles Herman Levy told me he was writing in which he showed how easy it is to build a philosophical theory on the wrong premises. In the Middlesex Hospital where we were patients, he gave me one of these articles which I still have. It was based on his own experience. He was due to lecture on a Saturday at the Kingsway Hall. He turned up on the Friday and found the doors locked, but was so convinced that it was Saturday that he felt angry and humiliated. He bought an evening paper and when he saw it was dated Friday took it back to the newspaper seller and accused him of selling yesterday's.

One day in April, after our return from Austria, I heard the screams and whining of a chain saw, the most painful to me of the new mechanical sounds, and went out to find two men felling the elm near the other end of the terrace. It has had Dutch elm disease and I knew it had to come down. I have seen many trees felled in the old way by one cut at the foot of the trunk, and at Woodbrook I used to help, and tried to learn how to use an axe exactly to make the tree fall precisely where you want it to fall. But here to avoid buildings, parked cars and the terrace wall, they cut the branches and trunk piece by piece from the top and lower each piece by rope. It is messy to watch and as painful as the sound. The axe and even the mechanical circular saws of the sawmills were low in pitch.

When Martina first heard that the tree had to be felled, she thought they meant the weeping ash outside our house, and dared not tell me. When at last she did tell me (she reminded me this morning) we went out to the ash and managed to find a disease.

They dug the roots of the elm out, leaving a hole like a bomb crater, but have since filled it and planted a sapling in its place. The thickest part of the trunk is the only piece still here. It is lying on the roadway and takes up the space of one car.

May 19th, Tuesday

Davy Sloan sometimes sits on the steps of the nuns' house in Oval Road opposite my window. Sometimes they give him a cup of tea, and that's what brings him there. But often he is waiting for me. He no longer comes to the door; in fact he used often to lurk round the corner on those steps and send Mary to beg from me. Today I was going to the market for milk. I didn't see him. He is so small and grey, the colour of those doorsteps, camouflaged. When he called 'Davy' repeatedly I looked round, not knowing where the sound came from – my sense of direction for sound grows worse. Then I saw him on the pavement, leaning on his stick, about to cross the road to me, but I signalled him back and went to him. He said he was going into the Royal Free next Wednesday and would I visit him, would I stay with him and not go away. I said I'd stay some of the time and come back. He must have seen a doubtful look on my face. He said

– D'ye mind the day when ye gave me money for the bus there? Well, I went.

May 20th, Wednesday

There has been a lot of rain this month, usually in showers, and afterwards the grass between the terrace paving stones shows up beautifully green. Was it an old prophecy, or a sentence in a Harrison Ainsworth book about grass growing in the streets of London? It was meant in a disastrous sense, but in London as a boy the thought cheered me up.

May 27th, Wednesday

Can it be? So near June. And hellish.

Had to see Pillicock again. Worse. And worse still because
I had to go to his disgusting flat. He's 'working at home
today'. I must learn to do my own tax – but that's hateful too.
Difficult to find Hanover Terrace. I thought it was the Camden
Town side of the park and those Nash terraces are long. You
go a hundred yards to see the name of the next one. So I
started walking the wrong way round, thinking, when I saw
what I'd done, is it quicker to turn back or go on? Saw ahead
of me a wavering figure in a long pale coat who stopped me
from turning back by holding a pair of gloves up in a
beckoning way. As we came near each other she said
– They are hounding the animals. Think of the poor animals,
don't let them hound you.
I didn't know what I could say to her and said
– Is it bad then, worse than it used to be?
She took hold of my arm rather gently and said
– They are hounding me.
We were as close as lovers for a second before she wandered
away. She had lovely eyes and a generous face and I liked her
clothes as well. She smelt of Joy, I think, or it may have been
Guerlain. Seventy more or less, I suppose.

You can hardly see Pillicock when he sits on one of his sofas,
cushions and other covered heaps of feathers hide him up to
the ears. But his record player gleams in the open like an
aeroplane, and sporting prints and cardinals, well framed, are
displayed. Had my eye on something even larger than the
aeroplane, a box with chromium doorknobs. He wasn't ready
to show its secrets but all the time he was yapping I thought
it was a cocktail cabinet. His napkinned clipboard kept rising
from the downy bed like a tray without glasses on it.

June 3rd, Wednesday

In Franz & Aliki's garden last night – Bulgarian red wine and
mint tea – they pointed out the tree next door where an owl
roosts. They often see it especially at dusk and they hear it at
night.

They have a little S-shaped pond made of concrete in the paved part of their garden. Newts and tadpoles live in it. Remembering how the boys used to catch tadpoles on the heath to fill our pond, I asked him whether his children had started the colony. But no: all the creatures in the pond came there of their own accord. He once cleaned it out and refilled it and next spring it became inhabited again. There are many toads and frogs in the garden; newts too, but he has never seen them out of the water. He finds toads in the compost heap and frogs in any damp place. The long quarter-moon of gardens between RPT and Gloucester Crescent has many trees and bushes and Ben on night work at the cinema finds it hard to get to sleep at dawn when all the birds are singing. When we first came there was a rookery at the Henlys garage end. I have still got a letter about it – from a woman protesting to the council and asking them to destroy it. A cruel destructive letter. Perhaps the rookery was destroyed. We never see rooks in London now. Only those big crows that walk in pairs on the grass of Primrose Hill. Are they carrion crows?

Another huge thunderstorm on Monday night, starting with a loud crack, very near, which Ben thought was a bomb. I too have recently found myself thinking of bombs before the thought of thunder occurs to me.

This time the lightning was almost ceaseless, one brilliant flickering following another so that the sky was lit up a whitish blue for several minutes, continually fading for a second only before it lightened again. M. called it 'an electric storm'.

Davy Sloan. I was at the Royal Free on Friday, May 29th, seeing Dr Benaim. Got there early so as to ask what ward Davy was in – thinking that he might have had the operation on Thursday. An Irish girl, with a sweet and serious face, at the admissions desk spent 15 minutes trying to trace him. It was difficult for me to hear what she said or even understand when I did hear:

– Has he an orthopaedic problem?

and I had to break off to keep my appointment. Came back later. His name was not even in the admissions diary for Weds.

On Saturday morning on my way to get bread, there he was limping briskly on his stick towards me with Mary clean and all dressed up beside him as though she was on her way to church with an unwashed son. She is much taller than him and has got hold of a light blue overcoat with a fur collar. He, on his grimy days, looks like an Indian chimney sweep. Even his clothes have turned almost black. They greeted me cheerfully. We shook hands. But as my right arm was loaded with milk I shook hands with my left hand. I would not have done that with anyone else, but remembered meeting him in Parkway long ago when I had hurt my right hand. I excused myself that day for offering the left and he said with Romanies it is a sign of friendship, very close and not to be broken for the left hand is nearest the heart.

June 11th, Thursday

When we came back from Edingthorpe on the Bank Holiday, May 25th, I saw the Tube Tatterdemalion again. He had just come up the Camden Town escalator, walking past the ticket collector (without showing a pass I am almost sure) and made straight for the staircase to go down to the platforms again – exactly as I had seen him do at St Pancras. But Camden has had no downward escalator for nearly two years.

June 17th, Wednesday

Passing fish and chip shop in Parkway a voice shouting
  – Excuse me, excuse me! above the rush hour traffic stopped me to look back. It was a boy of 12 or 13, his voice still unbroken, coming out of the shop with a tall black youth. He had a round, healthy, happy face and was smiling as he came up to me.
  – Can you lend me 10p? I can't get home.
  His friend, much older, stood at a distance as though to dissociate himself from this.

June 20th, Saturday

Mrs MacQueen – it makes me happy to think of her. I spent from 3 to 4.30 with her in her flat yesterday and was intrigued by all she said, refreshed by listening to her and looking at her healthy countrified face. She's not Scottish after all, only she married a 'Highlandman' and lived in Lanarkshire for many years. She was born in India and brought up in Hampshire. After she told me that I began to hear a trace of Hampshire in her speech. She is 87 and except for slight arthritis which makes her waddle a bit, very active – open in manner, uncomplicated, giving; and although she has had a very hard life and plenty of sorrows, some recent, she is the converse of neurotic, no bitterness, not even a grudge borne against people who have had easier or richer lives.

She has 17 children – 11 sons, 6 daughters – 36 grandchildren and 51 great-grandchildren and is expecting 2 more this year. She was married in 1916 and had '55 years of married life'. Her eldest boy was just 21 in the June when Margaret, 2nd to youngest, was born and he came to her christening. One daughter married a man who left her because of her children. He did not want them. She was going to put them into a home and get him back, but a brother went as soon as he heard about it and took them and adopted them and brought them up with his own. One girl is married to a Maltese, one to a Greek and one to a Jew and Mrs MacQueen herself is half Jewish –

– It's quite international, the family.

I said

– So was David – half Jewish.

– Was he? Well, I always thought so but he said no he wasn't, not at all. It would be on his mother's side then?

– Yes.

I told her about his friendship with Jack Winocour and how they discussed their Scottish-Jewish background as something rare in Scotland. I was greatly surprised to hear that he had denied this to her, but she said nothing more about it. Our conversation turned back and forwards, all the time I was there, between her recent years and friendship with him and her old days with her husband and the children, and now she spoke of Lanarkshire where most of them were born. They had no running water in those days and she would be up till after midnight washing every night. Some nights she never got to bed at all. A young girl used to come in and light the boiler for her for a penny, and she would do the rest alone, starting on it as soon as she had fed the children and put them to bed. She said she was 23 when she got married in 1916 and now I have worked it out I see she must have been well into her forties by the time the 17th was born. They had moved to London some years before that and were living in Tottenham Street. She worked in Foley Street, nearby, at the Middlesex Hospital's nurses' home, where for 17 years she started work at 5 a.m. While the last of the children were young she would get the nurses' coffee ready before two assistants came at 6.30, then go home, get the children their breakfast and see them off to school. Then back to work till dinner time when she went home again to feed them. And then to work again. You hear of women worn out by almost annual childbirth or by hard work alone and there she is, blooming and happy at 87, with '139 in the family and two more coming along this year'. She hopes the next two great-grandchildren will be boys, 'to keep the family name going'. She had nine brothers and six sisters herself. David Laing, she said, had none. He was an only child. He hadn't many friends – at least while she knew him – and he was lonely, a lonely man. To my surprise she had not known him long. She had met him first at lunch at the Hillwood in 1976.

– When I first knew him, he didn't really know God, but I think he turned to God.

We were having tea facing each other one at each end of the little kitchen table, the tea things on a tray between us on a lace cloth. She went through the hall into another room and came back with a book he had given her – a godly book called *The Way to Happiness* or something.

– He gave me this book, she said, but instead of showing it to me she laid it on the formica top by the cooker, a thin brown book obscurely published which I picked up and looked at later.

She said

– He would be alive now if he had married me.

It is true I'm sure – if he had caught flu it might not have developed into pneumonia under her care and if it had she would certainly have called a doctor in good time. She didn't hear of his death for several weeks, and this was the only moment during our conversation when she showed distress.

– I don't know whether he was buried or cremated, she said, and when I told her that the council had paid for his funeral she was shocked. I knew she was thinking of the disgrace of a pauper's funeral and of the desolate lack of ceremony, the absence of mourners, his loneliness drawn out symbolically even after death.

I described the funeral, the service in the chapel and at the graveside. She had thought there would be no service and was glad, glad too that the two girls and I were there, and about the flowers.

– I would certainly have been there if I had known, she said, and I would have baked a cake and brought you home with me afterwards.

She now thought she had seen him on the day he caught the cold that led to pneumonia. It was a day in October, when he had arranged to visit her. She had told him she would be out till one o'clock, but there he was shivering outside her door. Her flat is in a low block with front doors giving on to an open concrete passage, with a parapet overlooking a grassy quadrangle. The wind and rain blow on it when they blow. He had waited there a long time. Someone had brought him a chair.

She had never seen anyone shake so much from cold. Thin he always was, but now his face had shrunk to skin and bones and his teeth were chattering. She took him in and gave him hot tea. She did not give him whisky because he was off the drink just then, but sometimes when he had a cold she used to give him a miniature and tell him to take it with hot water.

When they grew to know each other well enough, he wanted to take a room in her flat as a lodger, but that she could not do, her husband being dead and she alone there.

Later on he proposed marriage but she would not marry him because of the drink. She was very fond of him and they had many good laughs together, but in drink he was horrible.

He made her angry when he came in drunk, but he was always well behaved.

She spoke angrily to me about his drinking but for a moment only and then softened as she remembered walking with him drunk from her block of flats to the Hillwood. There was a reason which I have now forgotten which made it essential for him to get there and the state he was in was such that he would not have reached it alone. But she would not hold him up.

– I was afraid he'd pull me down with him. He was walking very straight one moment like someone on a tightrope, not natural at all, and the next second swaying and taking long strides askew. Then he'd stop still and suddenly plunge forward as if he'd fall on his face, half running till he stopped and stood again. And he'd try to catch on to me to steady himself, but I wouldn't have that, but it's wonderful how he did keep his feet. And when I think of it, it was quite something for me to let myself be seen with a drunk on the street with all the neighbours watching.

Usually when I opened the door to him and he'd had some, I'd say: You sit on that chair till you get sober and then go home. I'm not giving you any more to drink.

Most days he wasn't like that at all and he'd never ask me for a drink unless he'd been in the pub. It was tea he wanted and he'd always like 'a bitty o' cake'.

The tea was strong and good and I said so.

– Yes, David liked it. He said it was the colour of his neck!

Which was to me as I took my next sip a rather disgusting image. She apologized for the cake which was still warm and soft in the middle, saying that she had only just taken it out of the oven, and I knew she had made it specially for me. There was something Scottish about it – brown, buttery with large juicy raisins – a kind I could not remember eating since my childhood.

I asked whether David had ever been married – it was one of many private things he never spoke of to me – and she said no, but he had been engaged to be married at one time and had lived with the girl for a long time. She gave two reasons with an interval between them for the breaking off of the engagement.

The first, which I thought more likely to be true, was that

the girl got fed up with him for going away frequently to look after his mother, who was old and ill. It was she who broke it off, said Mrs MacQueen, and he was glad in the end, because if she resented him for taking care of his mother, she couldn't be much good.

The second reason, given after Mrs MacQueen had been talking of many other things, was that David eventually saw that it was 'wrong in the eyes of God' to be living with this girl the way he was – 'if she doesn't want to marry, it's wrong'. He walked out.

Perhaps both reasons were joined together. Mrs MacQueen has a way of expressing different aspects as they come to her mind. When she spoke for the second time of her own reaction to David's proposal of marriage she said

– I just laughed at him.

June 24th, Wednesday

On Saturday evening crossing Parkway at about half past six I saw a small man in a leather jacket and blue bell-bottomed jeans, standing on the pavement opposite me, facing the street. It was Davy Sloan. I had not recognized him in those clothes – clean, and fashionable among young men – but his face was covered with a two- or three-day grey stubble. In spite of the money business, which I know is one thing that makes him eager to see me, he is genuinely pleased and friendly, and I like him more and more. It is difficult to say why one likes anyone. But one thing about him is genuineness, lack of pretence, to me at least, and his lack of that awkward class-consciousness which Davy Laing, who was far nearer to me in education, had and which MacL. even now that we know each other so well still occasionally has. Tim, Luke and Ben have none of it.

I said

– I didn't know you in those clothes.

– I got myself cleaned up.

We talked for a bit but he was pretty drunk, his speech slurred and hard to understand. I asked what he had in a bulging plastic bag under his left arm.

– Potatoes. I picked up some cabbage and potatoes in the market.

There is always a lot thrown away to waste in the gutters. I said

– Have you anywhere to cook them?

– The people next door cook them for me. I won't have a fire.

– The Simon Community?

– No. That's finished.

He still lives in a derelict house in St Pancras Way near where it was, but he lives alone (he prefers to be alone, he says). And I guess he has stopped having fires, because when some other squatters set fire to a house while he was drunk asleep he was the one to get arrested and accused.

When I touched his leather jacket and said

– That's a good coat,

he said

– It is a good one, aye,

and thinking it was from the nuns' or another charity I asked where he got it.

He told me how, and smiled and held out his hand for me to take as a pledge of understanding that I wouldn't think ill of him. It was black leather with a zip up the front and studded pockets. The black dye was worn out in places showing a yellowy green.

I thought, what with his leg and the drink, he won't last long. I felt sad about him and said as we were parting

– You shouldn't drink so much.

About five yards away he turned his head towards me and said

– Ye'd do the same, Davy.

June 26th, Friday

Yesterday, I saw the last bit of the Bedford Music Hall – a wall by the passage from Cam. High Street to Arlington Rd. Only this side wall is left with EXIT ONLY painted black on white on the bricks of the old arched gateway which has long been bricked up with newer bricks.

It has been closed up for years and allowed to fall into ruins recently, but for a long time there was a hope that it would reopen as a theatre, cinema, dancehall or social club. For years people dossed in it. The last show I saw in it was Marie Lloyd's daughter doing her Mama's stuff. I'm sorry it has gone. Next door there's a little shop with clothes hanging outside and a notice pinned above: 'Denim and Cord Dungs'.

June 27th, Saturday

Outside Piccadilly Theatre *Educating Rita* – couldn't hear – left M. there after interval and wandered looking at people.

I passed a young Indian with two beautiful children, a boy and a girl – I looked at the prices and a flattering *Time Out* notice on a tandoori restaurant, at the menu of another place, wandered looking at everything; hesitated outside the theatre seeing next performance was not till 8.40. Hovered, I suppose. The Indian family came near. The little boy tapped me on the arm and gave me 20p; pressed it into my hand.

I looked at him and tried to give it back, said
– Thank you, but you mustn't give it me.
I looked at his father, appealing for help, and said
– You take it.
He smiled in a really friendly way and said
– He wants to give it to you.
I saw I should take it, held the little boy's shoulder and said
– Thank you. I'll remember it all my life,
which is true. The child was pleased.
Before I said that, I said
– Well, thank you. I'd like to give you something, but I've nothing to give.

They crossed the road (Bedford St) towards Piccadilly. The two children had been holding their father's hands, all the time. The boy his right, the girl his left.

June 28th, Sunday

The Indian children and father looked happy, lovely to watch as they stood by me and as they walked away. It wasn't until I was with Martina, telling her about it, that I began to think I looked poor. The father was noticeably well dressed in rather 'informal' European clothes, the children neat and colourful.

I was in a light fawn summer jacket, which looks a bit creased I daresay, light corduroys, olive green, and canvas shoes that were once blue. The shoes do look faded and their string soles flat and ragged. Perhaps they thought I was hungry too – looking hungrily at one menu and passing to the next – finding all too dear for me.

A poor old man!

I had felt old in the morning too, when at the 'Old Gentleman's' stall, I got in a muddle trying to stuff the vegetables into M.'s green bag, fumbling I suppose with its two openings. The woman (his wife) broke off from her next customer, and said

– Come on, dear, let me help you. Now, you hold it open. That's right. Now there you are! That's all right then, ain't it? Mind how you go!

as if to a child who can't get his books into the school satchel. I didn't like that as I liked the Indian boy.

June 29th, Monday

I was in the public bar talking to Bob about his friend whom he wants me to talk to about the General Strike. There were about eight other people there all working class and, among them, one of the OAPs who from his talk sounds communist. Bob finishes his dustman's job about 10.30 or 11.30 and always comes into the Spread Eagle on his way home to dinner. He was on a stool at the end of the bar with his back to the wall and I on another facing him. Suddenly I heard a deep, blatant, public-school voice behind me of the kind that says: 'I'm a leader of men, I know what's good for the world.' The voice said

– Did you say the General Strike? I remember that!

Bob was hoping to stop him because he had more to say to me.

He said

– My friend is writing an article about it and . . .

VOICE: – I remember it very well. I was on the buses. We had a canteen in Park Lane.

To tease him, I said

– Were you on strike?

– No, no I was a blackleg.

Bob finished his beer and left saying

– See you later

to me.

D: – Were you driving a bus?

– No, I was a conductor. It was on a 31 to World's End – the same route as it is now.

D: – Was there any fighting?

– No trouble at all – everyone enjoyed themselves thoroughly.

When I reminded him about the fights at Chalk Farm garage, between police and pickets who were trying to stop the blackleg bus crews, he said the 31 only came as far as Swiss Cottage. (I think this must have been to avoid the trouble.)

He was 21 at the time and on holiday in the country from Wye (Rye?) agricultural college. Someone had given him a lift up to London; he had wanted to see something of the strike. In London he saw a recruiting poster and went and signed on for the buses – he did two days – no, 1½ days at the normal pay for a conductor. It was in shillings – ten or twelve a day – he couldn't remember –

– It doesn't sound much, but remember you have to multiply by 10.

I had remembered that, and also that he didn't need any money.

– The drivers were all older men. It was easy taking the money, giving change. We didn't bother too much – just handed out the tickets. We had a policeman with us. The passengers were all laughing. I think someone threw a stone at us once, that's all.

D: – You enjoyed it?

– Oh, it was great fun. Of course we beat the strike. The mistake we made then when the unions' power was broken was not to crush them absolutely. Baldwin was advised to do that. Old Baldwin was too kind, too nice a man – He said 'No, we can't do that.' If he had crushed the unions properly – it was just the right moment – we wouldn't have the trouble we're having now.

As he left he asked my name and introduced himself as Smith, with extra barrels – Somebody-Something-Smith. Then he excused himself for talking so much and I said I liked it, 'So few people talk in pubs' – to strangers I meant.

He said

– I'm afraid I do. And then I've got this terribly loud voice, which was the nicest thing he had said altogether.

I met Bob again an hour later. He asked how I got on 'with that man'.

D: – He's a high Tory.

– We don't want any of that! He shouldn't have interrupted our conversation in the first place.

July 3rd, Friday

A spate of letters from Philip. M. loves them. So do I. Funny and sad. But usually I don't answer so he doesn't know we like them except when she writes. At the Parkway crossing that day in March when he came to lunch a man beside us spat into the gutter. Philip said

– I hate people spitting but I spit myself, isn't it funny? Yes.

I hate the sight of old people but I am one. We should all be issued with yashmaks on the first day of the OAP and sentenced to life imprisonment if caught without one on. The sentence would be merciful and for most of us short. Dylan Thomas used to cover his face and sing sweetly 'Lady! Take off your yashmak', uncover, pull a horrible face and shout 'Now put your yashmak back!' I copied him to the children and they made it one of their games.

6 July, Monday

That Mr Somebody-fformidable-Smith the other day reminded me obliquely of Sam, because the only time I thought Sam muddle-headed was when he talked about the General Strike, which he so often did. He said it was caused by a few trouble-makers whose dupes those millions of strikers were. He was glad that it failed and believed it should have been put down even more forcefully, put an end to within two days. Yet he himself had taken part in the police strike only a few years earlier and was glad of the slight improvements he and his comrades won by it, although their main object – to get their union recognized – was not achieved.

Sam's most vivid memory of the General Strike was the seizure of the secret printing press of the *Young Striker*, a little news-paper called by the magistrates a circular, which was distributed daily by hand at the Chalk Farm and Cressy Road tram depots, Bowman's Drapery shop, the Penny Bazaar, at the corner of Delancey Street where Woolworth's now is, and to passers-by in the street. The office and press were in Camden Road.

Sam was one of forty policemen who arrived at the *Young Striker* premises in a furniture van at night. They were supported by several vanloads of special constables, students, businessmen and ne'er-do-weels, who were armed with chair-legs instead of batons. The specials wore civilian clothes. They ranged themselves behind the uniformed police against the walls of the building, out of sight of the windows and the front door. After long and patient knocking, a solitary policeman persuaded the newspaper men to open the front door and at his signal the whole posse rushed it, batons drawn, with the chairleg brigade to back them up. There was a savage fight. The newspapermen, unarmed, outnumbered, had been taken by surprise. Several were arrested, but most of them escaped through the back and side doors of the building. They lost all their secret files, stocks of ink and paper, every piece of equip-ment including of course the printing press. George Miles, the publisher, was one of those who escaped.

The episode enthralled Sam. He often described it with glee as a schoolboy might who has been allowed to dress up in uniform and join a gang of older boys in a daring prank at dead of night.

The glorious snatch of the printing press salved the chagrin from which his section was suffering for although the *Young Striker* was printed about five hundred yards from the Camden Town section house in Arlington Road, it was a sleuth from Scotland Yard who located it: one Cosgrove by name, Detective Inspector of that ilk, who made another coup immediately after the raid. An informer directed him to a house in Malden Road near the tram depot. In it he found 1200 copies of the dangerous rag, each of which bore the name of the publisher George Miles. Having placed these in the custody of the Camden Town police, he went immediately to the office of the Young Communist League in Great Ormond Street where he captured George Miles without trouble.

Miles was an engineer, aged twenty-four. He said in court that he took full responsibility for the publication and distribution of that paper, that no one else was involved. He was remanded on bail of £100, the equivalent of at least £1000 in 1980s money. Sam knew him by sight but not to talk to.

The *Young Striker*, the *Workers' Bulletin*, the *Workers' Weekly* and more than a hundred other 'disaffected publications' gave strikers courage by informing them of the progress of the strike in other parts of the country. Without these special papers each community on strike would have felt isolated. Without them there would have been no antidote to the government propaganda paper, the *British Gazette*, whose editor Winston Churchill made light of the strike and weight of arrests, imprisonment and fines.

Penalties for possessing or distributing 'disaffected publications' were harsh. Mrs Pollit of Highgate, whose name appeared on the imprint of the *Workers' Bulletin*, was fined £50 with five guineas costs or three months' imprisonment in default. Robert Stannot was fined £100 plus costs or three months' imprisonment. Sarah Span, twenty-six, a book-keeper, and her sister Bessie, a tailoress, were bound over. Shaphurji Saklatvala, the communist MP, refused to be bound over and was sent to gaol for two months. In Hyde Park, on May Day, just before the strike began he made a speech which the authorities considered to be seditious. Among other fearsome statements he had said, 'The Union Jack has for generations done nothing but protect fools and rogues. We want to tell the army boys that they must revolt now and refuse to fight, and then they will be the real saviours of their homes and the workers'. I want the navy boys to march beside them.'

Saklatvala had been the most popular of all MPs since 1922 when he was first elected. The police loved him because he had successfully supported the police strike. Sam knew him personally and liked him very much. He thought it wrong that 'in the course of duty' he should be commanded to join the small posse that went to arrest him.

From the government's point of view Camden Town was one of the worst trouble spots in London. It contained a hornets' nest now known as the Chalk Farm bus garage – a vast high building which was then laid out with tramlines and points but had ample room for buses as well. It had also a wasps' nest, smaller but vicious, in Cressy Road, Hampstead, from which tramlines ran to King's Cross. The hornets and wasps sent messengers to all the other London transport depots to exchange news peacefully, but when angered by scabs they stayed at home and fought.

There had been some fighting at the tram and bus depot every day since Tuesday, 4 May, the first morning of the Great Strike. On the Saturday the London General Omnibus Company announced that they had managed to keep eighty buses on the streets, forty-seven of which were seriously damaged by 'strikers or evilly disposed persons'. The British and the Thomas Tilling buses were similarly lamed but kept going until Sunday, 9 May. On that day there was a riot which the local police failed to restrain.

Anyone who saw Camden Town on that day and who had read descriptions of the excited crowds in the Paris streets in 1789 would have thought that the second English Revolution had begun. All streets from the depot to Camden Town tube station were blocked with people from pavement to pavement, a surging, roaring mass which, after swelling at the crossroads where it staunched the flow of traffic in Kentish Town Road, Camden Road, Park Street and Chalk Farm Road, spread thickly again from pavement to pavement, swarming, seething all the way down Camden High Street to the statue of Cobden at Mornington Crescent where it swelled once more and trickled out into small angry groups in Eversholt Street and the Hampstead Road. Sam, whose eye for crowds was practised by annual duties at Ascot and Epsom, said there were five thousand people around the tube station alone.

For several hours no trams or buses could leave the depot. The police fought the pickets but had to retreat. Then they sent to Hampstead for reinforcements.

A fleet of motorcars filled with chairleg specials arrived from Hampstead police station. The Kentish and Camden Town police, who had already suffered many casualties, beat a lane through the crowds with batons and one by one the cars ranged themselves in front of a tram or a bus. The procession started at walking pace towards the West End, fighting all the way. Stones, sticks, bricks and lumps of coal were thrown at them. Sam was on a bus sitting beside the driver protected by wire netting. He told me he just lashed out with his stick at anyone he could reach. The blackleg conductors were also armed with sticks. And of course there were no passengers, for who would be so foolhardy as to run a gauntlet of that kind?

As in all wars this nine-day war between the strikers and the allied forces of blacklegs and police grew more vicious in action and more bitter in emotion as the days went on. Mass meetings were permitted by the Emergency Powers Act. Marches were forbidden. Sam was on duty with eleven other constables at the largest of the Camden Town meetings, which was held near Cobden's statue at the end of Crowndale Road. The crowd of angry strikers filled the streets from the Working Men's College at one end across Camden High Street and down to the Hampstead Road railway bridge. When the speeches were over the strikers began to march.

'We broke them up. They never marched. We went into them and hit them with our sticks, right and left, and chased them down the side streets hitting them when we got the chance. And there was only twelve of us.'

The General Strike or Great Strike as it was called at the time had begun at midnight on Monday, 3 May 1926. It ended inconclusively on Thursday, 13 May. It need not have ended in defeat as it did. The morale of most of the unions was higher than it had been on the 3rd and 4th and many of them remained on strike in spite of the TUC's advice. They were angry. It was as though their staff officers had capitulated at the very moment when victory was in sight, for even in those days the high-ups of the TUC were out of sympathy with their members.

Of the three million strikers a vast majority of two million had come out not to improve their own lot but to support the miners whose wages were to be reduced in May when the government subsidy to the mine owners ceased. The miners had refused to accept the reduction and were locked out. By the beginning of the second week the government was known to be shaky. It had bolstered itself up by putting armoured cars on the streets and by publishing lies worthy of Goebbels in the *British Gazette* and on the BBC – lies for example about massive returns to work,[30] which had not happened. The TUC paper, *British Worker*, corrected such falsehoods in a deliberately mild and humorous manner, but the BBC would not broadcast the corrections they offered.

For a government to resort to threats and lies is a sure sign of weakness. I believe, as most of the strikers then believed, that Baldwin could not have held out much longer unless by introducing martial law and curfew, methods that would certainly have appealed to Lord Birkenhead (F. E. Smith) and Churchill who published in his *British Gazette* paeans of praise from Germany for Britain's firmness in dealing with the workers. The weakness expressed itself in a mean and deceitful offer to the miners, which they refused. The TUC told the miners' leaders that the other unions could not continue to support them if they refused. They then advised all their members to return to work. Their decision was a misfortune for the people of Great Britain who had to wait almost twenty years for the mild measures of socialism – the health service and some essential nationalization – to be introduced by Attlee. But the Great Strike did some good. Ensuing governments were scared lest it should happen again and the memory of Winston Churchill's attitude to the people throughout the 1920s and 1930s ensured his dismissal in 1945.

If 'disaffected' means what I take it to mean – rebellious against injustice – then Sam was disaffected within the police from his very first day when he signed on after the Peel House training course. Vanboys, who rode at the back of delivery vans, were earning £4 or £5 a week. He earned £1.

'But even on £1 living was good at the section house, quite good. You got your bed, breakfast and tea or supper all paid for. You cooked your own breakfast, all in one kitchen with gas rings; some would be having rashers of bacon, some kippers. I got into trouble with my first dinner there. There was a cook, a woman, got all the dinners ready and left them in the oven till you got in. So I got in. No one much about, and she was washing pots, the other side of the room. And I said, "Is my dinner in the oven, Cook?"

' "Help yourself."

'I took the first plate out I came on – top shelf.

' "You can't have that. That's Detective Inspector So-and-so's."

'I put it back and took another one.

' "You can't have that. That's Detective Inspector Such-a-one's."

' "What can I have, then?"

' "Down below."

'So down I go to the next shelf, but always she's got eyes in the back of her head.

' "You can't have that. That's a CID dinner."

'The CID dinners there – they were piled high. The PCs' down at the bottom, I'd say half the size. Now they got the same pay as us and we paid the same as them for dinners, so I thought to myself: "I'm having this" and I sat down and ate it. And she was wild. But I finished it up and it was very good; I can remember that dinner now. Well, that was the first trouble I got into in the force, because I wouldn't let that dinner business go: I got talking about it at a meeting. What business was it of mine, the sergeant said, and nobody else said nothing. But of course the old constables knew about it for years and I took the feeling they was on my side a little bit, because the CID were getting a plain-clothes allowance which didn't go most on clothes and gave the cook a few bob for bigger dinners. I thought: "There they are sitting in a warm office and we come in cold and wet off the beat."

'I didn't hear no more about that, good or bad. But when it

came to darts, that was my trouble, and that was in the second war, the Blitz time. There was cricket and the inspector was in the team and if there was a match he'd change the rota and let anyone in the team go on early shift and be free the afternoon. I was pretty good at darts and the captain of darts was only sergeant. That inspector wouldn't allow him to change the rota and give us a chance to play a match. I brought this up, too, at a meeting. Nothing was said, but next thing I was transferred to Somers Town police station away from friends, all strangers there to me and a long walk home to my old lady where we lived in Albert Street. The inspector knew I lived with her at home in Camden Town.'

He redeemed himself by bravery during the bombing of King's Cross Station and was taken back to Camden Town. From the moment he fell in love with his 'old lady', who was then aged twenty-three, Sam was determined to find a permanent and private home and after two years in the celibate section house he was earning enough, together with a police rent allowance, to take the top floor of a three-storeyed house in Albert Street a hundred yards away. There were two rooms on each floor and a lavatory for everybody on ground level.

'Thirty-two steps up and thirty-two steps down I have gone every morning with the slop pail for fifty-seven years. The police never dreamt I'd cost them so much in pension when I retired in 1945.'

We were in the Edinburgh Castle as he told us this, he on his high corner stool and Rosie, one of the nicest barmaids ever born, behind the bar listening. She loved listening to him. He had been a kind of father to her ever since she was a little girl.

'They say there's more violence in London nowadays, but I don't think so. The difference is we settled things on the spot – with the old Charlie Wood (baton) if it got bad. I never saw a prisoner beaten at the station but once, when a man was brought in fighting drunk and one punch on the chin was enough to quieten him. I think it's a habit that's catching. I think the young police have got somehow scared. And that comes from not knowing who you're up against – so much going about in cars.

'Well, I've been scared in the General Strike and often in a pub fight when a hundred men gang up on you, but the most scared I ever was was my first confinement, about three in the morning on the beat down Royal College Street, great long street badly lit in those days and no one about, and I saw this young woman leaning against the Vet College wall in the pouring rain drenched, and she wouldn't say nothing when I spoke to her, only sob. I said, "What's up, girl?"

'She said, "I've just had my baby."

'And there it was in her knickers – big old-fashioned knickers, not like the panties girls wear now. I took off my cape and laid her down on it. I lifted her skirt and shone my torch and the baby was attached to her. But it cried and I knew it was alive. They usually have to slap them first to make them cry out and breathe. Then I blew my flute (whistle). No policeman heard it. But when I blew it again and once more, a window went up opposite and a man came down, and across the street in his dressing gown. Back for blankets to cover her and the baby from the rain. Then I told him to run to the doctor's. I knew the address. And I told him run on to the station at Holmes Road. That was a mile, and he was out of breath when he reached there, and couldn't tell them to get the ambulance – couldn't speak, to say I wanted help, till after some time. The doctor came first with his surgical bag and he cut the cord and gave me the baby to hold. I had to shine my torch for him. I said to my missus next morning, "How does that ever come into shape again?"

'The rain was streaming down my neck inside my tunic. My shirt and trousers was so you could wring them out and fill a pail. I threw my cape on the floor when I got home and my missus said, "Are you hurt somehow?"

'The cape was covered inside with blood and stuff.

'Well, we had another long wait for the ambulance, me with the baby in my arms and the mother covered as best we could outside the Vet College under that high wall. You never knew such rain and cold rain. Well, that was all right at the finish. We all went to hospital in the ambulance – me, the doctor, mother and baby. And that was a mile and a half back for me to the station to make my report, just about the distance that girl was trying to walk on her own when her pains came on.

'I was so long with her that night I never forgot her face and a year and a half later when I was on day beat one morning in

Camden High Street I saw her with this little boy in her arms, standing talking to a friend. She was looking at me, and I heard her say, "I'm nearly sure that's him."

' "Good morning, ma'am," I said, "and how's your baby?"

'And I said to her little boy, "You don't remember me, but I was the first person you ever saw besides your mother."

'She had called him Robert after the policeman.

' "But my name's Sam," I said.

' "You didn't tell me your name that night."

'I've known them ever since, passing on the street, I've watched that baby grow up into a fine lad.

'And you see this young lady,' said Sam to me about Rosie, who had been listening as she served the beer.

'She used to hold my hand, most every day. She won't look at me now she's got her own young man.'

'Crossing the street to school,' said Rosie, 'it was always the girls' hands Sam took.'

The pocketbook came out – it usually did come out – to show what a fine-looking man Sam was in Royal Field Artillery uniform with his two horses. The snapshot made him and Rosie laugh but he laughed most at the police certificate in which it was wrapped: 'This is to certify that Samuel Humphries, District of Marylebone Division, joined the Metropolitan Police as constable, 7.8.1919 and retired 31.12.1945, having been pensioned on completion of service. His conduct was exemplary.' It had a blue embossed seal on it, signed by the Commissioner of Police of the Metropolis.

'There was a good many things he didn't know about me,' Sam said.

'I was lucky with my inspector, that's all, and lucky on duty at Ascot over seven years in front of the Royal Box. The first thing that happened when I was young was a terrible thunderstorm, the course a foot deep in water and all racing stopped. One of the bookies was struck by lightning, not twenty yards from us and we ran to him, four of us, and carried him off to hospital. We knew he was dead, the lightning struck him on the neck below his ear and that came out big as a turnip. Next morning on parade at Holmes Road, the Super comes. We thought to ourselves – "What's up?" He had a telegram which he read out to congratulate the Kentish Town police on their promptness for going to the rescue of this man, which he'd watched. And then my inspector. We weren't allowed to put a bet on in uniform, but we had to look round the paddock and see everything was in order before the race. And I knew horses from long before, knew the form, had in my head the odds from patrolling the bookies' stalls. I often guessed the winner. Between races we sat down behind the bookies, sitting on the rail. I'd tweak his trouser legs; he'd bend down and take my stake and I'd whisper Number 9 so-and-so, and get my bet on. Then back in front of the Royal Box.

'One day, I just got my bet on when my sergeant comes and sits beside me on the rail.

' "What are you on?" says the sergeant.

' "Number 9 so-and-so."

'But before he had time to get his money on up comes my inspector and the sergeant says, "Better go! Quick about it."

'We walked off. My inspector calls me back.

' "What horse are you on, Humphries?"

' "No horse, sir. I'm on duty."

'Next morning after parade he says to me on the quiet, "Come on, Humphries, I know from the men you picked the winner."

' "Number 9, sir."

' "You cunt. You could've told me."

'I was all right with him after that, and it was him who got me drunk on night duty the winter after, the time I was acting sergeant on a snowy night in Camden Town – a salubrious street; it may have been Gloucester Crescent, I forget. I was snow all over my tunic, helmet and all, and I couldn't feel my hands. There was a woman going home into her house and she said, "You look like Father Christmas."

' "I feel like Father Christmas, madam."

'She went in. A minute later out comes a young man, her son, with a bottle of whisky.

' "My mother says that'll warm you up."

'Well, I went and stood in a little doorway, dark, and I had some. Then my constable comes past. I call him, but quiet like. He thinks something's up.

' "What is it, sergeant?"

' "Come back here in the dark. Here it is."

'We drank the whole bottle between us. We were supposed to be looking after people. I don't know what we'd have done. And I was all right to go on on the beat till morning. Cold sobers you up, doesn't it? But when I was passing the brewery, down Jamestown Street, still snowing, a hand comes out of the door and grabs my arm. It was my inspector.

' "Come in. You need something to warm you up."

'He was as bad as me. What he'd got warm on I don't know but it was whisky when he took me in.

'You see things are different for young policemen now. I can't imagine a lady sending out a bottle of whisky now.'

'They'd bolt their door at the sight of him,' said Rosie.

'This lady didn't know me. But most did. The beat, you see, and always being seen in public like at Ascot every year. There was a young lady there, a smasher. I'd never seen one like her. Beautiful and cheeky. I was full of vim and vigour then in my young days. I was thirty-one years of age when I moved her on. No photographs allowed in front of the Royal Box. We had to move them on, and we were stood there. She stood by me with her little camera and I said, "Move on. You can't stand there with that."

' "You're standing there," she says, looking up at me, teasing.

'I said, "Don't do what I'm doing, do what I tell you," and I showed her off the course.

'Next year, I felt someone behind me, not pushing, but you might say pushing a bit. I didn't budge. I turned my head a little and it was her. She said, "Don't do what I'm doing, do what I tell you. Come and see my parents."

'Her parents came down from the Royal Box and I gave them two winners. After that she came up to me every day at Ascot for seven years. I had good teeth then. I kept them so white people said, "Are those false teeth?" And I always believe, whatever a man looks like, good white teeth are the main thing for girls. I kept mine good all the time in France in icy water.

'Well, then I was lucky again with an accident in front of the Royal Box another year, and this girl watching. The carriages with four horses and postilions used to drive round the course before the first race and the near leader of the last carriage – I don't know who they was in it – crossed his legs and tumbled, just off me. The postilion had turned his horse too sharp. I didn't wait for orders. I leapt the rail, got hold of it struggling and sat on its head. I loosed his harness, got him on his legs all right; he wasn't hurt, nor was the postilion; he was tossed off down the course rolling over and over. When he came back, I was harnessing his horse in again – the harness is the same as the Artillery – and he said, "I'll do that."

'But I'd done it. I lifted this little man up on the saddle and away they went. The whole Royal Box was watching.

'I think all good and bad that comes to a man comes by chance and often you think good is bad and bad good. Because another time at Ascot, my Super's car stopped by me, him and his chauffeur staring out of the windows at me. I thought, "What am I doing wrong?" And next day I saw the chauffeur in the Camden Town section house canteen. I said, "You're the very man I want to see. Your car drew up in front of me and you and the Super squinneyed at me. What had I done wrong?"

'He said, "Don't get swell-headed. The Super saw your starched gauntlets and your buttons polished. He said: 'If all my men turned out like that, I'd be proud.' "

'Of course, it was my army training – the buttons. I just couldn't get out of it. But the gauntlets was my missus. We'd only wear them at special times, white oversleeves on the forearms and she used to wash and iron and starch them. She took a pride in me. No one else starched them or got them so white. I know I didn't when I was living in the section house before I was married.'

When he first came to Camden Town Sam was shocked by the sordid poverty of people whose rooms he had to visit 'in the course of duty'. Sometimes he blamed the people for the mess they lived in and often his comments enraged MacL.

'It don't need money to keep clean and tidy. Only self-respect, that's all.'

'What kind of respect is that?' MacL. said nastily.

'It's the same as respect for the dead,' Bill Campbell said.

Sam's wife died early October 1974, at the age of seventy-nine. I had not seen him for a fortnight but had heard the news from someone and when he came into the Edinburgh I said, 'I'm sorry to hear your sad news.'

As I said it I knew I should not have. By sticking to the convention I nearly reduced him to tears. She had died of a heart attack after a week in hospital.

'I'm glad she went that way. No long illness. People looking after her, not like laying ill at home.'

I asked if he was managing all right on his own. 'Does your son come?' and as he told me about her, about nearly sixty years of marriage, he became cheerful, smiling, even laughing.

'He comes. Now my old lady, I told you before, was a trained cook. When I was in the force I used to go on at six and she was up at five in the morning and when I'd be finished shaving there'd be two rashers and eggs on the table and two cups of tea. That would set you off for the day. In those days it was point duty – no traffic lights they got now – eight till four in the afternoon at the crossroads Camden Town, rain, sleet and snow, and when I'd come home about five a beautiful dinner. You never seen such. She was like that till she had to go. She never let me dust my shoes, she laid out my clothes every morning ready.

'Well, I was the same if she let me. I'm all sorts now. I'm cook, housekeeper, laundryman. I get up in the morning, make the bed, run the carpet sweeper over. I do just what she used to do. I take everything off the mantelpiece, dust them, dust it. We've got one of those big old-fashioned wardrobes. I polish that. I take the top off. Those have a top that will come off. I polish that. On top she had laid out all with newspaper. I took all that down to the dustbin and laid new on.'

July 10th, Friday

Wild privet. I like the sound of it, but couldn't believe it ever was wild until I looked it up and saw that common privet is native, which means that it grows wild or once grew wild in England, which the rhododendron didn't. In the woods at Mrs Pym's near the river at Nairn the rhododendrons looked wild and if wild privet was there in the tangled growth beneath the trees it was invisible; its leaves and flowers are small, its stem comparatively spindly; untended rhododendron bushes would smother it, I think. Its strength comes only by cultivation, from the close-packed density artificially produced by planting hedges and keeping them firmly trimmed. It is this that has made me think of privet all my life as a tame and orderly plant.

Our hedge became wild this summer. It has taken two years of neglect for its leafy twigs to reach over the pavement in front of my window, swaying in the wind, bowing with the weight of rain and springing up again, some stretching halfway across our front door. At night, when I forget it is there, it brushes my face as I open the door and frightens me for a second. The flat, rectangular top of the hedge – that green platform which looked from above as though you could walk on it – is no more. Three or four long twigs have grown upwards towards the sky, tapering from their thickly leaved base, into three-pronged forks that wave above the roof of the house opposite in Oval Road.

I cannot remember ever before seeing a privet in flower, the constant snipping aborts the flowers. But this year our hedge was covered with white flowers, a little longer than loganberries and the same shape and each breathed out a honey smell.

Branches from the old horizontal twin of the weeping ash now make a roof over the roadway, too high for most lorries to touch and in the wind flick the privet in the tiny part of a second in which two butterflies touch. The weeping part touches the black iron railings. You have to push it aside, or bow down to get past, but in a few weeks the dark, full August leaves will weigh it down, leaving a clear space for people to pass in single file. To go by the privet and then the ash is like going through a wood. The old sunny place by our doorway where I often used to read and drink in the deckchair, my bottle of wine on the doorstep, has been in the shade all this summer. I have seen tall unkempt trees of box. Perhaps some of those that formed the St Pancras cemetery grove were box trees. The Box Hill we used to visit near Guildford in Surrey took its name from the wild box trees that grew on it. But from childhood when anybody mentioned box, I thought of border-edging – 6 or 8 inches high.

July 28th, Tuesday

We hear very little of black white, white black hatred in Camden Town. Martina heard Tommy Sweet telling one of his customers in the market to 'get back up them trees' and once on a sunny hot day I watched the ancient lemon man drive away some stately robed Arabs from his tiny stall, then hobble after them to the fruit and vegetable woman to whom they went across the pavement, calling to her not to serve them. The other market people laughed at him. She served the Arabs.

August 7th, Friday

A week ago, on 31 July, I went to the Hillwood to see Brenda Rivett. As I was leaving, Mrs McQueen came in to say she was going to the doctor and would be back soon. It was about 10.30. Brenda's reply asking how she was was not fussy, nor patronizing, but familiar in the true sense of 'family', and again I thought afterwards how good she is and how the job suits her. She is her own boss and is not bossy.

Mrs McQueen remembered me without a hint from Brenda and invited me to come to tea. The trouble about fixing a day and time would have prolonged our meeting anyway – I was unable to remember the engagements I had and she was insisting on the Tuesday because her niece was coming and she had to be in anyway – but the muddle of deafness lengthened it still more.

D.: – Would Wednesday suit you as well?

Mrs McQ.: – Yes. It's my best day, Tuesday.

D.: – All right Tuesday, only I'll have to leave about ½ past 4.

Mrs McQ.: – Then you'd better come about 1 o'clock if we want to have a talk.

D.: – I couldn't get to you till 3.

Mrs McQ.: – Come any day you like.

With a few more roundabouts we understood each other and settled for Tuesday at 3.

On Tuesday I walked up the open concrete staircase, past a pram and bicycles, to the first floor and along the balcony. It was very hot and sunny and across two corners of the courtyard hung bright washing – coloured sheets and garments. Mrs McQueen was standing on the gallery outside her door, resting her elbows on the parapet and crumbling bread which she threw down to the pigeons on the grass below.

– They know me, she said. Sometimes they come right up here to my door. I don't believe they give children diseases.

There was a small group of pigeons – 15 or 20 – walking about unhurriedly to pick up the bits of bread. When I left I saw they had finished it all.

It was very still and hot. She led me into the kitchen as before down the short passage to the right where coats are hanging from hooks – many coats left there I suppose by her children, all middle-aged now, or her grandchildren. The little table in the kitchen was laid with a tray and a tablecloth for tea for two. She apologized for not having baked a cake and I said it's too hot, it feels like thunder.

– You know I'm still frightened of thunderstorms, and I shouldn't be. I've always done as much good as I can and God has been good to me. Look how He saw me through the bombing. The house next door to us was bombed down, a heap of bricks and dust, nothing left, all dead. Ours was all right. Not one of us had a scratch. That made me think. He brought us safely through two wars. In the 1st, the factory at Greenock blew up. In the 20s and 30s, in Ayrshire, all families of 5 or more like mine, got free milk and free oatmeal or flakes. Quaker Oats, you know. Real oatmeal's more nourishing. I took that. [She makes porridge for herself every morning even now.] My husband was a good man altogether. He was a miner. We didn't get a penny when he was out of work – no dole, nothing. I used to go for herrings when there were some – 5 for ¹/₂d. That would give the family one feed. And he made cat's whiskers, and sold them for £3. You remember the old cat's whiskers wireless set? On outings with the children he used to hang one from a tree – a magic tree he used to say, with music coming from it.

Mrs McQueen said she used, in Scotland, to pay ¹/₂d to the club and that gave one day's holiday at the seaside. They'd set off in the morning with a bit of a picnic and the cat's whiskers – her husband always brought that – and come back, often just as it was getting dark.

– That was nice. And times were very bad then. But even when there was no work – for years in the 30s there was no work and you'd find it hard many days to get any bit to eat at all – all through the difficult times God was good to me. I pray to God every day all day long – well, not all day but it's seldom He's not in my mind. I thank Him for the day and for the night, for bringing us through the night, for the sunrise and the grass and trees all day, and the evening.

She says God has been good to her, yet in the next breath describes the cruel hardships of her life, her children's tragic misfortunes and her sympathetic suffering.

Inverness Street market is a parable of dawn to dusk, birth and death, a daily rebirth ending in mess and dissolution. If I were as full of faith as Mrs McQueen I would thank God for it when I am in a good mood and curse it when I'm unhappy. But when she is unhappy, I suppose she would believe God was smiting her with it for her sins, so close is his personal interest in her that he kills her neighbour and saves her.

One Saturday evening, about a year ago, I met Loup-the-Dyke on a 53 on my way home from the London Library and took him into the Windsor Castle. I don't think it was his first visit to a pub but it was his first to a working-class one. It happened to be dirty too, uncleaned after the crowd of Saturday lunchtime, and it smelt stale. He hated it. We left by Arlington Road on our way to RPT, and he stopped to look down Inverness Street just as the market was collapsing. The last of the barrows were being wheeled away, piled high with boxes, exposing heaps of paper mixed with cabbage leaves and fruit. At the top end, opposite the Mixer, two piles of debris, one taller than a man, had been gathered waiting to be loaded on to the old trailer that stands there. Soft vegetables, bananas, oranges had been squashed into wet muck by wheels, and papers fluttered above our heads in the wind. Three refuse men led by the great black dignitary had begun to clear it away but the whole length of the market was still splashed and strewn with stalks and scrap and cast-off leaves. The few barrows that were left stood askew on the street like boats in the mud at low tide. Three drunk and ragged men were sitting on the pavement, dazed, with empty bottles of VP wine beside them.

– What is it? said Loup and stood looking at it as one might look helplessly at the disgusting rubble of an earthquake.

– The market.

I knew he had often passed it in his car, but then a car is a good protection against smells and sights.

– The rubbish street, he said and that is what he has called it ever since, as though he had seen a miner only once at the end of a shift before his bath, and believed that all miners' eyes and teeth glared out of darkness all life long.

August 11th, Tuesday, 1.20 p.m.

Couvade – The word came to me just now as I opened this book forty minutes before Martina's driving test. It is I who am nervous. I had been trying to remember the word all morning at odd times since shaving after breakfast when, looking at the messy shaving soap in the mirror, I cleaned my face stroke by stroke, questioning all the time the power of prayer – Mrs McQueen's faith in it, Father James's quiet and philosophical certainty. To pray to God to let her pass the test is something I would not do. It would be like praying for a new pencil box or bicycle as a child, for one of my premium bonds, now, to win a prize. But I can believe in the power of a state of mind induced by prayer, that if I could induce a calm confidence in myself I might transmit it to her, and that even in her absence I might imbue her with it. While she was with me I was calm and so was she. We planned to walk across Primrose Hill, but near the railway bridge she decided on a 74 to the Baker Street tube, and in waiting there looking for it to come round the corner we talked of other things, and when it suddenly came, I forgot the magic words 'Good luck'. The rest of the morning in a stupid anxious state – which I hope has not been transmitted. 1.50 p.m. If my moods are transmitted to her, it's all right now. I mean I am calm and confident and shall remain so. 2 p.m. Her test is starting. To perform the couvade properly I should get into a parked car, sit at the wheel, try it for shakes, the road being icy, gravelly, slippery with oil, hold the car on the clutch, change down from top to bottom, and watch out all the time for my greatest danger: the pedestrian.

Martina is lovely and funny as she recites her knowledge to me when we're walking together. Last night it was safe distances from the car in front at various speeds. We guessed to the next lamppost and 'paced the land'.

It's 3.15 and she hasn't rung up. I think she would have if she had passed. The only hope is that she didn't want to keep the BSM man waiting. She has to drive him back to Harrow from Hayes – about an hour. Then the tube to Finchley Road and a 31 home.

Next day Weds. She arrived about ½ an hour later. I had turned back to write about Mrs McQ. and forgotten her, my head down in this book, till she called through the open window. I couldn't see, didn't wait to see the expression on her face. Nor could I tell from her voice, ran to the door and there she was with a sprig of privet in her mouth.

– What's that? Does it mean yes?
– It's my laurels.

I took the leafy part between my lips and kissed her, but wouldn't believe it till she said yes, she had passed. She said it with the privet between her teeth.

We went to dine on red mullet and retsina at the Kolossi and it was a beautifully warm light evening for the celebration, smelling and tasting nostalgically of Greece.

August 14th, Friday

Went to Milia's for wine – wrote cheque and was searching for my credit card, because it was a new man who brought me the wine, when Madame Milia called from her place at the till.

– No card! I know him twenty years.

I had not remembered it was so long but now do because she and most of the Cypriot people who now live in Camden Town came here at the time of what she calls 'the troubles' of the 1960s. Both her parents were killed in that war. She still has a brother and a sister living in Cyprus. She says she found happiness again in the shop. Her real name is Christoforou.

We say Madame Milia because that's what's written on the shop.

She had a tiny shop at first. I've forgotten it – which street it was in – but remember how our wine used to be delivered by a boy with a barrow. When they moved to Pratt Street they stopped retail deliveries and I asked her how much I had to order to get it sent.

– Sixty dozen! with a regretful smile.

We have always liked each other. When I was younger I thought of her as the primordial goddess, the Great Mother of ancient Cyprus, later as someone's ideal wife and as the perfect mother of her own children. She has a big generous face and a big generous body and she always dresses in the Greek fashion of neat black.

She often looks sad when she's not aware of anyone watching. But normally she looks happy, especially when she has her granddaughter on her knee by the till. And she has a lovely sense of humour.

On one hot summer day I made her laugh a lot, and all the young men serving behind the counter laughed, when I asked her to go swimming with me in the Highgate ponds.

– But I can't swim! she said.

August 19th, Wednesday

I was thinking this morning about Mrs McQueen's magic tree, again; how children's minds are constantly dealing with magic and finding real or imaginative keys to unlock its secrets with. But all inexplicable sounds, smells and sights, anything that shocks you with surprise whatever age you are has a similar effect; you search, you worry it out. I must have been nearly 60 when I first heard a talking motorbike. I was on the pavement of Parkway among many people walking to and fro. None of them stopped to listen, but I had to. I could not go on without searching for that harsh voice. I had passed it before I turned back. There it stood in the gutter, a motorbike without an owner near it talking to itself, giving instructions to itself about where to go next, abrupt instructions, the name, the number, the street, clipped rudely off and repeated again and again. Of course I knew what it was. The childlike wonder lasted only a few seconds. But the miracle persisted. Its own voice, through a voice box built into it, was telling it what to do, but it was not its own voice. It was a ventriloquist's.

I was writing at the open window here this morning when a sudden voice shook me out of it – a belly-based voice that said 'Electricity meter'. I looked up of course and it said it again and there was a rubicund man with yellowy-grey hair and a huge white moustache which hung down on either side of his mouth like those bushy bits of sheep's wool that hang in the wind on barbed-wire fences, tapering to points. As I let him in he said

– You've been sitting at that window for some years.

He knew his way to the basement where the meters are. We went down the stone staircase together and he talked as we went. He said he hadn't been to this house for eight years and that I was sitting at my window just the same then. He had been working at the same job for twenty-five years. It is just about as long as we have lived in this house and I filled in for myself his unspoken words: how could I sit there for twenty-five years? His voice kept booming in the hard-walled corridor. He loves listening to it, like many deep-voiced men. His big red face was cheerful.

In the end he thanked me overmuch, as though I had done him a favour, and went out. I watched him from my window. His self-confidence was enviable, pot belly, wide fat shoulders and thin legs covered in reddish-brown tweed all went along with it in high spirits.

When Martina came to see me I told her what he had said and she laughed a good deal about me sitting here so long; and I added

– In front of the same sheet of paper with half a sentence written on it.

August 27th, Thursday

In the middle of Parkway, at its junction with Camden High Street, there stands an island which divides the one-way traffic into two streams. It is fenced on three sides by iron railings ornamented at the top with hoops in groups of four enclosed by horizontal bars. From its open end, which faces the crossroads, a steep flight of marbled stairs leads to a lower world beneath the street. It is, so far as I know, the only memorial a grudging Camden Town ever raised to George Bernard Shaw (though there is a plaque on his house at 29 Fitzroy Square). His name is not on it. It has one inscription only, the word 'Ladies' in bold black letters on white plates, one on either side below the hoops. This island has been boarded up for five years or more. Huge beams of wood, one of which forms the winos' grandstand, facing the High Street and backing on to the stairs, lie on the ground all round it. A hoarding painted red and white encloses the memorial but wire-netting windows have been made in it through which you can see a part of the sloping banisters which were once gleaming brass and are now painted black. Mary and all the other ladies have for all these years, in peril of their lives, had to cross the main road and enter an orange coloured horsebox or showman's van which blocks the way into the tube station.

How can it take five years to refurbish a lavatory? It took less than a year to build it, once that dreaded decision was reached, to excavate the site by spade, before mechanical diggers hastened that kind of work, to fit it up and tile it. But more than six years of angry argument, in which Shaw took a strong and humorous part, preceded the decision. In 1927, at a meeting on behalf of the Cecil Houses Fund, for dosshouses for women, Shaw said

When I went into active municipal life, and became a member of the Health Committee of a London Borough Council (St Pancras), the question of providing accommodation for women, which was part of our business, was one which I conceived to be pressingly important. And you can have no idea of the difficulty I had in getting that notion, to a limited extent, into the heads of the gentlemen who were working with me on the Committee . . . I talked and talked to get proper sanitary accommodation for women, I found it impossible for a long time to get over the opposition to it as an indecency. A lavatory for women was described as an abomination. Exactly the same feeling stands in the way of providing for women what is popularly known as a 'doss-house'.[31]

Such notions stay for years and years. We accept women's lavatories in the middle of our streets just as we accept pedestrian crossings and traffic lights, but nothing so far has persuaded us to provide for homeless women. Lord Rowton thought only of men. And so do all of us, except for a few devotees of small and impoverished charities.

Bernard Shaw was not the first person to advocate the building of public lavatories for women. There were a few in St Pancras and in other parts of London before he was made a member of St Pancras vestry in the spring of 1897. In October he became a member of the health committee, on which he served for a second time after the vestry became St Pancras Borough Council. He was on the vestry and council for six years. He liked it.

On 28 May 1897, he wrote to Ellen Terry excusing himself for not answering her letter by giving a long list of the work he had to do 'and on top of it all the Vestry with its two weekly committees'. She replied in a cross but affectionate letter, 'Don't write to me for a month . . . I can see you are busied to death (and a little worried, I think) . . . A Vestryman! You! You will glory in it.'[32]

He took it very seriously. But he did glory in it. There are no verbatim accounts of what he said at meetings, but nearly all reports, in the third person, are interrupted by the laughter of other members, and many of them show his wit, the individuality of his mind, his love of shocking people.

Shaw wanted more women's lavatories, he argued successfully for more pay and more days off for lavatory attendants and he supported a proposal that one place in each women's lavatory should be free. Mr Fitzroy Dell opposed the motion, saying that in the parish of St Giles free places were used by the flower and watercress girls to freshen up their flowers and watercress. (Loud laughter and cries of 'Nonsense'.) Mr Bernard Shaw held that to him that was the strongest reason why these places should be kept clean, and was the best argument in favour of free accommodation for women (laughter).[33]

The motion proposing free places was defeated, but as in many cases including the controversy about the Park Street site, the argument for it made public in the local press became effective years later.

In 1900 an obstruction, so called, was built on the site as an experiment. It is described much as I would describe the wooden structure that now surrounds the ladies, but being no wider or longer than the proposed iron frame it allowed more room for traffic on either side of it. The buses were narrower than present-day ones, the horsedrawn lorries much narrower than juggernauts, yet it was thought by the bus companies to impede their trade. Their representatives in the two deputations which attended the vestry that summer were more influential than the Park Street shopkeepers and house-holders, who hated the thought of such a thing near them and said it would lessen the value of their property. Shaw who was present on the second occasion when the largest deputation came said that 'as this was a woman's question, and as there was no woman on the deputation, he moved that it be not received.' But the chairman overruled him and his motion was not put to the vote.

A Mr French led off for the bus companies, saying that the bus runs of the London General, Tilling, Waterloo and Camden Town, and the Bayswater omnibuses up and down Park Street were one a minute, that the model obstruction had proved itself a danger – hardly a day had passed since its erection without some accident and only on Tuesday a very serious casualty had nearly occurred – and that if the convenience were built the police would be obliged to move the bus stop higher up the street where it would be inconvenient and cause even more serious congestion.[34]

At a later meeting Shaw said, 'Does not so much traffic make lavatory accommodation all the more urgent?'

The St Pancras Gazette found it difficult to understand how 'any healthy-minded man or woman can object to such quite smart looking erections as have been put up already in various parts of the parish.'

When eventually it was built it did not diminish the value of the buildings near it nor, even in the days of two-way traffic when we first knew Park Street, did it cause bad traffic blocks. The worst congestion in the 1920s, Sam used to tell me remembering his point-duty trials, was in the middle of the junction of five roads where trams had to stop to change points and shift their poles from cable to cable. Trams, buses, brewers' drays, horse- and motor-lorries, coal wagons, pair-horse carriages, slow, hooded oil carts, newspaper vans and butchers' two-wheelers which wanted to go fast in spite of the danger to everyone else became inextricably tangled at some time every day because there were not enough policemen to govern traffic coming from so many directions. And on top of it all were the costers' barrows lining the west side of Camden High Street, as parked cars do now.

In the 1900s between the Britannia pub and Paradise Passage there were six fish stalls, which infuriated Bernard Shaw because of the filth they scattered on the pavement – entrails, heads, tails and bones of filleted fish. When another councillor, defending the fish costers, reminded him that cans were provided, Shaw said, 'They prefer the pavement.'

He tried to promote cleanliness everywhere, in public baths, libraries, streets and I suppose that on his way to his Park Street bus stop he had to step through this slippery, bloody patch.

Others complained of cat's-meat men, eel-skinners and the dissection of rabbits. One councillor had forced a coster to move when the smell through his bedroom windows above his shop became too much for him. But most of the shopkeepers on the west side of the street, the side nearer the park, wanted the stallholders to stay. They attracted crowds and the crowds brought trade to the shops as well. The shopkeepers on the other side wanted them removed.

Shaw was the chief advocate of their removal to little side streets such as Inverness Street where their few survivors still trade, which was unlike him because during his six years on the vestry and council he spoke so much for less fortunate people, women and underpaid men. Now it was he who complained of congestion. But the costers depended on crowds and the side streets suggested would not hold half of their barrows. Their leader told the council that if there were no buses and trams there would be plenty of room for the stalls. The costers had stood there years before traffic obstructed the High Street. They had a right to stay.

Their lives, at the end of this argument, were made more difficult than before. They were nominally driven out of the High Street but those who failed to find a stance in one of the allotted streets remained, moving inch by inch if a policeman came near, for legally they could only be accused of obstruction if they stood still. It was tiring to keep moving. Tommy Sweet who now works in Inverness Street had, like most of them, a two-wheeled barrow shaped like a wheelbarrow but longer and wider which he would keep moving with his knee as he sold vegetables, took money and gave change. And at times when the police were strict he had to wheel his barrow as far as Kilburn High Road, selling when he could, and back to Camden Town after dark. Those times were few. Even when they stood still men like him were too numerous to be prosecuted, just as cars parked on yellow lines are now. Sam, after giving a warning, would get a handshake and feel a half-crown on the palm of his hand. His old lady always had free vegetables. But occasionally his inspector would order a raid and then dozens of costers would be led with their loaded barrows to the station.

Most of Bernard Shaw's proposals were turned down: proposals to raise the working age of children from twelve to fourteen, to make building a municipal monopoly and so exclude private contractors who built mainly for the rich, to start a crematorium in St Pancras, to make the mayor and aldermen pay for their own gowns and badges – regalia which he ridiculed – but to pay the mayor a living wage so that those without a private income could take office.

But when his term of office ended in 1903 the council was unanimous in praise of him, applauding his efficiency, his grasp of administrative procedure, his practical sense in dealing with routine business, all of which had struck some as improbable at the start when they heard that a playwright, a habitué of theatres, had been appointed as a colleague. Some of them had made fun of him. He admired most of his colleagues, especially a bootmaker and a Methodist minister who became his friends. He grew to believe in municipal government as complementary to Parliament. He believed it to be more democratic than Parliament because its members took part in the work of the community they ruled. (It is remarkable to read in the debates about the costers that many of the councillors knew each by name.)

By Shaw's time the local government of St Pancras had enormously improved. For half a century it had broken the law, committed local malpractices and failed to practise work for which it took money from the ratepayers. The paving boards and the directors of the poor were the most culpable. Both had formidable powers to use or misuse.

The paving boards, by Act of Parliament, were supposed to pave the streets. They were also responsible for lighting, water supplies, refuse, watch-houses, lock-up cells and green-yards. In the Camden Town district in 1850 there were fifteen self-elected commissioners to look after four and a half miles of road. £408 17s went on salaries and £366 on paving. In winter, roads were deep in mud and impassable, in dry weather deep in dust. Refuse was collected by private entrepreneurs, called 'Flying Dustmen', who took only the valuable parts. The perishable and most offensive stuff was thrown into the road. There were no lamps and, worst of all, no public pumps. The commissioners were £11,000 in debt.[35]

This was not the kind of thing to provoke a hullabaloo in the national dailies. The deportation of pauper children was.

On 18 January 1851, the *Morning Chronicle* and on the 23rd, more powerfully, *The Times*, roused Parliament and people all over the country by discovering a practice that had been going on privately for years in St Pancras.

Within the last few days the attention of the Poor Law Commissioners has been directed to a practice which, it seems, has been for some time in existence among the guardians of the poor of the extensive parish of St. Pancras of deporting numbers of children of tender age, varying from 10 to 11 years, to the Islands of Bermuda.

The circumstances were first made known to the commissioners by a novel application being made, upon the 17th inst., by Captain W. B. Burrows, of the brig James, to the guardians of the adjoining parish of St. Marylebone, for a number of children of that parish to proceed by his vessel to the Bermudas on the 25th inst. . . . Captain Burrows stated that he could convey the children to the Bermudas for 6L per head, and he led the board to infer that this would be a cheap and convenient mode by which the parish could relieve itself of a great amount of juvenile pauperism . . . he added that he had taken out 60 children of both sexes belonging to the parish of St. Pancras.

It was only because Captain Burrows's juvenile cargo for 25 January had fallen short that the Poor Law Commissioners found out what had been going on between him and the St Pancras board of guardians. The St Marylebone guardians rejected his request and wrote to Somerset House about it.

The Poor Law Commissioners wrote from Somerset House to St Pancras a stern letter asking 'to be immediately informed whether it is the fact that any children have been sent, as alleged, from St. Pancras workhouse to Bermuda under the care of Captain Burrows, and, if so, that they may be furnished with the particulars of the proceedings in the case.'

St Pancras replied admitting that the allegations were partially correct, but that

40 and not 60 children have been sent from this workhouse to Bermuda at three different times . . . Every necessary care was taken, and strict enquiries were made by the directors from persons well acquainted with Bermuda before the children being sent. Good situations with respectable persons at Bermuda were obtained for the children previous to their leaving England, and most satisfactory accounts have been received of and from them.

The Poor Law Commissioners made a thorough inquiry during the next three weeks under the direction of one of their senior inspectors, Mr Hall, and in their letter to the St Pancras directors of the poor they said that they, 'after deliberate consideration of the evidence', were satisfied that the directors were influenced by humane and benevolent motives in the course which they adopted. But they could not ignore the fact 'that the provisions of those Acts of Parliament which relate to the emigration of paupers were wholly overlooked . . . The expenditure out of the poor rate was therefore illegal, in regard to the whole of the emigration.' Also, because many of the children were under sixteen and some were also orphans or deserted children, consent in the petty sessions ought to have been obtained with a certificate from two justices. The Commissioners then thanked the directors for the frank and courteous manner in which their inspector was aided in his investigation.

In his report Mr Hall said that no child whose relatives could be found had been sent to the islands without their relatives' consent; that the emigrants were furnished with a suitable and sufficient outfit; that every precaution was taken for their moral and physical welfare during the voyage (boys were kept separate from girls on the brig *James*); and that they treated these children with great kindness and attention and obtained for them on landing in the colony situations in families of known respectability. Letters from some of the children were produced during the inquiry, all of which indicated the same spirit of contentment and happiness . . .

I have read many of those children's letters. Hints of unhappiness in them are rare. But as I read them I remembered that some pauper children could not read or write at all and I thought would the St Pancras directors have sent any of the unhappy ones to the Poor Law Commissioners? The letters now in the Public Record Office at Kew are those which were sent to Somerset House. Most of them are copies made in the same handwriting, with perfect spelling, by one of the St Pancras workhouse clerks. Some of the originals must have been dictated by the children to adults in Bermuda and all, I suppose, had to be shown to the child's master or mistress before dispatch; you could not secretly slip one into a letterbox. Letters had to wait for the brig *James* to arrive with its next batch of emigrants and be handed personally to Captain Burrows by B. C. T. Gray and Son who acted as employment agents.

Some letters, defending pauper emigration, were solicited by the St Pancras directors from men who knew the islands well. Mr Gray himself was in London at the time, suffering from a long illness. On 27 January 1851, he wrote:

My dear Sir,
    I had heard, previously to your Note of today, that there was a discussion in the public papers, respecting the emigration of certain pauper children to Bermuda, and but for my own confinement to the house for nearly 14 months of indisposition, I should probably have either called on or written to you upon the subject. As it was by me I apprehend that the attention of your Board was first called to this subject about the Autumn of 1849, and as upon that occasion you appeared to me to take every reasonable precaution for the

welfare of the children committed to your care I should have felt pleasure in tendering my testimony to that effect had not my aforesaid indisposition rendered me incapable. I can only say that after several personal interviews with the Master (I believe) of your Workhouse, sometimes in the presence of the Chaplain and always in that of the boys themselves, unto whom everything relating to the voyage and their situations afterwards was fully explained and written, 5 or 7 . . . eagerly availed themselves of the offers made to them . . . I have no reason to believe that any of these boys were disappointed with their places, and from my intimate knowledge of Bermuda I have no doubt whatever that they are infinitely better off there than, in ordinary circumstances, such children would be in this country. Thanking you for the three Papers herewith returned.

    I remain, etc. etc.

    B.C.T.G. by A. W. Gray.

On the same day Mr Osmond Jones of 6 Richmond Grove, Islington, wrote to George Birmingham Esq. at Morton Villa, Kentish Town, saying that since they last met and spoke about the Bermuda emigrants he had seen Lt Col Reid who was for many years Governor of that island and who 'will be happy to confer *personally* with any Gentleman who may be appointed by your Board of Guardians and to give him any information on the subject.' Osmond Jones's family had been settled in the island for many generations. His father's and his uncle's families were still there, he himself was connected with it from birth and resided in it for more than eleven years. He could therefore confirm Captain Burrows's report

that the convicts have no opportunity of associating with the other inhabitants and that they are not allowed to remain in the colony when their term of transportation has expired. The latitude of Bermuda is the same as that of Madeira and the climate is very salubrious, the inhabitants are proverbially 'Poor and honest' and as far as my opinion may be worth anything I think that the advantage to the emigrants is incalculable . . . they have a fine climate . . . and a chance of bettering their condition instead of being apprenticed in England, and sometimes as I have heard returning, *with their Masters* to the Workhouse when their apprenticeship expires . . .

    I am etc. etc. Osmond Jones

In February 1851 the *Weekly Dispatch* published a letter from a man who had stayed in Bermuda and then left for Canada. Speaking of the children, he says:

> They were sold like slaves. Immediately upon landing, the ship was boarded by Bermudians, who seemed anxious, all of them to have some of the boys. Five times the number would not have supplied them all; the children were, therefore, quickly disposed of, the Captain receiving at the rate of £1 and over each per head. They are, all but two, apprenticed to these men for whatever terms the men choose. They are to labour in the fields or gardens, or at any other work their masters put them to for any time or any hours, for merely their board and lodging, which is very poor indeed. They are to have no money whatever for their several years' labour, nor learn any trade so that they might as well have worked for any one by the day; but no, the sham apprenticing is the selling of the children. In one of my journeys I one day saw a John ——, who was sent out with Mr. Mann in the first lot; he was then living with a Minister of the Gospel; he was often beaten unmercifully, half starved and kept in rags and barefooted, and was made to labour in the fields from daylight till dark for his food and lodging; he had six years and a half to serve under the treatment when I first saw him. Another boy of the first lot who came out, James George, brother of Charles George, in the house, I saw him after walking about 14 miles purposely, he told me he was very much ill-used, scarcely a day passing without his being beaten. He showed me his person, which was covered with bruises of long standing; he was a little better fed than some of the others; he did not like the place, nor did any of them. One of the girls named Gardner, is living with a Mrs. Cameron, opposite Paget Church, Bermuda. Before she was one week there, her head was cut open with an iron key, and she is much beaten. Nearly all the children are in this way treated. I hope you will name this treatment of the children to someone, in order to prevent any more being sent out, as when the ship left the mate had customers for a great many more to be disposed of for a great deal of money – I say again to sell them like slaves.

George Barron, aged fourteen, wrote from Bermuda to the workhouse in November 1850:

My dear Friends,
    the 'James' leaves tomorrow and I must write you a letter to beg of you to send my sister here as I am sure she will be well situated. My Master would like her to come to him as he is certain of a good

place for her – a lady living near us is in want of a girl . . . My Master and Mistress are very kind to me. I see Sam Thelwell very often – he is in a very good family, his master and mistress are very kind people . . . and the Captain was very kind to us and got us all very good situations. I must conclude now with my best respects to you and love to my sister.

I am etc.

[No date]   Kennedy Hall, Pagat Parish,
                                                                     Bermuda

Dear Uncle,

I have taken this opportunity of writing you these few lines – hoping to find you in good health and I put this piece of brush in to let you know that I am in Bermuda and my Master is very kind to me and shew it to the Schoolmaster and Bermuda consists of 365 Islands, and I like the place very well – and I suppose you think it very strange that the heat now of the sun is as strong here as at home in the summer and we have two harvests in the year in this country.

From the Boy – James Combley

[No date]   Hamilton, Bermuda

Dear Friend,

I take this opportunity of writing these few lines to you hoping to find you in good health as it leaves me at present and will you send a little girl named Jane Richards to Mrs. Trimingham for she will be well treated in every respect and live in the same family that I do and I have got a good situation . . . and I have got a kind Master and Mistress and I am treated very kindly indeed and I am bound for 7 years with free will . . . and give my 'affectionate' love to my 'Governess' and thank her for what she has learnt me for I find it was for my own good so no more at present from Caroline Boyd. 'excuse bad wrighting' –

This letter is one of the few with spelling mistakes crossed out and corrected – the gh in 'wrighting' is crossed out – which makes me think she wrote it herself with some help. The phrases 'my master and mistress are very kind to me', 'I have a good situation', 'I am very happy' appear in almost every letter from both boys and girls, some of whom appear to have been used as recruiting officers to supplement the efforts of Captain Burrows and Messrs Gray.

Bermuda Islands, June 16th, 1850

Dear Friend,

I take up my pen to address these few lines to you . . . We had very calm weather that is the reason I could not write before – we were out six weeks on the sea. I was seasick two days. I am very comfortable where I am now, thank God for it. I have a very kind Master and Mistress and they say if I be a good boy I shan't want a friend – there are several Gentlemen want boys and I hope some of them will come – please give my love to all my schoolfellows . . . Please give my love to Mrs. Hammond (and etc. etc. of the Workhouse) – so no more at present from

George Channon

22 November 1850

Dear Mother,

I now take my pen up with the greatest of joy writing these few lines to you hoping to find you in good health and dear Mother I am very glad to inform you that I have arrived quite safe thank God – dear Mother I hope you are quite well – I have not forgot you and I am very much obliged to Mr. Eaton [the Workhouse Master] for the comfortable place he has got me. I have got a good place and a good Mistress and Master and my Mistress wants a woman and a girl and I would be very much obliged to Mr. Eaton if he would let you come – and I am very happy and you must not fret . . . and dear Mother do come if you can for I think Captn Burrows will ask Mr. Eaton for you for he said that the place would do for you nicely and Mother do not go and live with Tom. If you do I shall not see you again and now Mother I hope you will be happy . . . and dear Mother give my love to all enquiring friends and Mother there is only a little cooking to do . . . please Mother would you answer this, then I shall know you have had it . . . I have only to be here 2 years and 6 months – So no more at present from your affectionate daughter Christiana Eliza Godwin.

A few adults did sail with Captain Burrows, but their prospect of finding employment was faint compared with the children's, who, as so-called apprentices, got no pay. I can find no mention of any trade to which they were apprenticed; the girls seem without exception to have been employed as domestic servants and the boys, where work is mentioned, as helpers in gardens and farms.

B. W. Mathew, a St Pancras pauper in his early twenties, who left the workhouse for Bermuda on the brig *James* in June

1850, wrote a long letter to Mr Eaton, the master, in August describing the difficulties he was experiencing.

> On our arrival the boys were immediately disposed of and had there been as many more they would have found employers [this statement contradicts the guardians' claim that situations were obtained for all the children before they left the workhouse], the men with the exception of myself and Nimmo were soon engaged to different persons . . . there is not the slightest chance of my obtaining employment in these Islands . . . With respect to employment generally in these Islands, I have no hesitation in saying that men who can turn their hand to Agricultural pursuits there would be no doubt of their obtaining immediate employment [*sic*]. Again – men understanding Horses would soon obtain employment, but wages are very low, but it is of no use for any person to come here, except they are acquainted with one or both of these things – with respect to the boys and girls there is a great opening but all will depend on themselves.
>
> A Gentleman here . . . is very anxious to obtain a woman about 30 years of age as Cook and a Girl say about 13 or 14 to wait at table etc. . . . Applications will be made to you by Captn Burrows of the James for the above to whom I have entrusted this for posting in London. . . . I am, Sir, your obed^t Humble Servt
>
> B. W. Mathew

In those days few people knew anything about the colonies, especially the smaller ones. Voluntary emigration was rare. Great Britain, like most European powers, had discouraged it in fear of depopulation which would weaken armies and navies and, in spite of the small government schemes which began in England in 1832 to send women, unemployed mechanics and farmworkers away with grants, few individuals went to settle in the colonies of their own free will. The tens of thousands who sailed to North America from Scotland and Ireland in the middle of the nineteenth century were driven from home by hunger and by rapacious landlords who tumbled the roofs off their houses and left whole families sitting on the roadside.

It was not until the 1870s that people began to think of emigration as something hopeful and brave. Sons and daughters from then on went off 'to start a new life in a young country', found opportunities unheard of at home, sent money to relatives and in a few cases made fortunes, news of which spread widely.

Knowledge gained through them of what life in the colonies was like removed much of the fear of the unknown. But until long after 1864, when the government gave way to the last of the colonists' protests and abolished transportation altogether, countries like Bermuda, Australia and Van Dieman's Land were associated with crime. The majority of ships sailing to their ports were convict ships, the majority of unconvicted passengers were warders, soldiers and officials belonging to the penal service or to naval and military establishments. Emigration seemed to most people in the 1850s a fate reserved for the wicked and for the starving hordes from Ireland where famine was still raging.

It was no wonder then that the strongest reason given in the newspapers against the export of children to Bermuda was that they would come in contact with criminals. There were two large penal establishments there, one at Boaz and one at the Ireland Island, which between them held a convict population fluctuating from year to year of between a thousand and two thousand felons, a high proportion of the European population. The prisoners at Ireland Island lived on hulks, those at Boaz in barracks on shore, but both lots worked every day in the dockyards, on the roads, at excavations and the blasting of rocks. It is unlikely that anyone, especially any child, had anything real to fear from them except when they mutinied as they did in 1855. But residents did avoid passing near them when they could. A distant sight of their straw hats with ribbon bands, their special blouses and coarse brown holland trousers made some turn back on the road.

> There are not even now [in 1857] warders sufficient to keep a constant supervision over the convicts while at work . . . They have been sometimes found chasing and pelting each other with stones. Few ladies like to walk out on Ireland Island till after working hours, even when protected by a gentleman, through such numbers of convicts; fewer ladies still have the boldness to pass through them unescorted. If they do so they must expect verbal insults, or disrespectful remarks.[36]

A more real objection, it seems to me, was that there was no way of proving that the children went of their own free will.

Inmates of any institution become submissive. Pauper children were imbued with the Christian principles of humility and obedience from an early age and it appears that they, and especially the many orphans among them, revered and loved individual guardians and masters with the loving fear they were taught to have for God. Their guardians knew what was best for them, no doubt. Nor is it certain, in spite of the defensive plea put by the St Pancras guardians to the Poor Law Commissioners, that no child was sent to Bermuda without the consent of relatives:

Extract from the 'Master's Report Book' dated 13 November 1849:

> Also – To a letter received from Mr. Gray as to the Boys he required for Bermuda . . .
> Also – That the Grandmother and Uncle of Charles Sersale aged 12 years object to that boy going to Bermuda.
> Also – That the Boys named be permitted to visit their friends on Wednesday.

> 21st May, 1850. The Master's Report was presented and read. Resolved that George Barrow, Mary Ann Gardiner, Charles Sersale (and thirteen other named boys and girls) be sent to Bermuda by the Brig 'James' under the charge of Captn Richardson, and that they be apprenticed and that they be apprenticed [sic] to him as Servants until they respectively attain the ages of 18 years, and that Henry James, aged 25 and John Buckingham, aged 27 be also sent to Bermuda by the same vessel and that £9 be paid for each Adult and £6 each for the Boys and Girls as agreed.

I suspect that these masters' reports were withheld from Somerset House or that the inspector, Mr Hall, shook them through the riddle of his memory as he sat down to summarize his inquiry, for there is in them something more generally deceptive and culpable than the case of Charles Sersale and that is the deliberate misuse of the term 'apprenticed'. All the boys and girls were apprenticed to Captain Richardson personally. He and Captain Burrows after him made three or four voyages to Bermuda every year. They must therefore have had about fifty new personal servants each, every year and continued to train them in their job for seven or eight years, acquiring by arithmetical progression as those years went on an unmanageable number of trainee chefs, pastry cooks, undercooks, commis, housekeepers, launderesses, ladies' maids, house maids, kitchen maids, scullery maids, butlers, wine butlers, table men, dressers, valets and bootboys. And most of the time both captains were at sea eating salt pork full of weevils.

For a child in those days the prospect of a voyage to the Bermudas was probably as thrilling and fearful as a journey to the moon would be now. The workhouse was home for most of them. It is clear from their letters that the workhouse nurses, teachers and guardians had become parents in their minds. They were snatched from home by a rough sea captain, an ogre to some, a stranger to all, and herded on to a swaying ship. School storybooks then were filled with shipwrecks and drownings.

Yet most of us nowadays would think that however terrifying the voyage was, and alarming the arrival among strangers, however lost and homesick they all were, the whole venture was worthwhile as the only possible escape from the shuttered course of workhouse life which ended for huge numbers only in death.

That is what Mr Osmond Jones and Mr Gray thought (Mr Gray had a financial interest in the venture it is true), and it is what I now think, after having been shocked when I first read of it as most people were shocked at the time. And suppose the improbable – that jobs had been found for the children in London; life for a domestic servant in Bermuda could never have been as hard and as unhealthy as contemporary accounts show it to have been here. Most pauper boys, if they were discharged in London, worked in factories where conditions were notoriously bad or were half-starved as match sellers, crossing sweepers and the like. If some were ill-fed, ill-treated by their colonial masters, at least they breathed good air in a healthy climate and were surrounded by a beautiful countryside near the sea.

But in 1851 very few people looked on the scheme with hope or approval. In their first letter, the Poor Law Commissioners did not use the word emigration; they referred to a practice of 'deporting' children of tender age, a word close to if not synonymous with 'transporting'. And as to the plea that deport-ation to Bermuda was preferable to an existence in a workhouse at home, you might as well have tried to convince people that transportation was preferable to imprisonment in hulks at home or hard labour on the treadmill in Brixton gaol. Next to hanging, transportation was the most dreaded punishment of all and yet the hard labour of even the Bermuda prisoners, whose regime was stricter than that of Botany Bay, was done outside the prison with much more liberty than the authorities approved of, as the field officer's stone-throwing story shows. John Mitchel's account in *Jail Journal*, 1856, of his own confinement in Van Dieman's Land shows how he was made a ticket-of-leave man soon after his arrival, allowed to travel about the island without supervision, and how he was given a grant of land. His voyage from Ireland in the convict ship had taken almost a year, it is true, some months of which were spent in the Bermudas. And being a political prisoner he was treated more lightly than others. But accounts by Ralph Rashleigh, who served his sentence in Australia from 1825 to 1844,[37] and by the prisoners quoted in *For the Term of His Natural Life*[38] show that, fearful as the punishments were for the slightest offence, tickets-of-leave with grants of land were given to non-political felons as well.

Relatives of transported convicts all over Great Britain must have had letters year after year describing their lives. Many invited their wives to join them and even sent the money for the fare. And yet the terror of transportation persisted in most people's minds. In the 1850s, more than seventy years after the publication of John Howard's *State of Prisons*, few respectable people knew anything about the horrors of life inside gaol at home.

Readers of the *Morning Chronicle* and *The Times* of 1851 probably knew less about what went on in workhouses at the time than we know now, just as their parents knew less about slavery in cotton mills here than about slavery in the West Indies.

I cannot find out what happened to the children – James Combley who sent a sprig of brushwood home to prove he was in Bermuda, Christiana Godwin whose letter to her mother is so homesick, and the other little castaways 'bound' for seven or eight years. Some must have died two years after their arrival in the epidemic which reduced the population of Bermuda in

1853, but others probably wrote to the guardians of the poor when their apprenticeship came to an end, when according to Mr Mathew's letter their prospects of finding work were dim. Adult labour, which had to be paid for, was always to be found, cheap and plentiful, among blacks and mulattos who had lived in the Bermudas for generations.

September 20th, Sunday

Martina turned to me in bed this morning, put her arms round me and said

– Why did you bring me to this horrible place?

We got back from Crete last Thursday afternoon and now I see she shares my sadness at the homecoming. She was most struck by the change of light, even inside the plane, as we reached England. Even above the clouds, the sun had dimmed since Greece – ever since we crossed the snowy Alps – then we went through clouds into the dull air of Heathrow. It is cold and here in the house the woven bag she bought in Heraklion has changed colour. It was dark red there among such brightness. It is still beautiful here: but a much lighter red.

October 13th, Tuesday

I look for the post anxiously these days expecting an answer from Proinséas but Dublin people can't write letters any more than Americans can. Saw the doormat from yards away scattered with dull brown envelopes that don't need opening. Electricity, gas, telephone – you know the amount within a pound or two and the final demand will tell you exactly what you must pay. There's a larger one, octavo I should say, without a window, addressed to me in ample feminine handwriting. I can read that too without opening it. It's from the Dept. of Health and Social Security. It is printed but someone has crossed out the Madam that comes after the Sir. It says

> Our records show that you will shortly reach age 70 and we should like to settle your burial grant whether or not you intend to die then. I am therefore sending you the enclosed application form

(BR 2) and a leaflet about burial grant. Please read the leaflet carefully before filling in the form.

The leaflet explains that burial grant is a once for all payment and that the sum allowed to each candidate varies according to his/her income and capital value of his/her property. The leaflet lists modes of corporeal disposal from which you may choose only one. It is recommended that you make your choice after forecasting as nearly as you can your probable resources at the time of the event.

Whether or not you are going to die, or even if you have not yet made up your mind, it is very important in your own interests that you should complete and return the enclosed application form quickly. A pre-paid envelope is enclosed for your convenience.

November 3rd, Tuesday

Today I heard a sound I had never heard before – the new American kind of police siren – police wailer rather – wee-oop, wee-oop, a horrible sound. I was near the Japanese school and before I saw where it came from I thought it must be the latest monstrous children's toy. It came from a striped minibus, packed with men in uniform, which swerved through red traffic lights towards Oval Road. Later I saw two more, one with an ordinary siren and in Delancey Street a silent one. Enough men to quell a riot but no sign of a riot. The burglar alarm at Henlys garage was ringing all weekend and no one took any notice. Soon no one will notice sirens any more. They are too frequent. And the reason there are so many police cars screaming past our house in the afternoons is that they are rushing back to the Kentish Town canteen for tea.

November 14th, Saturday

Davy Sloan has defeated the doctors again. It must be three years since they threatened to amputate his leg, and now he has even given up his walking stick. I thought it had been broken or stolen by whoever it was who beat him with it – in the first of two incidents that might be chosen as proof that Fate is ironical.

First, to be beaten and have two ribs broken by strangers with his own walking stick, the one he had shown me saying

– I'll need this all my life.

Second, that he was taken to the Royal Temperance Hospital – not UCH which was just as near.

– I walked out. Ye'd do the same, Davie.

Our relationship has changed completely ever since I stopped giving money to him and Mary. (I stopped giving anything to them some time ago when I was fed up with everyone.) This means that I no longer come when I'm called or spend time talking on the pavement, and as I pass them with a mere greeting he looks hurt – not resentful or threatening as some have been. Perhaps he thinks, and perhaps truly, that I have broken our friendship pledged as he said by shaking hands with the left hand.

December 10th, Thursday

On Tuesday morning I noticed it was lighter than usual when I looked at my watch about 7.30. I got up and drew the curtains and shouted 'Snow!' The first snow just after daylight is always a shock of delight. I remember it from childhood at Nairn. And here from the back of the house, the semicircle of Gloucester Crescent roofs are like the banks of a deep white pool that lies among the trees below our bedroom window. The nursery bars outside our window bear even white coats on top and show up blacker than before. (On Wednesday, after Tuesday's slight midday thaw each bar had a row of icicles below the black.)

At breakfast from the kitchen window – delicate filigree on the long narrow twigs of the Japanese willow and on the terrace in front of the house, the weeping ash is in filigree too, every twig and branch picked out in white; a thin ridge of snow lies on each branch about an inch deep and the terrace roadway is like a farm track, only one cart has been down it – the dustcart. The grass and trees pure white, untouched.

The privet hedge has bowed towards the pavement – white tyres thick on each bowed spray. But on Wednesday after a second fall of snow, the sprays are no longer to be seen – it is like a bank covered with snow – smoother and more steeply bowed, and the part nearest the house is like a sagging thatched roof. London is clean and silent.

December 11th, Friday

On Wednesday morning the sky above was dull but a pale low sun shone down the terrace turning the snow on the privet hedge to thin gold, but the light rose upwards from the ground.

Fine snow when M. and I left the house this morning but now at 11 a.m. it is heavy and thick like cottonwool. The terrace pure white again – several people including me had cleared their pavements and the cars had blackened the roadway. From a distance trees that have bunched branches look like clouds of mist. The two thick slanting, twisting stems of our ash are thickly coated with snow on the top side and even the upright trunk from which they branch is coated on the windward side.

The snow on the pavement turns to lumpy ice as people trample it. Outside the Co-op, near the bus stop, it is very slippery. A fat woman, dragging her trolley behind her, fell just in front of me.

I noticed how people always lie still for a few seconds when they fall. I bent down at once to help her up, but until I pulled her from beneath her arms she lay quite still. Then she made a good effort to get on to her feet, but I had the whole weight of the upper part of her body.

This heroic Christian act was barely over when I was dismissed by an even fatter woman of the same age, fiftyish, but this one was Life's Manageress. She would never have fallen. She told the fallen one to come in to the Co-op doorway. With her trolley in one hand, I helped her in. Life's Manageress helped her morally and probably she was right – you need a few quiet minutes to recover even from a small shock. The fallen one was stroking her left forearm – the part she had fallen on – and as she stroked it she turned from the Manageress who was still giving instructions; she turned to thank me and I had my first glimpse of her face which was plump and kind. I said

– Did you hurt yourself there? (the forearm) and she nodded.

Then I left them standing in the Co-op doorway, the Manageress looming over the fallen one.

I went to the post office for money, stepping more carefully than before on the bumpy ice which is brown and yellow here near the crossroads. The road itself is a black river between discoloured rugged whitish banks. I crossed it at the lights when I left the post office and crossed the double river of Camden High Street by the white island of the gent's public lav whose railings are decorated with dainty frills of snow, to Martina's bank which has installed new sheep-dipping rails for its customers. Instead of queueing up in several queues – one for each cashier – everyone faces the end wall and you make a dash for it one by one whenever a cashier is free. It is to prevent you from seeing how much money your rival has got.

On the way out, I held the door open for a man who was limping slowly along behind me on a stick. I was thinking how stupid I was to hold the door open for him – that he could easily open it himself and I remembered how annoyed people get if you help them when they don't want to be helped. As soon as he reached the door I started to go down the steps. He called me back

– Just a moment – would you mind taking these? No, in your left hand! I want your right hand. My tricycle is just round the corner and when I get there I'll be quite all right!

There are four or five steps from the bank to the pavement but they had been cleared of snow. I took his two plastic bags in my left hand and ranged myself beside him for the descent. I put my right hand under his arm. He had been dictatorial from the start, but now he was irritable.

– No. No. I want your right hand.

He clasped it. His was warm. I did not much like the clasp of Christian fellowship nor the bossiness that went with it and I was relieved to see his tricycle by the end wall of the bank, quite near. When he had said 'round the corner' I imagined walking hand in hand all the way to Greenland Street or even Bayham Street.

A strong feeling was transmitted to me through his hand, an intimacy that I found repellent. But when we reached his tricycle and let go, I didn't want to rush off. He took the bags and arranged them fussily in the wire basket behind the seat; then undid the lock, and said

    – I'm not going to ride it – not on these icy roads.

    – Why did you have to bring it out?

    – It's a walking frame. It's very useful and that's why I'm glad I didn't buy a bicycle – that would have been no use at all.

    When I asked him whether he had far to go he said

    – Only to Friends' House. I've to be there at one o'clock. It's not far.

    It seemed to me rather far with his lame leg in the snow all that way down Camden High Street to Mornington Terrace, the whole length of Eversholt Street, past the Hillwood Centre, to Euston Road. As soon as he mentioned Friends' House, I knew he was a Quaker – the good, determined face and manner. God is right and I am right. You can't think of it as complacent, because Quakers are aware more than most people of the suffering of others. And yet all the Quakers I remember meeting have had a look which says 'I know better.'

December 18th, 1981, Friday

Hard frost for the past two nights, all day yesterday and today very cold north wind blowing from the old goods station.

    Plumbers on our roof putting on new lead took extra trousers and jerkins out of their car this morning and put them on over their other clothes. They don't wear gloves – I suppose they can't handle tools in them – but the younger one, whom I spoke to, said he didn't mind the cold so long as it is dry. It has been dry. Patches of snow trodden hard here and there remain on the pavements – on the terrace pavement there are two stumbling blocks where people piled up the snow to make a footpath. And from our bedroom window we can see two deep patches, pure white, one under the eaves of the Little House and the other on the roof of Mr Shaeff's garden shed. These are so securely hidden from all eyes except ours and tucked away from the sun, south and west, into the darkness of north and east walls where they shine bright, that they might be used to hide treasure in.

I broke off for a while daydreaming about *Treasure Island*. It is going to be produced at the Mermaid again for Christmas and seeing that in the paper made me remember the book. I suppose of all stylists, excluding several pre-Victorians – I still admire R.L.S. the most, and even as a boy parts of the book, Blind Pew for instance, enthralled and scared me more than the play could.

Was that why I wrote that treasure might be hidden in that hidden snow? Or was it because of the thief I had heard of in Norfolk in the hard winter three years ago who buried some crates of whisky in the snow, intending to fetch them next day, but could not get near them or find them because the snow had drifted during the night?

Or perhaps I was thinking of Enoch the thief. I did once meet him on a snowy day, in that very winter probably, when he held me freezing on the pavement opposite the convent on his way to Primrose Hill with that fierce dog he always led about and spoke for, explaining on its behalf that it could not help frightening other dogs and people because it was half Irish wolfhound and half Alsatian. People think him ill-natured, he would say in a tone which deprecated the ignorance of people but with a smile to show his kindly tolerance of the mists of error that most of mankind wandered in, but he is doing his best according to the gifts God gave him. When he jumps up at you snarling he thinks he is protecting me. When he sees me talking to you he is your friend. The dog's nobility was more difficult to perceive when it tried to savage a cat or a Pekinese, but Enoch always held it on a lead and his voice rose above uproar in its defence.

His Cardiff accent had been somewhat flattened by a long residence in England, but a pleasant intonation remained with the persuasive eloquence, and pure vowels.

But in the Edinburgh Castle the dog lay still for hours with its chin on its paws like a sheepdog in church and it was there that one could listen to Enoch in peace, there and only there that he spoke calmly. He was seventy-four when he first spoke to me and must be now about eighty-six, but like everybody else who walks the pavements of Camden Town, or watches through a window, I had observed him curiously long before that for he was distinguished wherever he went, as he had intended to be all his life, by the spotless excellence of his dress. Wintry weather subdued it, it is true, but only in colour; no one else outside the city, at that time, wore stiff pinstripes, glossy black shoes, leather gloves, or a close-fitting overcoat of black worsted. His had an astrakhan collar – imitation I think – and on top of all that he wore a proud bowler hat.

It was his summer suits that took my memories back to boyhood and youth in the 1920s and 1930s. I would have been rather afraid of him then, for people of my upbringing would have called him 'flashy' – one to be wary of, as at later ages we were wary of 'drones' or Teddy Boys.

Enoch's summer personality was set off by hat and cane. He had a connoisseur's variety of straw and light trilby hats all very much too small for him by modern standards and worn tilted in Burlington Bertie style. The straw ones, which I remember best, were soft, narrow-brimmed and pale, almost white, with a grey or bright red band; and on top of his strong head and thick short body they would have been absurd had he not possessed a natural grace of movement, an agility both in gesture and gait that enabled him to make them a part of him as necessary as spectacles and worn without self-consciousness. Summer and winter he wore a buttonhole, a carnation or rose with its stalk kept moist in a silver holder beneath his lapel.

His cane was much thicker than Burlington Bertie's and he carried it without a swagger. But of this portable ornament he really was conscious and never hid his pride in its silver knob which was heavy enough to transform the whole length of polished finery into an ugly weapon.

He looked at its head very often as he spoke or listened and at his fingernails which were always clean, polished I think, but not varnished. His fingers were short and thick, his hands broad and hard, and were the only outward show remaining of the prodigious strength of his body, for his face had lost its clarity with age, red puffy flesh had covered the cheek and jaw bones, with small white patches here and there. From this disturbing mask small clear blue kindly eyes looked out.

Sitting beside him one evening in the Edinburgh on one of

the red upholstered window seats, thinking of his exacting job as pot and cellarman in a nearby pub, I complimented him on keeping his clothes so spruce and he said with his usual candour, as though he had nothing surprising to announce, 'I was a thief.'

I thought at once of pickpockets in fashionable places, but it was 'smash and grab' – an expression I had not heard used since the thirties.

'I never did any harm to anyone,' he said. 'I'd have nothing to do with that. I always was well dressed. You had to be – kid gloves, doctor's bag, press the button on top and it opens, then snaps shut.'

He pressed the top of his cane with his thumb to show me then suddenly snapped his fingers.

'No one knew who I was. I had style. In the hotels they called me "Doctor". You've got to go steady. You've got to be sure of yourself on the job and off it, keep your cool, as the young people say now. If you can wait for a lorry it screens you, especially in a traffic block – wait and smash your window when it revs up, it'll drown the noise of glass. The corners are the weakest part of a window – always go for the corner where the cream is.' (He meant the best jewellery.) 'You have to be quick. Walk away, don't run. Once I went into the same shop next day like a customer to see what more they'd got, and did them again two days later; they never expected that.

'Of course, I never did nothing in my own town. I did most up in Lancashire, time it if I could for the night train, sleeper to Euston, and see my fence early next morning. Or the truth is I never did see him. In all those years I sold him stuff, he'd never let me see him – only his woman and wait, you had to be patient. It would be a long wait till he went over them with a magnifying glass and tests. I knew what he was doing. He knew jewellery and he was honest. You could trust him. But I wasn't a bit afraid of being seen. I once took a bus, when I'd done the job, to a country pub, stood drinks all round and late to bed; a fine bed and breakfast, I'll never forget it, bed and gammon and egg for three half-crowns. The landlord said in the morning, "If anyone else had shown that bundle at the bar, Doctor, he'd have been robbed."

'He wasn't quite right there, you know but you could trust

people more in those days – pull out a bundle with everybody looking and no harm. Of course, they didn't know what was in my doctor's bag.'

He was always fond of girls, he told me, and had to have money, but when I asked if he had married one of them he let the cane slide through his hand to bang the floor and looked at me sternly.

'Someone looking at you when you put your coat on and: "Where are you going?" "To the pub." "I'll come with you." You can't have that.'

This made me laugh and he laughed too, but only because I laughed. He glanced at me trying, I thought, to find out whether I agreed with him or not and fearing that he might have offended me, for he had often seen Martina with me in the pubs. But I had laughed only because I guessed he had spoken from experience – that someone had tried to come with him and probably succeeded and because I was thinking of Scotland and Ireland in my youth where women were excluded from pubs ostensibly on moral grounds but really because men wanted an exclusive meeting place, a poor man's Athenaeum or Reform Club. Also I remembered visiting a married school-friend in my own bachelor days whose wife was a stranger to me and how, after allowing a long enough time for impersonal conversation, I suggested a walk to a pub. She came with us and I parted with him that night without a word about love or sex, which had always been our chief subject of talk, anxiety and laughter.

The Edinburgh Castle was filling up and the sight of several people distracted my attention. A man I knew who had just come out of gaol six months after a daring theft of whisky sat down on Sam's stool in the corner, usurping the old policeman's throne with absolute confidence, and a huge woman like a black rhinoceros, white-faced and agitated, kept staring at him, angrily edging nearer and nearer to him as people ordered their drinks and moved away. She was, as all of us knew who had not been in gaol, the first usurper and when she found anyone on Sam's stool she raged and fidgeted, unable to enjoy herself or even speak until she had ousted him. Usually she went into reverse to accomplish this, pressing with her back and buttocks, stretching an arm as thick as a tree trunk between the intruder and the person he was talking to, always with her face turned away. The whisky robber was alone. He made a counter-attack with jolly talk until he made her smile. Her depredations ceased but he did not relinquish the stool. They spoke to each other, amiably perhaps, but I could not hear what they said. It was before I went deaf, but the pub had grown noisy by then.

Enoch greeted friends as they came in and out. It seemed that he was popular, not only renowned as a man of character but well liked as several told me for his fairness of judgement and easy-going ways. His wide range of acquaintance grew not only in the pub where he worked and lived but from a part-time job collecting 'rents' for the council from the market stallholders, and of course from the encounters forced on strangers by the dog.

The dog had risen, turned round twice in the narrow space between our legs and the table, and was now asleep by my feet, the only creature in the place oblivious to the noisy throng which increased every minute by trickles of young people who wound their way like water among rocks to join their own pool at the farthest corner of the bar. There were several pretty girls among them to draw Enoch's attention and mine.

After an unusually long silence, he turned to me and said, 'If I had my time over again I'd be as I was. I wouldn't want it different. I wouldn't be able to change if I wanted.'

He told me he had been apprenticed as a mason from the age of fourteen to twenty-one and had come to London looking for work just after the General Strike, slept out in Trafalgar Square and found no work, 'not a smell of it', for weeks and every night the 'Silver Lady' came there to the Square – 'a con woman; as good a con as the Salvation Army and Billy Graham – she got her money and handed out a little bread and dripping and bed tickets.'

'Everyone looks down at you when you're down,' he said and laughed. 'Otherwise they wouldn't be able to see you, would they? Specially women – they just can't see you at all. But when I was in work for a while – well! If you walked down Commercial Road with your bag of tools women would run after you. You were a living. None of the women had a living except chars.'

He had seen me smiling about the bag of tools and laughed again, then looked at the young people in their corner.

'Now men run after women,' he said.

I thought there had always been a good deal of running on both sides, although women hid their footsteps more carefully in the past and the nicer ones were obliged to sit on sofas and watch their mothers running for them. Certainly no one ran after me when I was young, and when I ran I used to push the pace so fast at the starting post that I often lost the race.

'Look at them there,' said Enoch. 'It's the girls that's paying. In my day it was always the fellow.'

In my day too; but I had never thought of myself as a 'living'. I looked towards a very young girl who was burrowing with both hands into her bag and said, 'Do you think her boyfriend regards her as a living? She's still at school, I'd say.'

'If she couldn't pay, he wouldn't come out to the pub with her, would he?'

He began to reminisce about money, saying that he had never been greatly distressed by physical wants when he was young; it was the blow to his self-esteem that wounded him.

'It's what people think of you that matters when you're young. I ought to know. When I was in work, I had friends, but casual work didn't last long at that time, during the Depression, and then you knew what people thought of you. I made up my mind to have money. And it wasn't easy, but I did it. My biggest job got me £350 – a lot of money in those days. I could have bought property but I didn't – all in gold sovereigns. I overheard people talking about those sovereigns in a pub. They were in a big country house. "Taffy was a Welshman. Taffy was a thief." Do you know that rhyme? "Taffy came to our house, and stole a rib of beef." Well, I came from a respectable Cardiff family. I was the only bad one out of six – four boys and two girls.'

January 6th, 1982

When I am unhappy all attractive women go into hiding. No one sees them in libraries, on buses or pavements. But when I'm happy, as I now at last am for a bit, they emerge from hibernation and in all this snow they are spring flowers. But you must not pick them.

I know I am absurd when I see flowers. M. knows it too. But Whose fault is it? It's just that I haven't changed since I was fifteen. I learn from autobiographies that people do change.

When I get on a bus I survey it and choose if I can a seat behind the prettiest head of hair which often – I can't think why – goes with a lovely face. If I can't sit behind her I sit near on the other side of the aisle, never beside her if I can avoid it, because if I sit beside her I can't help turning towards her all the time, which is embarrassing for both of us.

If it's a girl with long hair down her back I behave even more stupidly. I clasp the hand rail on the back of her seat. That's what it's meant for I suppose, but I've never seen anyone else clasp it. And as she moves her head her hair touches my hands. Once some such beauty tossed her hair back and it fell over my arms which were bare in short sleeves. It was one of those rare hot days. Hair has no feeling in it. It only hurts if you pull. I pushed the rest gently towards her neck and stroked the part she had given to me. Assault, I suppose, in legal terms.

Last Eastertime when I was staying with Marie and Seamus in Merrion he drove me to Joyce's tower. I had seen it when young. It is now a museum. We didn't go in, walked instead to the bathing place where Buck Milligan teased Stephen Dedalus as he shaved himself by a rock. The bathing place is for men only, for nude bathing Seamus said, with huge women's protests scrawled in white paint on some rocks. The rocks are rounded and exceptionally sexual in shape – buttocks, breasts and the delightful cleft. Seamus remarked on it as I was thinking of it. (Martina and I had similar thoughts in the days when we hired horses at Lewes and rode over the South Downs.)

I said
– Almost every object is sexy.
– Yes, thank God, Seamus said.

January 30th, Saturday

All the furniture and clothes and carpets, pots and pans are
rushing about the basement as if carried by flood water, and
some have risen up the stairs to the ground-floor level, settling
down for a while in the hall. The great long sofa landed in the
garden and settled there, its broken springs resting on the
grass. This has happened because John moved out last week
after living in the flat for two years.

It was the flotsam that had risen to our hall and among the
things that we found floating near the front door was a small
leather case, the kind of thing young women carry the dainty
parts of their clothing in, a neat case about one foot wide by
eighteen inches by six. You often see them queuing up at bus
stops or dangling from ladies' fingers on the street. The top,
where the opening clasp is, is curved and has a golden lock;
and over the top there is a strap handle which does not droop.
The base is flat with a few gold studs. There is probably a
name for this thing but I don't know it.

Martina filled it with little garments and left it in the hall
for me to give to Rita, but she has been calling less and less
often this winter and I thought it would land up at the Oxfam
shop. Instead she came as if by instinct the next day, calling
loudly at me through the window. She knows I can't hear the
bell, but even I can hear what she says ten or twenty yards
away, for like many country people, especially County Leitrim
people, she cannot speak quietly. She doesn't shout; there is
no forced effort in her voice; the phrases come out of her with
natural modulations but loudly enough to be heard across the
broadest waters of the Shannon above Carrick where her home
is. She speaks rapidly in a hard clear voice, and she sounds
harsh at times and yet by nature she is gentle. She looks wild
as she hurries on her splay feet about the street, her brown
coat flapping, her hair like a forkful of hay in the wind and
two or three plastic bags in her hands bulging with old clothes
which she picks up here and there and sells to small
secondhand shops. But she does not look so wild as she did
ten or fifteen years ago when I first met her, for in those days
her own clothes were ragged; she had no place to keep them
clean and seldom a place to wash her hands which made her

face sooty whenever she pushed the long strands of hair away from it; and though her hair was beautifully brown it frightened people, who thought, I suppose, that she was as unruly as it. When she came up to me in Parkway that first time, as I was looking at the headlines on the rack outside the newsagent's, she gave me two pennies and asked me to go in and buy her a packet of Polos.

– They won't serve me in there, she said.

She moved out of sight as I went into the shop, but walked all the way down Albert Street with me, though as it turned out she didn't want to go that way, and talking all the time about her parents and sister and the small mountain farm they lived and worked on. She was delighted to hear that I knew the Leitrim Mountains when I lived at Woodbrook only fifteen miles away across the county border. I told her how I had watched their changing colours every day from the lakeside fields and garden and from the windows of the house.

– But ye never was in it? she said.

– Yes, often with the bicycle to Drumshambo and along by Loch Allen, under Slieve Anierin. It's beautiful, isn't it?

– But ye are not Irish?

She could not believe me. I told her I was Scottish but had lived in Ireland for ten years.

Several times after that first meeting I saw her gesticulating outside the baker's window, peering through the little cakes on glass shelves, while I was waiting to be served with bread, and one of the girls would be sent out to her to give her a loaf. I guessed it was yesterday's but am not sure.

She spent the whole year saving bits from the little money old clothes won her to visit her parents in Ireland, and now that they are dead she still goes to her sister when she can.

When she came to the door last Thursday she was trim in a clean brown overcoat, a pale yellow guernsey and black skirt, and her face, which is round with bulging blue eyes and a large thin-lipped mouth, was fresh and healthy.

– How are ye? And the mistress? Is she at home?

She makes a balloon out of her cheeks and the words come pounding out of it. She herself was 'not so bad, not bad at all'. She was staring avidly at the flotsam in the hall.

When I gave her the case she stroked it and turned it every way to look at it.

– That's grand, that's lovely. I'll bring that with me when I go to Ireland.

– Martina put some things in it.

She did not open it. She told me how she had spent Christmas at home with her sister, and about the long journey, the rough sea crossing, the train slowed down by snow, the roads blocked with snow, but no snow on the way back, and then she looked down at the case again and burst into tears.

I held her hand while she was crying or rather I laid my hand on the back of hers which was clutching the handle of the case. Hers was warm but rough and chapped. She cried for a long time, sometimes sobbing as she spoke, and whatever I said to comfort her started her off again. We were standing on the doorstep and glancing at her face in a new way because I was upset I saw how much thinner she had grown since I last saw her. Now her voice creaked and shrank.

When I said

– Will you go again in the summer? she nodded and told me how she had no one in the world only her one sister; the brothers were gone to America and some she didn't know where and the other sisters were married away. Her Leitrim sister wants her to come and live with her, but she must wait for the pension; the pension in Ireland is nothing, only a few pounds.

– How old are you, Rita? I said. I was surprised to find her thinking of the old-age pension.

– I'm only just gone 50. That's ten years to wait.

It made her smile and she recovered from her tears. She says she has no friends in London. Nobody. She has a council flat, very nice, after seven years waiting for it.

When she had told me all, I asked how long she had been in England.

– I came over in 1956. Too long.

She said goodbye loudly, in her normal voice, and walked away fast, both arms straight and laden, her gait energetic as it always is, but this time, for the first time, it made me sad to watch her go away.

1956 was the year we moved into this house.

She came again a few days later to ask for Martina, cheerful but very disappointed not to find her here.

– Tell her the shoes is lovely. Tell her they're lovely – they fit me just right.

She doesn't sell anything she likes, keeps it to wear.

– Tell her there's comfort in them shoes.

February 13th, Saturday

MacL.'s father seeing his black fingernails and grimy shirt at breakfast said

– Try to look a bit more Protestant.

– How can I when you won't let me off mass?

– Well, you'll need a job, won't you? You'll be twelve next year and with a name like ours you can cod them, make them think you're a Proddy.

– Why, Da?

– Mac. There's lots of Macs in Scotland.

His father died just before he was twelve. I think he loved him but in that tight Belfast way he now pretends not to have. And his father and their poverty was an embarrassment at school. The children were supposed to bring a halfpenny a week to pay for the ink. His parents could seldom afford it, so his father made his own ink out of acorns – a process he knew – and when MacL. brought in his homework the teacher said

– What kind of ink is that?

And then there was their dog on which his father depended for most of their food. It was a large lurcher, awful for city people to look at but a fast and silent hunter at night, the ideal beast for any poacher to possess. I never thought Belfast was a beautiful city, even before the British Army turned it into a shambles, but it shares one delight with Dublin; you can see mountains from the very centre of both cities and a short bus or tram ride will bring you into the foothills, which means that Dublin and Belfast dwellers are not exclusively townspeople in the sense that many Londoners are. Which made it easier for old Mr MacL. to take hares and pheasants from several rich Protestant demesnes. Then he kept on selling the dog and it was so devoted to him that it ran home each time to the Falls Road. He locked it in a shed in the backyard at those times and when its new owner, who had just paid for it, arrived to say it was lost he always advised him to offer a reward on a card at his local newsagents. Of course he never sought the reward himself; the dog was too valuable to him.

And he always had a live ferret in his topcoat pocket and often a bag of newly dead rats to sell to the anatomy classes at Queen's.

On the day after he left school MacL.'s mother found him a job in a hotel. She said

– Always stick to kitchen work all your life. It's the only thing a person gets enough to eat on.

And he has, except that in the summertime nowadays he sells ice creams from a barrow in Covent Garden, which he likes better because a kitchen porter's work is exhaustingly hot; the cooking pots in places like the Ritz, Savoy and Claridges are huge and heavy and you have to turn them over and over to clean them and the grease on your hands and clothes is disgusting. And then in the mornings you have to carry heavy carcasses in on your shoulders from the delivery vans.

When I first met him in Michael Donovan's days at the Edinburgh, that pub was a gathering place for kitchen porters. It is casual work for most of them. You find jobs if you can day by day by queuing early in the morning outside the back doors of the hotels and in the Edin. news was exchanged – the most likely hopes for next morning. Bill Campbell was always in a black suit – you have to look fairly well done up – some chefs, like the old slave-buyers, go down the queue feeling men's muscles, glancing at their teeth and ears for dirt. I guess that's why Bill looked like a stockbroker all his life. He too lived in Rowton House. MacL., whom I used to call the Vicar of Bray, was then a convinced but inactive communist, just as I used to be, but he bought all his clothes at the Conservative Party shop in Albany St. He once found two pound notes in the pocket of a coat he was trying on there, took them and put the coat back on its hanger. He says the Labour Party clothes are dreary.

Jack Winocour, always more sociable and talkative than I am, introduced me to MacL. and Bill.

– Haven't you met the Black Campbell and the Red MacL.?

It struck Jack as funny that two men from the Six Counties, a Proddy and a Mick, should always be huddled inseparably at the bar. They were friends but often shouted quarrelsomely at each other, and sometimes when I spoke to one or the other alone they said unpleasant things about each other. It was never about religion or Irish politics; both had given all that up long before.

Bill's family was not so poor as MacL.'s. He was born and brought up in the country on one of those small farms in Co. Tyrone where the soil is sparse and grass and crops meagre. But he knew country life as well as MacL.'s father. He loved Regent's Park and walked round it a lot, day and night. He was neurotic, tense all the time except when he found someone to talk to, and he had a horribly loud voice which with Tyrone accentuation is as distressing to me as a juke box. He once gripped my arm with iron claws and shouted

– Relax! Relax! Don't look so worried.

He fed the Regent's Park ducks and the younger geese every day until some got to know him and came when he whistled. He had a way, which many Englishmen know, of whistling or imitating birds' and animals' mating calls. You can draw a hare to your feet like that or by voicing distress or pain, and if you are a good mimic it will sit at your feet until you pick it up and kill it.

One Saturday night I was drinking by myself in the Engineer a hundred yards or so from Primrose Hill when Bill came in. It was after half past ten, near closing time. He hadn't had a drink all day. He had just come from Regent's Park lake, hoping to get to the Engineer before it closed. We had time for a pint or two together. He looked ruffled with the wind and his face was redder than usual. There was mud on the sleeves of his black topcoat. He said

– There's some very bad people get into the park at night. There's ways in when it's shut and no keepers about. David, you won't believe me when I say what they go in there for. I've seen some – you know two of them well, but I'm not saying – and I've seen them at Claridges next day and with carrier bags. They get the job if the chef spots the bag and they get enough to keep anyone for a sennight for what's in the bag, and get the day's work as well.

– What's in the bag then?

–Wild duck and sometimes young geese, but geese are nasty. You can get hurt.

We spoke of other things but when we were thrown out with everybody else at closing time he picked up a bulky Tesco carrier bag which I hadn't noticed when he came in.

St Patrick's Day

M. said at breakfast that she's learned lots of good things from me and when I said

– What for instance? she answered

– Spending money.

She means she's picked up my careless ways. In fact I only taught her two things – how to smoke a cigarette and how to have a bath. She had to smoke a cigarette on the stage. I forget which play she was in then, but she used to hold the cigarette as though it was going to sting her, then screw up her face with her eyes shut and back away from the clouds of smoke she puffed out.

Then she never used to wash herself in the bath. She thought that if she lay in the hot water long enough she would be clean without soap. I discovered this one morning while I was shaving and she luxuriating in the bath beside me. Also when she has a bath at night she jumps into bed all wet, preferring the warmth of my body to a towel. She has bubble baths nowadays and emerges covered with froth which, she says, is better than soap. I like the smell.

April 8th, Thursday

It must be *nostalgie de la boue* that draws me back to the White Hart so long after joy died one of his frequent deaths in it. I was near, it is true. I was on the way back from the boneyard having found the grave inscriptions indecipherable. But there was no need to go in. I was punished for it in the gents where I went as I was leaving. Graffiti in huge black ink.

– Kill all black babies at birth.

– No blacks at pool tables if whites want to play.

April 10th, Saturday

Last night, Good Friday night, at the bottom of the escalator
at King's X tube, a weasel-faced man in uniform was sweeping
up rubbish with a wide broom, drink cartons, cigarette packets
with all the dust and filthy scraps of the day which he pushed
towards an elegant long black glove that was lying there. I
expected him to pick it up as I would have – I thought of
picking it up, but was too late. He smothered it in a wide
sweep. It seemed to me extraordinary and shocking that he
had no feeling for it. Several images went through my mind,
a symbolic hand, a dead blackbird, an ornamental bookmark
fallen from a lectern Bible – any once-precious relic being
tumbled in the dirt. As I went up the escalator I remembered
the Tatterdemalion whom I haven't seen for months and
thought of his body, if he were to die in the tube, being
tumbled about with the rest of the thrown-away rubbish.

Notes

1. F. S. Williams, *Our Iron Roads*, Ingram, Cooke & Co., 1852, pp. 73–4.
2. *Personal Recollections of English Engineers by a Civil Engineer*, Hodder & Stoughton, 1868, pp. 34–7.
3. Charles Dickens, *Household Words*, vol. 4, no. 81, 11 October 1851.
4. Thomas Roscoe, *The London and Birmingham Railway*, London, 1839(?), p. 18.
5. Roscoe, op. cit., p. 43.
6. Williams, op. cit., p. 130.
7. Robert Rawlinson, *Papers Read Before the Statistical Society, Manchester*, Manchester, 1846, p. 46.
8. Rawlinson, op. cit., p. 47.
9. Williams, op. cit., p. 132.
10. Williams, op. cit., p. 129.
11. Rawlinson, op. cit., p. 49.
12. Rawlinson, op. cit., p. 45.
13. Rawlinson, op. cit., p. 49.
14. Edwin Chadwick, *The Sanitary Conditions of the Labouring Classes of Great Britain*, 1842.
15. Anon., *A History of Inland Navigation*, 1779; quoted by Anthony Burton, *The Canal Builders*, Eyre Methuen, 1972, p. 156.
16. Herbert Spencer, *London's Canal*, Putnam, 1961, pp. 40–41.
17. *Illustrated London News*, 10 October 1874.
18. Maxim Gorki, *Fragments from My Diary*, Philip Alan, 1924.
19. Doris Lessing, *The Memoirs of a Survivor*, Octagon Press, 1974; Picador, 1976.
20. *The Times*, 3 October 1980.
21. Richard Farrant, 'Lord Rowton and Rowton Houses', *Cornhill Magazine*, vol. 89, pp. 835–44, June 1904.
22. James Joyce, *Ulysses*, Bodley Head, 1960, pp. 375–6.
23. Sylvia Plath, *Johnny Panic and the Bible of Dreams*, Faber & Faber, 1977, pp. 223 et seq.
24. Pascal, *Pensées*, 1670, p. 139.
25. Walter E. Brown, *The St Pancras Book of Dates*, Town Hall, St Pancras, 1904, p. 7.
26. John Brown, *A Memoir of Robert Blincoe*, J. Doherty, 1832.
27. Terry Coleman, *The Railway*

Navvies, Hutchinson, 1965; Penguin Books, 1968.

28. *Railway Bell*, 5 September 1846.

29. *The Times*, 26 September 1846.

30. G. D. H. Cole and Raymond Postgate, *The Common People*, Methuen, 1971, p. 582.

31. Bernard Shaw, *Platform and Pulpit*, edited by Dan H. Laurence, Rupert Hart-Davis, 1962, pp. 175–6.

32. *Ellen Terry and Bernard Shaw: A Correspondence*, edited by Christopher St John, Constable, 1931, p. 210.

33. *St Pancras Gazette*, 8 September 1900.

34. *St Pancras Gazette*, 21 December 1901.

35. See William Booth Scott, *Saint Pancras, 1890*, The Vestry, 1890, pp. 16 et seq.

36. *Bermuda: A Colony, a Fortress and a Prison*, by a Field Officer, Longman, 1857, pp. 210–11.

37. *The Adventures of Ralph Rashleigh*, Jonathan Cape, 1929.

38. Marcus Clarke, *For the Term of His Natural Life*, Macmillan, 1907.

MORE ABOUT PENGUINS, PELICANS
AND PUFFINS

For further information about books available from Penguins please write to Dept EP, Penguin Books Ltd, Harmondsworth, Middlesex UB7 0DA.

In the U.S.A.: For a complete list of books available from Penguins in the United States write to Dept DG, Penguin Books, 299 Murray Hill Parkway, East Rutherford, New Jersey 07073.

In Canada: For a complete list of books available from Penguins in Canada write to Penguin Books Canada Ltd, 2801 John Street, Markham, Ontario L3R 1B4.

In Australia: For a complete list of books available from Penguins in Australia write to the Marketing Department, Penguin Books Australia Ltd, P.O. Box 257, Ringwood, Victoria 3134.

In New Zealand: For a complete list of books available from Penguins in New Zealand write to the Marketing Department, Penguin Books (N.Z.) Ltd, P.O. Box 4019, Auckland 10.

In India: For a complete list of books available from Penguins in India write to Penguin Overseas Ltd, 706 Eros Apartments, 56 Nehru Place, New Delhi 110019.

Also by David Thomson in Penguins

WOODBROOK

Woodbrook is a house that gives its name to a small, rural area in Ireland, not far from the old port of Sligo. It had been owned since the seventeenth century by the Anglo-Irish Kirkwoods. In 1932 David Thomson, aged eighteen, went there as a tutor. He stayed for ten years.

This book grew out of two great loves – for Woodbrook and for Phoebe, his pupil. In it he builds up a delicately lyrical picture of a slow pre-war society, of Irish history and troubled Anglo-Irish relations and of a delightful family. Above all, his story reverberates with the enchantment of falling in love and with the desolation of bereavement.

'One of those books which . . . leave marks in the memory like the scars of personal experience' – W. L. Webb

'An enchanting story' – *Hibernia*

'Combines artistic skill and wisdom . . . a masterpiece of historical writing. The book has moved me deeply and I greatly admire it' – A. J. P. Taylor

'A marvellous conjuring up of a past age, of a beautiful decaying house . . . an innocent and idyllic love' – *The Times*

A Choice of Penguins

LONDON IN VERSE

Edited, with notes and illustrations chosen by
Christopher Logue

Poets from Shakespeare to Spike Milligan, from Byron to John Betjeman and Adrian Mitchell trace a route through the streets, sights and characters of London.

For this anthology the poet and actor Christopher Logue has provided an entertaining commentary, and included all kinds of verse. There are nursery rhymes, street cries and the epitaphs of some eccentric Londoners; there is Blake's dark vision of the 'chartered Thames', and Dunbar's sweet lover's declaration – 'London, thou art the flour of cities all'.

'A lively and thoughtful selection, full of small marvels' – *Guardian*

'Logue's own wit presides throughout, calling on our laughter, pity or astonishment ... a rare and delightful book' – *Country Life*

THE PEOPLE OF PROVIDENCE

Tony Parker

'It is just about impossible to overpraise this book ... Tony Parker has taped a series of interviews with a cross-section of the inhabitants of a London housing estate, from the window-dresser in his high-rise penthouse to the local soak, "Billy Bottle" ... from the single women with children to the self-made men – BR official, union activist, freemason ...

'It is a fascinating microcosm of working-class life ... and it can be read like the best fiction: it is as true to life as that, and as gripping' – Anne Smith in the *New Statesman*

'A triumph, capturing vividly and movingly what urban life is like' – Peter Willmott in *The Times Literary Supplement*